"In all the wide world of Christian missionary enterprise there is surely no project more fascinating in its inception or more thrilling in its results than that being carried on in the fabulous interior of Dutch New Guinea—the Shangri-la Valley where only a short while ago was discovered a completely Stone Age people. Here is a moving account of this Christian mission written by one who spent weeks on the scene."

—CLARENCE W. HALL,
Senior Editor, *Reader's Digest*

CANI

CANNIBAL VALLEY

By RUSSELL T. HITT

Stone Age Savagery

CANNIBAL VALLEY is the thrilling account of the spiritual advance into Dutch New Guinea by intrepid Christian missionaries who daily risk their lives to bring the gospel to Stone Age Dani tribesmen.

The Spiritual Challenge

The "valley that time forgot" was first discovered in 1938. Sixteen years later, after several attempts, American mis-

(Continued on back flap)

CANNIBAL VALLEY

RUSSELL T. HITT

HARPER & ROW, PUBLISHERS

NEW YORK and EVANSTON

FIRST EDITION

H-M

Library of Congress catalog card number: 62-14577

To DEBORAH

missionary to suburbia

. . . your young men shall see visions, and your old men shall dream dreams. . . .

Acts 2:17

And this gospel of the kingdom shall be preached in all the world for a witness unto all nations; and then shall the end come.

Matthew 24:14

. . . ye turned to God from idols to serve the living and true God; and to wait for his Son from heaven. . . .

I Thessalonians 1:9-10

CONTENTS

11. YEARNING FOR HAI   163

12. THE DANIS RESPOND   173

13. STRUGGLES IN THE BALIEM   182

    Picture Section   *following*   192

14. OTHER VALLEYS HEAR   202

15. THE PROPHET JABONEP   216

16. THE FIRES AT PYRAMID   224

17. MARTYR OF KULUKWI   234

18. DAWN OF A NEW DAY   247

    Acknowledgments   255

    Maps   *back endpaper,*   86

CANNIBAL VALLEY

1

INTO THE FORBIDDEN VALLEY

In the flickering rays of a kerosene lantern, Lloyd Van Stone, a tall young missionary from Texas, sat in a tent in Dutch New Guinea writing a letter to his wife:

"Darkness is just settling on the valley of mystery. I can look out the tent door and see the mountains across the valley silhouetted against the stormy sky not yet drained of all its light. We are on the banks of the Baliem River, not fifteen feet from the water's edge. I would like to relate the events of the day that brought us here at last.

"I awoke this morning at 5:30, had brief devotions, and then finished last-minute things. At 6:00 I was over at Mary Lewis' [fellow missionary] for breakfast, followed by devotions. By 6:45 we were in the hangar; 7:05 in the plane, and 7:10 in the air.

"Is it a dream? Can this really be true? Are we at last in our field of service with a goal to work for? No more delays? No more hindrances? No more sickness? No more trouble with the plane? Can it really be possible that we are on our way?

"How hard it is to face the reality. No, it's not hard at all. The truth of what is taking place does not come as a surprise. The

13

enemy has been working too hard to hold us back any longer. Too many at home have prayed, have cried, have besought the gates of heaven for these Dani people. The doors could not remain shut any longer. Too many were pushing. The doors had to give and so the first wedge was made.

"The plane circles over the airfield just once, tipping its wings gently to those watching below. It rises steadily, passing through fleecy clouds, climbing above the heartaches, disappointments, and discouragements. Can we look back? Our hands are on the plow and we dare not look back. We close our eyes, sometimes praying quietly, sometimes thinking, sometimes gazing at the distant horizon.

"The mountains grow larger moment by moment; the air becomes cooler. Our hearts grow more anxious. Clouds are everywhere, but through the rifts we can see everything below. . . . We can't get there a moment too soon.

"At 8:10 we can see the mountains before us. Sentinels of time. How long have they endured the attacks of time? Never once have they relinquished their tenacious hold on this Shangri-La. They have borne the attacks of the ages, but have never once given in. Their wounds show that.

"8:16—We've come through the pass. Look at the gardens! This is a valley that is one of the many that open into the Grand Valley. Villages that stir one's heart with such a deep longing. Will I ever be able to walk in that village and tell them 'unto you a child is born' and 'his name shall be called Jesus' for he shall save you from your sins?

"Deeper and deeper we fly into the land of promise. Stone fences that grace that garden like a white collar on a lovely golden dress. There's the river winding its brown path like a walkway through the flowered gardens of a king.

"Can words ever express the thrill, the joy, the inner tingle of a strange sensation that goes up and down your spine, making side trips around your heart, making it to beat a mile a minute?

"Aren't you afraid? Yes, before the trip we thought of all that could happen to us. We had heard about the atrocious Danis; how they rob you while they are looking right into your face. The

Kapaukus [another tribe] told us how mean they were. That's why they filled their carrying nets with trinkets. They said, 'We have a gift for the Danis. They won't hurt us. Tuan [teacher], when we land on the river, it won't be near a Dani village, will it?'

"O airplane, don't let us down now! Father, help us to alight upon the river and give us a safe landing. That river doesn't look too wide from here. Wait, we are going down. There's the landing site before us. Round the bend and the plane wings its way. Look there, two men in some kind of boat. Or is it two logs tied together? Both of the men are standing up, pulling the boat, I believe.

"We are flying over the landing site to check for hidden logs. Is this river ever big! Our plane is like an Austin on a four-lane highway. Now we are coming in to land. Fasten safety belts. A light flashes the warning that we are almost down. Splash! The first bump on the water. Keep settling, old girl, you've got to go down a bit more. Whoosh! Waves cover the window, hiding the shore from view. It's 8:40 A.M.

"Ed is out of the cockpit, tying a rope to the nose of the plane. He holds the rope in his hand ready to jump when the plane approaches the shore. What is in our mind as we follow Ed outside the plane? Only this: Praise the Lord! Glory to God! Hallelujah!

"Working our way to the eastern bank, the weeds are too high to penetrate—at least so it appears. The plane taxis across the river. Watch that tree as you jump ashore! The current is too swift. The plane must be tied to a tree. Ed's up to his chest in water. Now I'm in up to my hips, pushing, stumbling, beating back the high weeds. We finally tie the rope to a tree.

"Here comes the equipment. Miko sitting on the nose. I'm in the water. Ed's on the bank and Elisa beyond him. Al passes the things from the plane and in fifteen minutes everything is ashore. The rope is released. The plane scoots down the river, now it comes rushing back, with its wings steady. Just a series of waves lapping the shore in its wake. It's airborne again. We're all alone. No— hardly. He promised never to leave us, never forsake us.

"What a job faces us! The ground has to be cleared of the grass that rises ten to fifteen feet in the air. It's long, canelike grass that reaches out to scratch your arm, slicing deep cuts in your hand if you grasp its knifelike blades. Sweat and hard work for three hours. Finally an area big enough to pitch an 8 by 8 tent is cleared."

Thus did Lloyd Van Stone describe the epochal events of April 20, 1954. On that day a missionary expedition made the initial flight into the Grand Valley of the Baliem River. A beachhead was established in what some of the missionaries called the Cannibal Valley of Dutch New Guinea! Entry into this hidden valley, isolated for centuries from the rest of the world, represented a long-forward step in the grand plan of the Christian and Missionary Alliance to bring Christianity to the Stone Age cannibals of interior New Guinea.

Van Stone's missionary vision had been awakened during World War II when he fought in New Guinea with the First Cavalry Division of the U.S. Army. After a stint in Bible school, and two years in the pastorate, he and his wife, Doris, had been dispatched to New Guinea to work among the Kapaukus. Later they volunteered to serve on the Baliem Valley project. Van Stone was alone now. Illness had forced his wife to return to the United States for medical treatment. She was recuperating in Houston, Texas, when she received the welcome news of the expedition's safe arrival in the Baliem.

Einar Mickelson, the "Miko" of the letter, headed the landing party. A stockily built man in his late forties, Mickelson for many years had been haunted by a compulsion to tell the neglected New Guinea tribes about Christ. He had faced death many times on lonely treks into hostile territory in vain earlier efforts to reach the Baliem Valley on foot. Starting out in 1935 as a missionary to Borneo, he was transferred in 1942 to the struggling New Guinea mission. After working for a year among the Kapaukus in the Wissel Lakes region, Mickelson in 1943 opened the first station among the Moni tribe in the Kemandora Valley, three hard days of hiking east of headquarters at Enarotali. Hardly had this been accomplished when he was forced to flee the country one step ahead of the Japanese invaders of World War II.

Also included on the initial flight was a family of Christian Kapaukus, converts of earlier missionary activity in the Wissel Lakes area, who had volunteered for the expedition. Elisa Gobai, a native pastor, and his wife, Ruth, accompanied by their two-year-old daughter, Dorcas, indicated by their presence to the fierce Dani tribesmen of the Grand Valley that their entry was a peaceful one.

Pilot Albert J. Lewis of Hamilton, Ontario, a former Canadian Air Force ace, and co-pilot Edward W. Ulrich, a strapping ex-U.S. Navy flier, had flown the twin-engined amphibian on the history-making air journey from the coastal airstrip at Sentani into the interior.

As soon as the beachhead was established and the airplane unloaded, Lewis and Ulrich flew back to Sentani for a second missionary party.

Van Stone continued to describe the events of that important day:

"Miko and Elisa disappeared after the plane left and did not appear for an hour and a half. They tried in vain to make a way through the high weeds and great casurina trees, some as much as three feet in diameter. They were unable to reach an area about a quarter mile back that seemed suitable for drops from the plane. It's swampland and it's filled with mosquitoes.

"At noon we stopped for lunch: Nescafé. One can of an Australian casserole steak. (That fancy name covers a multitude of sins, I think.) A can of date bread sent for Miko's birthday.

"Hacking away, we cleared the bush from the river front so the plane could come in safely the next day. Then we cleared a path to string up the 100-foot radio aerial. It had to be stretched full length for a radio contact.

"No sight of any Danis but we felt they were in the forest and tall grass across the river, watching every move we made. Nightfall came quickly. Supper so soon. Yes, we were tired but happy. We really hoped a Dani would visit us.

"For supper: a can of cheese and a big pot of chocolate. I had an imaginary piece of cherry pie with a slice of cheese on top for dessert. Elisa, Ruth, and Dorcas in the pup tent. Miko and I in the umbrella tent. What an invasion party! But it is 'not by might, nor by power, but by my spirit, saith the Lord.'

"At 6:00 P.M. Al gave us his reasons over the radio for not making a second trip. The weather had been against it. He said he would come in tomorrow with Myron Bromley and two more natives.

"7:00 P.M.—Ruth, Elisa, and baby come in for prayer. Ruthie prays first, then Elisa. How burdened our hearts are for these people! I prayed for the first time in Kapauku. I'm sure it was full of mistakes. My vocabulary is so limited. The Lord knows what I wanted to say: 'Give us these Danis for Christ.' Einar closed in prayer.

"Back to letter writing. It was 8:30 and we were all ready for bed. Looking at it from the outside, the tent glowed with a greenish light. I hope soon we can bring the lamp on the outside to penetrate this valley. Just now we're a light shining dimly.

"Tomorrow we move across the river to a drier location. Smoke signals rise from four or five places on the mountain across the river from us. They are not too far away so we'll probably have visitors soon. Keep praying."

Night with its eerie stillness enveloped the tents. This first day of exciting adventures had ended without the appearance of a single Dani. But from the smoke signals on the hillsides and along the river, the "invaders" knew their arrival had not gone undetected.

On the following morning the radio brought news that pilot Al Lewis was winging toward the Baliem from Sentani, Hollandia's huge airport and the mission's coastal headquarters, from which the expedition had departed the day before. Mickelson and Van Stone had scarcely cleared away their breakfast dishes when the gleaming Sealand amphibian dropped down with a swoosh on the waters of the Baliem. First ashore was Myron Bromley, the round-faced, fair-haired young bachelor who would serve as linguist. He greeted Mickelson and Van Stone warmly. Accompanying him were a Biak islander named Adrian, and Topituma, a Kapauku, who aided with the unloading.

Bromley, who was from Meadville, Pennsylvania, had been trained at Nyack Missionary College, principal school of the Christian and Missionary Alliance; Asbury Theological Seminary; and the graduate school of the University of Minnesota. His big task would be to surmount the language barrier that stood between the missionaries and the people they hoped to befriend.

With the landing of the second flight, the missionary party was brought up to its full complement and the work of establishing the new station could now begin in earnest.

The long months of waiting for the expedition to materialize had been particularly trying. Mickelson's wife had been forced to remain in the United States because of a heart condition. Mrs. Van Stone had been flown to Texas for emergency surgery. Jerry Rose, a husky barrel-chested Southerner who had expected to be a member of the Baliem party, had taken ill, and with his talented wife, Darlene, had returned home.

An earlier flight had to be postponed when virtually everyone in the missionary group had been stricken by illnesses and injuries. Even Mickelson had been hospitalized with a high fever. It seemed as though the invisible forces of hell had been unleashed to block the conquest of Cannibal Valley.

The strain of being separated from their loved ones had told on Mickelson and Van Stone. Mickelson, usually reticent about discussing his experiences, became quite garrulous as he talked endlessly of his pioneering adventures of earlier years in New Guinea. Van Stone, concerned about his wife's condition, and dreadfully lonely, was moody and quiet, often leaving the group to brood by himself. Then, too, Mickelson and Van Stone had no illusions about the dangers that lay ahead of them. The Danis who ruled the Baliem Valley had a reputation for being hostile, arrogant, and tricky. What kind of a reception could they expect from these cruel cannibals whose cycle of existence had been warfare and violence? How could they communicate with men whose language and culture were still unknown?

What about the perils of flying over trackless jungles and swamps, of groping one's way through the jagged peaks of the narrow pass, shrouded most of the time with clouds and buffeted by sudden storms and fierce winds? They knew there was only one air corridor into the valley—the pass that broke into the Baliem from the north. Perpetual banks of clouds resting on barren, rocky slopes normally prevented entrance into the valley from the east, south, and west. What about the perils of landing on a virtually unknown river with its sandbars, logs, and swift current?

Mickelson later admitted that he felt he was virtually giving his life. "There was a momentous feeling of speculation about what tomorrow would bring," he said, "yet we had no sense of being heroic."

There had been no easy way into the Baliem Valley. Mickelson and others had learned through painful experience that it was not practicable to travel the two hundred miles overland from Enarotali, the Alliance station in the Wissel Lakes area. There were no roads or trails that led from Hollandia on the north coast. High mountains and swamps were formidable barriers from east and south. Officials of the missionary society were quick to recognize that the only means of reaching the hidden valley was by air. Furthermore, they had decided that there was one man to fly the missionary airplane—pilot Al Lewis.

A key figure in the Baliem project, Lewis had left a successful contracting business in Hamilton, Ontario, to serve as a missionary pilot. With his neatly trimmed mustache, his brusque military manner, and his air of self-confidence, Lewis had won the respect of everyone. He had a no-nonsense personality coupled with Christian dedication and intensity of purpose. His perfectionist demands for safety and his long experience in aviation impressed his colleagues with his competence.

During the greater part of the war, Lewis had served as a flying instructor for the RCAF. Upon his discharge from the air force, he returned to Hamilton. It was not long before he was engaged in a prosperous undertaking, but he was plagued with the realization that his aviation skill could be employed in the service of the Lord. Even though he was older than most missionary candidates, he presented himself to work overseas as a pilot. His first assignment was in Indonesia, as the Dutch East Indies had come to be known.

Officials of the missionary society at first had hoped that a single airplane, piloted by Lewis, could serve both Indonesia and the expanding operation in New Guinea. But Indonesia, so recently freed from Dutch colonial rule, clamped down on travel of all sorts to New Guinea, which was still administered by the Netherlands. Separate flying programs were therefore required for the two mission areas.

Other circumstances precipitated the decision to assign Lewis to New Guinea. Flying from Borneo to Jakarta, he had stopped for fuel at a small town on the northern coast of Java only a few miles short of the capital city. He tied his amphibian to a pier and went ashore to look for the filling station attendant. Meanwhile, a band of Indonesian insurrectionists cut his aircraft adrift from its mooring. Lewis returned to find it had foundered several hundred yards from shore on a shoal in the Java Sea. All his efforts at salvage were unsuccessful, and within a few hours, heavy seas had rendered the amphibian useless. With this abrupt ending to the Indonesian air operation, Lewis was available for the hazardous New Guinea assignment.

The absence of airfields in the uncharted, virgin interior of New Guinea dictated the use of amphibian aircraft. Two tentative plans for reaching the Baliem Valley by air had been developed by the missionary society. One called for alighting on Lake Habbema located at an altitude of eleven thousand feet in the mountains. Richard Archbold, wealthy American explorer who discovered the Baliem Valley in 1938, used such a landing. However, this would entail a long overland hike from the lake to the floor of the valley. The other possibility was to land a plane on the longest straight stretch of the Baliem River in the lower end of the valley. The latter plan was favored by Lewis and it was the one he later employed.

Lewis urged the use of a Sealand amphibian such as the one he had flown in Indonesia, even though some had questioned the use of an aircraft costing one hundred thousand dollars. Lewis, with his concern for safety, maneuverability, take-off distance, and payload, convinced church leaders that this was the proper equipment for the New Guinea project. Accordingly, an intensive fund-raising effort was launched by Alliance churches in the United States and Canada. The Baliem airplane project far exceeded the demands of the normal budget of these missionary-minded congregations noted for contributing sacrificially. However, it was given high priority and met with such warm response that the funds were eventually subscribed.

After many months of waiting for the delivery of "The Gospel Messenger," as the new amphibian was named, it was finally turned over to Al Lewis at an impressive dedication ceremony held on November 13, 1953, at the Belfast factory of Short Brothers and Harland, Ltd. Lewis and Ulrich, his co-pilot, flew the airplane first to London where additional radio equipment was installed, then ferried it across Europe and Asia to New Guinea. It was February, 1954, before it reached the hangar and base that had been prepared for it.

The all-metal airplane was equipped with wheels for airstrip landings and pontoons for the water. It had the flying characteristics of a plump pigeon rather than of an eagle or a swallow. But it looked beautiful to the missionaries in New Guinea who had waited so long for air transportation.

With the landing of the Christian task force in the Baliem Valley, Lewis felt that he had been used of God. With this sense of "mission accomplished" on that April morning, he flew back to the base at Sentani.

Now the Baliem missionaries turned to the job before them. Joined by Bromley and additional native helpers, Mickelson manned a rubber dinghy, which had been brought in by Lewis, and paddled across the river to locate a better camping site. He had landed Van Stone, Bromley, Ruth, and tiny Dorcas on the opposite bank, and was recrossing the river with Adrian, Elisa, and Topituma when he heard a commotion in the original camp. A band of Danis had arrived and were making a careful inspection of the expedition's supplies!

As soon as Mickelson and his companions touched shore, they

9.5
H

were greeted by naked Danis, armed with bows and arrows and huge spears, and led by an elderly man who was weeping and wailing. Mickelson was familiar with this type of greeting practiced by other New Guinea tribes. The leader, later identified as a witch doctor, and those with him, shouted *"Nahp! Nahp!"* This was their way of expressing a peaceful welcome.

Mickelson seized the hand of the weeping old man, who then threw his arms around the missionary and burst into tears. There could be no question about the welcome now.

Meanwhile, across the river, over a ridge behind Van Stone, Bromley, and Ruth Gobai, there appeared a strange sight. Limned against the sky, they saw a long column of Dani warriors in full regalia standing erect and holding fifteen-foot spears aloft like so many palings of a picket fence. Some of them wielded stone-headed battle axes and others were armed with bows and arrows. Suddenly their leader gave a hoarse order, weapons were lowered, and the whole group approached the missionary party with warm smiles and shouts of *"Nahp!"* The missionaries echoed the greeting with a great sense of relief, shook the extended hands, and submitted to the hearty embraces of the friendly men whose bodies had been smeared with pig fat.

The missionaries in subsequent letters credited their peaceful contact with the natives to the "volumes of prayerful intercession for us by faithful groups back home."

The Danis, of above medium height, were dark-skinned Melanesians with brown eyes, strong aquiline noses, and thick lips. Soot had been rubbed into their faces to give expressions of fierceness. Their kinky hair, saturated with pig grease, was stuffed into fiber hairnets. About their necks were long strings of white cowrie shells and strings of beads. Boar tusks were inserted through the septum. Long yellow gourds, assuring their modesty, completed their wardrobe. As they moved about in their excitement, their sweaty bodies gave off a strong odor resembling smoked bacon.

The Danis were as curious about the ways of the white men as the missionaries were about them. Flashing wide smiles, they crowded close to examine the strange white faces and arms. They pinched and rubbed the strangers' skins until they were raw to see if the "paint" would come off.

Mickelson found the Baliem Valley anything but a peaceful asylum. First there were the chores of getting settled at Minimo, as the new camp was called, directing the moving of supplies that were dropped almost daily by the Sealand, and attendance at a pig feast, to which "Weepy" the witch doctor had invited him. The veteran missionary was amazed by the friendliness of the Danis and the fact that thus far they had stolen none of the outsiders' equipment.

Van Stone had spotted a low range of hills to the north of their station. From his first contacts with the natives he heard that beyond the hills was another hidden valley, quite cut off from the Baliem. He was curious to know more about the mysterious area. He decided that at his first opportunity he would find out what was behind those hills. "I call it 'Magic Valley,'" he wrote to friends in the United States, "because it has been like a land of wonder to me. From the first time that I laid eyes upon it, it has drawn me back again and again like a magnet drawing a piece of metal. . . . The waters that drain into the valley from the surrounding mountains drop off into a large hole and go underground for perhaps a mile or more. The river comes out again just a short distance from our camp and empties into the Baliem River."

Mickelson, accompanied only by carriers, made a twelve-day trip up the Wamena River Valley and located the route from the Baliem to Lake Habbema high in the mountains on the southwest rim of the Grand Valley. Although he experienced some brushes with unfriendly natives, he accumulated information that would be valuable to subsequent expansions of the thrust into the interior.

The exploration trips of the missionaries were important because they thus located population concentrations. Getting acquainted with the valley was a pleasant task.

Some of the romance, however, connected with their camp location began to wear off as the missionaries learned more about the war patterns of the region. Indeed, it wasn't long before they realized that they had been granted box seats at a battleground near their camp. "Our camp is situated in a very strange place," Van Stone wrote. "This is no man's land . . . between two groups that are enemies. The foes met in battle one Sunday afternoon right behind our camp. They faced each other from opposite mountain slopes, with about two hundred yards separating them. Chills went through us as we saw a bunch of warriors go charging up the hillside. It was something to see twenty or thirty men adorned in feathers and fur headdresses, with their faces blackened, waving huge spears above their heads, as they rushed toward their opponents.

"Then the battle royal began. We heard one man on our side yell out murderous threats as he bounced up and down on his toes and shook from head to foot. He waved his spear, furiously brandishing what appeared to be a feather duster. From across the battle line came an echoing yell, filled with venom and poisonous oaths. Then a spokesman from the opposite side waved his spear, jumped up and down, and also shook with violent emotion.

"If words could have killed I'm sure the battlefield would have been filled with corpses. As it was, the verbal feud continued for about thirty minutes, then both sides retired because darkness was closing in on them. It was an interesting way to fight a battle."

Two men had followed Van Stone as he left his mountain vantage point. They asked him whether any of their foes were visiting the missionary camp. Van Stone volunteered to proceed to the camp to see whether they were. After checking, he signaled for them to come. Soon the camp was swarming with Danis from Magic Valley. They wanted to stay overnight with the missionaries, they said, but Van Stone told them that there was room for only two of them. The others would have to return home. He described the task of informing their chief of the limits of missionary hospitality:

"Can you imagine what it is like to try to tell someone something when you don't know his language? . . . We have discovered a new form of conversation without using the voice.

"To get a point over is one thing, to get the Danis to move was another. Only one thing to do—drive them home! We picked out the two who were permitted to remain, and then I started the cattle drive, with a flashlight in one hand and a canteen in the other. If the natives tried to hide in the brush, I turned the flashlight on them, causing them to scamper in a hurry. This game lasted all the way to the top of the mountain. Every so often a couple of Danis would hide behind a bush, and as I approached they would rush at me with wild yells and spears drawn. It was fun for them, not for me.

"At the top of the mountain, things changed. Threats or no threats, they were not going to move until they were ready. I was told to sit down. Fifteen men stood around me with long spears. . . . Finally one of the men motioned for me to follow him. We started descending the opposite side of the mountain . . . toward Magic Valley.

"The trail down the mountain is bad enough in the daytime. You have to pass two large limestone sink holes and sometimes the trail is very slippery, and it is a long way to the bottom. Here we were walking around this hole by moonlight and the dew on the ground made walking more difficult. Whenever I started to slip, a Dani in front of me, or behind me, would grab my arm and help me along. Finally one gave me his spear to hold while he held the other end.

"In the moonlight I could see a long line of men in front of me and an equally long one behind me. We had to walk single file. They were all very quiet. Any necessary remarks were made in low tones. I'll have to admit I was scared. I was praying all the way, 'Perfect love casteth out fear.'

"We reached a village about midnight. I was taken to one of the round houses and asked to enter. It was at this house on my second visit to Magic Valley that they had killed a pig for me. On that occasion they had conducted a long ceremony in which they rubbed my arms and face with pig fat and had me share meat with them. Then they placed my hands on a long belt to which cowrie shells were attached as one of the chiefs made a long speech. Apparently this was an induction into their clan.

"These round houses have two floors. The lower floor of this house was about fifteen feet in diameter and about four feet high.

A fire was burning in the center of the combination living room and kitchen. Under the roof was another floor, the communal bedroom for the men. The upper floor was made of long beams over which was laid a flooring of long cane poles about one-quarter inch in diameter. The cane poles were covered with soft grass that served as their inner-spring mattress.

"About thirty men gathered on the ground floor of the house and talk went on for quite a while. Apparently they were going over the events of the evening. The air was thick with the smoke from the cigarettes and the wood fire in the center of the room. Gradually I realized that my fears were unfounded and I was getting sleepy. Since sleep was impossible on the ground floor because of the mosquitoes, I crawled upstairs. Three men were already lying down. I found that they sleep with their feet to the center like spokes in a wheel. I stretched out in similar fashion. With the fire below, the upstairs was like a warming oven. First I took off my sweatshirt, then my shoes. No blankets were needed here. My eyes and nose and throat were burning from the smoke and other strange odors. Other men came upstairs and crawled over me. Finally, from sheer exhaustion, I fell asleep.

"In the middle of the night I was awakened out of a dead sleep by a piercing yell. I raised with a start and bumped my head against the roof. Where was I? I broke out into a cold sweat, fumbling for my flashlight. I found I had twisted around until I was on the other side of the house. It was twenty minutes to three and one of the Danis was having a nightmare!

"It was difficult for me to get back to sleep. Every now and then one of the men would stir and I'd feel a hand reach out and touch me to see if I were still there. The fire below was still going and I felt as if I were slowly cooking. . . . Morning finally came. Others were getting up, so I followed suit. I just had to smell fresh air again. The moon was still shining in the west and dawn was breaking in the east. I told my friends that I must return to Minimo. They wanted assurance that I would visit them again. I quickly agreed to this, then started back over the mountain toward home.

"As I reached higher ground, I turned and looked back across

the valley and wondered how much longer these people would remain in spiritual darkness. When would the gospel light dispel the
darkness of sin?"

As time went on the campers at Minimo found themselves involved as noncombatant first-aid men to warriors from both sides
of the battle line. Far too much time was given to dressing arrow
and spear wounds and administering penicillin shots to those with
infected injuries.

Another large segment of missionary man-hours was spent in
attempting to rid the area of mosquitoes. Einar Mickelson confessed that he had never encountered such swarms of the insect in
all of his previous New Guinea experience. The missionaries tried
to drain the swampy spots in which the annoying mosquitoes bred,
and cleared the riverbanks of trees near the approaches to the
river landing area.

Meal preparation was a shared responsibility. The concoctions
prepared by the amateur chefs from North America had their
appeal at first. After a time, however, the fare served by the
"widowers" of Minimo made all of the "victims" long for the
women's cooking.

The Stone Age Danis, who ate with their hands and had no
kitchen or dining utensils, were fascinated by the prepared cake
mixes and canned goods which made up the varied diet of the missionaries. After all, a Dani's diet consisted chiefly of sweet potatoes
served steamed or roasted, according to the native mood. There
were a few extras such as taro, another edible tuber, and a sort of
local spinach. There were also cucumbers, beans, and bananas.
Sometimes the protein-starved Danis enjoyed such delicacies as
caterpillars, beetles, and occasionally a bit of crayfish, a miniature
marsupial known as the cuscus or mouse opposum, and every two
or three years the ceremonial pig feasts which sometimes lasted for
three months, or at least until the supply of decaying pork was exhausted.

The time came when Mickelson had to leave. His furlough had
been long overdue. Thus, soon after he returned from his explora-

tion trip he asked Al Lewis to fly him out to the coast. When the Sealand landed on the river, Lewis realized that the water level had dropped too low for safe landings and take-offs. The Baliem River, fed by mountain streams, ran swift and violent or slow and sluggish according to the season. The water level had reached a dangerous low.

As Van Stone and Bromley now waved good-by to Mickelson and the pilot, they little knew that they would be marooned in the valley without another airplane visit for four and one-half months! For them it would be a trying experience but not an insurmountable one. They could rejoice like Mickelson flying back to Sentani on his way home, rather that the long-awaited conquest of the Baliem Valley had begun.

2

VISION OF THE LOST TRIBES

New Guinea had long attracted missionary societies because it was one of the most remote, dangerous, mysterious, and primitive regions left on earth. The interior was inhabited by savage tribes practicing cannibalism, multiple marriage, and cruel customs. But vitally concerned with the goal of ultimate evangelism was the Christian and Missionary Alliance.

Throughout the centuries New Guinea has sprawled like a huge bird in the waters just north of Australia. From its beak pointing westward toward the Indonesian archipelago it stretches eastward fifteen hundred miles toward the wide expanses of the southern Pacific.

There was good reason for New Guinea's isolation from the rest of the world. More than half of the Netherlands side of the island consists of virtually impenetrable swamp, especially the forbidden south coast inhabited by crocodiles, poisonous snakes, and head-hunting cannibals. The remainder of the terrain is made up of craggy mountainous country that defies access by ordinary means of travel.

30

New Guinea was first discovered by Portuguese seafarers back in 1511, but Portugal never bothered to absorb it into her growing empire. The Spanish explorer, Ynigo Ortiz de Retez, sailed along the north coast in 1545 and stopped off long enough to lay claim to the island for the king of Spain. But Spain, like Portugal, never did anything about it. Because de Retez thought the people resembled the Negroes of the Guinea on Africa's west coast, he gave the island its name, Nova Guine [New Guinea]. That appelation stuck until the Indonesians, under Sukarno, named it West Irian. It is the second largest island in the world, next to Greenland.

Although the Dutch East Indies Company had been granted a trading monopoly which they exercised during the seventeenth and eighteenth centuries, New Guinea figured only vaguely in this sphere of influence. It was not until 1828 that the Dutch formally proclaimed the western portion of the island as a Netherlands possession. Dutch Protestant missionaries started work on the coast and nearby smaller islands in 1855, but a permanent government administration was only established in 1898.

Until recently many knowledgeable people confused New Guinea with Guinea in Africa or British Guiana in South America. A handful of intrepid explorers had conquered the swamps, jungle, and mountains to probe into the interior. Nature had made the island a fortress many times more formidable than Alcatraz or Devil's Island.

It wasn't until trustworthy airplanes had been developed that entrance could be made into the hidden interior. In 1938, Richard Archbold, leader of a full-scale scientific expedition, discovered the lush Baliem Valley as his aircraft was crossing Dutch New Guinea. The Archbold Expedition, sponsored by the American Museum of Natural History in New York, had two main purposes: to gather flora and fauna specimens from the north slopes of the Snow Mountains that form the spine of Dutch New Guinea, and to make the first circumnavigation of the globe by air near the line of the Equator at the world's greatest circumference.

Archbold, accompanied by top scientists from the United States, flew from San Diego June 2, 1938, in the *Guba,* a huge twin-engine Consolidated flying boat. When he arrived at a prearranged base at Hollandia, Dutch New Guinea's capital, he was joined by Netherlands scientists, Army officers and soldiers, and a labor force of convicts and Borneo Dyaks used as carriers. They swelled the number of the expeditionary force to one hundred ninety-five men —a massive army fully equipped for the advance up the rugged terrain. Archbold's men pitched their first camp on the marshy shores of the Idenburg River, thoroughly frightening thousands of crocodiles with the roar of the *Guba's* engines.

His next goal before heading out for Mt. Wilhelmina was to land his huge craft on the waters of Lake Habbema, situated at an altitude of eleven thousand feet and surrounded by threatening crags of the Snow Range. In the thin air of the highlands, it was questionable whether the flying boat could land and take off from the lake. It was on the first exploratory flight, June 21, from the Idenburg camp toward Lake Habbema that Archbold and his crew discovered what he called the "Grand Valley of the Baliem." They correctly estimated from the air that the hidden valley was about forty miles long and ten miles wide and contained a population of sixty thousand natives of Negroid origin until that time unknown to the outside world. A Dutch explorer, J. H. G. Kremer, had crossed the headwaters of the Baliem River en route to Mt. Wilhelmina in 1921, but he missed the Grand Valley by several miles.

Archbold reported years later, in the March, 1945, issue of the *National Geographic Magazine,* that as the *Guba* flew over the valley, the well-laid-out gardens criss-crossed with irrigation ditches and surrounded by stone walls looked like a scene from the farming country of central Europe.

Before long Archbold found that he could land and take off from Lake Habbema, so he established it as his main inland base. Even as the party entered the Baliem Valley on foot, some of its inhabitants greeted the first white men to enter their domain. On July 31, showing neither great fear nor amiability, two naked men, wearing distinctive yellow gourds to cover their genitals, and coarse mesh hair nets over their hairdos, gravely shook hands with the leaders of the expedition. They were followed daily by scores of others, who were fascinated with the strange giant bird that had landed in their midst.

The expedition's scientists gathered all sorts of specimens of birds, animals, and plant life. The botanists found twenty-five species of rhododendron, orchids, tree ferns, buttercups, daisies, gentians, and alpine flowers. Ornithologist collected rare species of birds of paradise, flycatchers, rock birds, pipits, and migrating snipes from Siberia. Others found rats three feet long, bandicoots, mouse opposums, and aquatic rodents that looked like small musk-rats, six species of butterflies, as well as moths, crawfish, lizards, and snails.

Later the party set up camp on the mountain slopes of the south banks of the Ibele River, and after several weeks camped on the banks of the Baliem River at the lower end of the valley in "a grove of sighing casuarina trees." For the first time in their history the tribespeople were sharing their secluded valley with strange white men who were able to fly where they wished in the bowels of a big noisy bird. The natives continued to be curious but showed no hostility to Archbold and his men. Archbold was amazed not only by the agricultural achievements of the valley dwellers but by their ingenuity in constructing rattan suspension bridges across their turbulent rivers. Twenty people could cross on them at one time. These bridges were built without the use of a nail or modern tools.

When Archbold left Hollandia to continue his successful globe-circling tour May 12, 1939, he knew that the greatest achievement of his expedition had been the finding of the Grand Valley of the Baliem River. His account of what he saw in 1938 was remarkably accurate as viewed from the vantage point of nearly a quarter century. His discovery of the populous Baliem Valley only confirmed the vision of a man unknown to him, Robert A. Jaffray, one of the great missionary pioneers of all time.

Jaffray was the son of a wealthy Canadian family. Early in his life he had come under the spell of Dr. A. B. Simpson, dynamic founder of the Christian and Missionary Alliance. Simpson had left the pastorate of a prosperous Presbyterian church in New York

City after becoming impatient with the smugness of his congregation. He forthwith launched a missionary society that within a few years was to become a world-wide organization. A tireless evangelist, Simpson was to New York what Dwight L. Moody was to Chicago. Without seeking to found another denomination, he started a missionary training school and a magazine. But his great interest was gospel outreach around the globe.

Defying the objections of his parents, Jaffray left his comfortable home and bright prospects for a successful business career. All this he gave up to enroll in Simpson's New York Bible school that had neither impressive quarters nor educational status. But it was there that the future missionary field commander learned lessons that shaped his entire life. From Simpson he absorbed the truth that the principal job of the church was to proclaim the gospel to the ends of the earth. He caught the vision of reaching primitive peoples by literally interpreting Matthew 24:14: "And this gospel of the kingdom shall be preached in all the world for a witness unto all nations: *and then shall the end come.*"

Jaffray, like Simpson, wanted to reach the forgotten lands that the main line denominations were missing. He was fired with the idea that by preaching the gospel to the very last tribes, he would hasten the establishment of Christ's kingdom on earth.

How theologians might interpret these prophetic Bible passages Jaffray cared not. His view of future events became the dominant motivating force of the missionary's life. This spiritual drive enabled him to establish strong church movements in three major mission areas.

Jaffray, described by Dr. A. W. Tozer as an "extroverted mystic," was a tall gracious man with great natural gifts of personal magnetism and leadership. He had the air of a man of the world, meeting dignitaries and government officers with relaxed ease. Assigned to China in 1897, Jaffray was soon elected chairman of the South China field. He became fluent enough in Cantonese to publish a periodical, *The Bible Magazine,* in that dialect. It became popular with missionaries and Cantonese-speaking Chinese throughout the Orient and around the world.

Under Jaffray's direction, a hardy band of Chinese preachers were soon being trained at the Wuchow Bible School. He was convinced that indigenous leadership was necessary for effective evangelization and the establishment of a vital church.

Against impossible odds he started a publishing house known as the South China Alliance Press. His struggling missionary society had only a limited amount of money, so Jaffray dug down into his own pockets for funds. Printing equipment could not be found in China. At great expense he shipped in presses from the States. Then he had to locate trained printers and compositors who could set Chinese Type. There was a short supply of suitable printing paper. But Jaffray never gave up.

Soon a torrent of gospel literature was pouring from the presses of the new publishing concern at Wuchow. The missionaries were supplied with tracts, booklets, and gospel portions to push ahead in their God-given task.

It was not long before he and his colleagues had established a chain of churches that stretched across Kwangsi Province.

But the thriving Chinese enterprise was only the beginning of Jaffray's lifework. When other men would have rested on their laurels, Jaffray had only started. In 1911, using Wuchow as his base, he launched a new missionary program in French Indo-China to the south. Through trying years that challenged Jaffray's diplomatic gifts, he surmounted a series of difficult obstacles. He nursed the young church in Indo-China through its formative days. In time a sturdy witness of Christ had been planted and others took over what he had begun.

Jaffray's twinkling blue eyes and sparkling presence concealed the fact that he was a lifelong invalid greatly handicapped in his working habits by diabetes and a serious heart ailment. But he never let anyone know. When lesser men would have retired from active service, Jaffray entered the third and final phase of his illustrious career.

After an extensive exploratory trip, he decided in 1928 that "God would have him minister to the unreached areas of the Dutch East Indies." Soon he had set up a new headquarters in

Makassar, principal city of the Celebes, and began to map out a campaign to spread the gospel throughout the vast archipelago.

Like a military commander he pored over his maps, plotting a campaign of conquest. He envisioned an army of trained young people who would reach such exotic places as Bali, Sumatra, Borneo, Java, and the Celebes. Suveying his domain that extended from Malaya to the South Pacific, he even dreamed of reaching tribes of men in the mountain vastnesses of New Guinea, far to the east of his base.

Jaffray's first major move was to start a Bible school at Makassar. Soon he was training Chinese, Malays, and even the newly converted wild men of Borneo. They had been brought to Christ in the far-ranging missionary activities of his aides. Before long natives of this island would be carrying the gospel back to their own peoples. The numbers being reached for Christ began to mount. In 1934 Jaffray reported that "no less than 4,347 souls have accepted the Lord Jesus Christ and have hurled their idols and fetishes to the bats." With MacArthurlike tactics, he directed island-hopping task forces set upon gospel conquest.

The first recorded hint of his desire to enter New Guinea is contained in a report he sent in 1933 to the head of the Alliance Foreign Department. This letter showed a map of the Dutch East Indies which then included New Guinea. Then word reached him that on December 31, 1936, a young Dutch flier, Lieutenant J. F. Wissel, had sighted a cluster of three beautiful lakes while making an aerial survey of the central highland of New Guinea for an oil company. Wissel also reported the presence of a large native population in the mountain areas adjacent to the lakes. The Dutch government promptly designated the area Wisselmerren, or Wissel Lakes.

Before the year of 1937 was over Jaffray and the Dutch government took action of different sorts. The Dutch authorities sent an overland expedition headed by Dr. W. J. Cator to inspect the new lakes area, and to establish a government post at Enarotali on Lake Paniai, largest of the three lakes. The expedition found that the newly opened region was swarming with thousands of tribesmen totally ignorant of the outside world.

Jaffray made a trip to Batavia, the capital of Java, and discussed with high colonial officials the possibility of opening up work in New Guinea. Right from the first Jaffray felt that the airplane must be employed to carry out the task properly. He had already ordered a hydroplane to be used on the rivers of Borneo.

In a letter to those in Canada and the United States who had prayed for him and supported his work, Jaffray told about the aerial photographs taken by Wissel showing the tribespeople of the interior.

"How do we reach them?" he asked. "We do not know, but we are sure that we will never find out by sitting here in Makassar. We feel an urge to go and see what can be done. These peoples are included in the 'every creature' of my commission. If men after gold and oil may go, why not the missionary seeking precious souls, even though he may have to fly to them?"

Jaffray had hoped he could undertake the survey trip to New Guinea before the end of 1937, but he did not go until early 1938. Even though he was sixty-four years old, Jaffray was no armchair general. He hopped a boat for Ambon, the administrative head-quarters for the area that included New Guinea. Briefed by Dutch officials, he proceeded to the first port in New Guinea, tiny Babo, an oil town at the extreme western tip of the Vogelkop, or Bird's Head.

Everywhere he went Jaffray found the ubiquitous Chinese shop-keepers who were always delighted to meet a Cantonese-speaking white man. Jaffray was at home with rulers and diplomats and with the humblest men who responded to his warm personality.

When he saw Borneo Dyaks laboring in the oil camp, it suddenly struck him that "wild men of Borneo," now Christian converts studying at the Makassar Bible School, would be the ideal workers for New Guinea. This idea did not work out as well as others. But later, Malay-speaking teachers and workers formed an important part of the peaceful invading forces. His vessel next put in at

Fak Fak, where he had a surprising encounter. He found himself in
the presence of Dr. Cator, the very government officer who had
made the first perilous land trek into the Wissel Lakes area. Before
Jaffray left Fak Fak, he had in his possession a great prize. It was
Cator's carefully drawn scale map of the trail from Oeta on the
south coast to the government post of Lake Paniai. This was a
priceless document showing the route into the previously uncharted
interior.

With a pocketful of notes, photographs, and every shred of information he could extract about the strange tribes of the interior,
Jaffray headed back to Makassar, his heart singing and his head
buzzing with practical plans for the penetration of New Guinea.

"It is a joy to feel that the Lord is leading us to new tribes, where
the gospel has not been preached," he jubilantly wrote the home
office in New York.

An already-planned trip to the United States fitted right in
with Jaffray's desire to lay an assault on New Guinea. He timed
his landing in San Francisco for the opening of the annual General
Council of the Christian and Missionary Alliance that was meeting
that year in Oakland. Jaffray, a capable platform man, stirred the
delegates with his plea for conquest of new tribes still unreached
and needy. Later, the Alliance home board, in New York knowing
Jaffray would get his way, okayed the plan to enter New Guinea
and promised financial aid and workers.

While he was in the United States, Jaffray fell seriously ill. For
a time it seemed that he might never get back to the Far East.
His grand scheme for reaching the people of New Guinea was in
jeopardy. But he finally recovered and by the fall of 1938 had
rushed back to Makassar. He called a meeting of his field committee to present them with his latest project. Members of the group
enthusiastically approved the plan to enter New Guinea. Like the
ancient church of Antioch which had sent forth Paul and Silas, the
missionaries at Makassar gave two of their finest workers for
the important task. The men chosen were C. Russell Deibler and
Walter M. Post.

Deibler, a brilliant young missionary from western Pennsylvania, with dark hair and flashing dark eyes, had become Jaffray's right-hand man and protégé. He had already demonstrated his abilities and gifts of leadership in performing a remarkable piece of work among the Dyak head-hunters of Borneo. The elder missionary had confided to friends that he hoped Diebler would become his successor in directing the mission.

While Deibler had been home on furlough in 1937, important events occurred which were to influence his future. During his deputation trip to churches in the United States he told about the wonderful things happening in Borneo. While in a country church, he met Darlene McIntosh, a beautiful young Iowa girl who had just completed her Bible school education.

After a whirlwind courtship, they were married. They set about immediately to plan their sea journey to the East Indies. But before they left the United States, they attended an illustrated lecture on Dutch New Guinea that fired their imaginations. This, they decided, would be the place of their future missionary work. Deibler wrote a lengthy letter to Dr. Jaffray, outlining their convictions about New Guinea.

At the same time in far-off Makassar Jaffray had written to Deibler, sounding him out about the possibility of making the initial trip into New Guinea. Their letters crossed in the mail, thus confirming both men in their belief that they were moving forward in the will of God.

Walter Post, proficient in both Malay and Dutch, had established a fine reputation for his work in the Celebes. In later years he was to serve as field chairman first in Indonesia and ultimately in New Guinea.

The Deiblers had scarcely settled themselves in Makassar when Jaffray besought his protégé to pack for the New Guinea trip. Because of the hazards of the initial journey, it was agreed that Deibler and Post would make the survey trip alone and would be joined later by their wives.

Characteristically Jaffray was delegating a job to men he felt would succeed in carrying it out. He knew that both Deibler and

Post shared his spiritual burden to reach the tribespeople of the neglected land.

It was nearing the end of 1938 when Deibler and Post sailed from Makassar for New Guinea. En route they stocked up with supplies at Ambon before continuing their journey in a government steamer. They reached the tiny town of Oeta two days before Christmas. Post returned by steamer to Ambon when the missionaries learned that there were not enough carriers available to accompany both of them into the interior. Deibler decided he would go it alone.

After a dull Christmas Day in Oeta, Deibler and his ten carriers boarded a government motor boat that took them four hours up the Oeta River. Darkness forced the boat to drop anchor for the night. By the afternoon of the following day the boat had reached a point where the shallowness of the river prohibited further travel. Deibler's things were transferred to canoes and taken ashore. But he chose to spend the night in the boat, feeling that the river breeze would help in the nightlong battle with swarms of mosquitoes. The following two days Deibler and his men headed upstream in a large canoe. The Papuans had little skill with the paddles, and on one occasion the missionary was forced to leap overboard fully dressed to save the canoe from capsizing with its precious cargo of provisions. After two days of paddling, they reached Camp Orawaja, the government base for supplies to the Wissel Lakes. The river was no longer navigable, so the journey up the mountains would be on foot. They spent two days preparing for the overland trip.

Deibler's carriers, now reduced to seven by illness, started off shouldering their loads in fourteen five-gallon oil tins. Nine of the tins held food for the carriers, the other five, Deibler's supplies. The carriers, it turned out, would eat two-thirds of their load!

How the missionary needed his New Year's Scripture portion, the Lord's exhortation to Joshua: "Be strong and of a good courage; be not afraid, neither be thou dismayed: for the Lord thy God is with thee whithersoever thou goest."

Arising at dawn on New Year's Day, Deibler and his men climbed a rugged trail that grew steeper and steeper. And for the entire first day on the trail they were pelted with a drenching rain.

"The second day was the most difficult I have ever experienced," Deibler told his friends later. "We climbed two mountains the like of which I have never seen. At times it was almost a perpendicular climb. Often we had to resort to the use of a crude ladder. Sharp stones cut one's shoes to shreds. There were boulders which, if set in motion, would destroy everything in their path. I shuddered as I peered down some of the precipices. About 11:00 A.M. the rain came down in torrents and continued throughout the afternoon. A number of carriers had to be helped into camp and one was injured when he fell under his load.

"The following morning, while preparing to leave camp, I learned that my carriers were conspiring to desert me in the jungle and return home. I could not blame them for their mutinous spirit, but abandonment here meant death. After much persuasion, they promised to travel another day, provided they could leave half the luggage behind. That made traveling easier for them the next day and they finally agreed to accompany me to the end of the trail.

"We decided to halt the next day for a rest while three of the carriers returned to bring forward the provisions left at the last camp. In the ensuing days we traveled through sparsely inhabited areas, walking some of the time through sweet potato gardens. The local natives came into camp at night to barter sweet potatoes for anything we had to offer. The altitude gradually became higher and the cold increased, adding to our discomfort. The carriers were so chilled, they cried. Now the sharp, stony path developed into a veritable mud hole and most of the time we were wading in mud to our knees."

On the eighteenth day of the strenuous trek, the Deibler party reached the last overland camp on the banks of the Oeta. They loaded their gear into two outrigger canoes and began the three-hour paddle upstream to Lake Paniai. Reaching the lake, they found it too rough to cross. They waited for six hours. At nine o'clock that night the wind died down and they started to paddle across the lake in the darkness. The lead canoe, containing all

Deibler's clothing and bedding, struck a rock and sank. Splashing around in the water, Deibler and those with him finally were pulled into the other boat. They continued on in the second canoe, paddling and bailing out water to keep afloat. It was near midnight on January 13 when they reached the government camp at Enarotali and disembarked. They fell into bed exhausted.

There was not much at Enarotali except the lonely temporary government post. There were a few wretched native huts made of wooden slabs and thatched roofs, but there was not much else. Yet the scenery was glorious. The site of the future missionary station was on a sloping hill looking out across Paniai. Surrounding the lake were the high mountains of western Dutch New Guinea which no white man had yet explored.

Lake Paniai, about fifteen miles long and twelve miles wide, was a strange body of water without fish. Its olive-green depths produced only one marine delicacy, fresh-water shrimp. Native women could be seen fishing for them with nets from crude boats made of big logs. At night the fisherwomen built fires in the bottom of their boats to keep warm. The lights of the fires made a romantic night picture.

But now in the bright sunshine, Russell Deibler looked across the lake and enjoyed the view. He had already met a few of the Kaupaukus, the shy tribe of short, slightly built natives which would be first to respond to the gospel in New Guinea. He studied them curiously and later described them thus:

"They greatly resemble the African with their brown skin, broad nose, and kinky hair. They are clothesless, dirty, well-built and seemingly healthy. Through a hole in the nasal septum they frequently wear huge white pig tusks. Their diet consists of sweet potatoes that, lacking cooking vessels, they roast in the coals of an open fire. . . . They are a most backward people, living still in the Stone Age."

"Upon meeting a friend, a Kapauku places his index finger between the index and middle fingers of the other person. They simultaneously pull their hands apart, which produces a snap. The louder the noise and the more often repeated, the more certain the signs of friendship. It is an interesting practice but decidedly irritating to the finger joints."

The missionary was surprised to learn that the Kapaukus "rolled their own," making cigarettes out of local tobacco which was enveloped in a dried jungle leaf about six inches long. He was amused by the Kapauku custom of carrying a spare cigarette in a hole of the earlobe.

"With a single cowrie shell, they can buy a half bushel of sweet potatoes," he said, "and with forty, a pig, or a wife—they seem to be of like value."

For years, Deibler mused, other East Indies tribes had called him a "white" man. The Kapaukus called him a "red" man, why he did not know.

Deibler, the first missionary to enter the interior of Dutch New Guinea, had made some friendly contacts with the Kapaukus. In the short time spent with them, he had picked up a few phrases of their language, but it would be a long while before he could speak fluently. It would be longer still before the Kapaukus would hear and respond to the gospel. But they would be the key tribe to New Guinea. The missionary base established among them would one day have great implications.

The young missionary had begun a movement in the Wissel Lakes that would spread through the remote valleys and mountains of the central highlands of New Guinea. One day it would reach far to the east into the Baliem Valley.

Now Deibler's survey trip was completed. He managed to obtain a ride on a government airplane to a port on the north coast. From there he returned by boat to Makassar to make a full report of his discoveries. Jaffray, the man who had conceived the idea of penetrating New Guinea, would be his most eager listener.

In March, Deibler teamed up with Post again. They were accompanied by three Malay-speaking Indonesians and twenty Dyaks, and headed again for New Guinea to set up the first mission station at Enarotali. The party disembarked at Oeta and soon were tramp-

ing inland on the difficult sixty-mile trip to Enarotali, bearing supplies for a six-month stay. When they arrived at their destination,
housing became the first order of business.

"Seldom is missionary work begun in a place where some sort
of house or shelter is not available," Deibler reported. 'Upon our
arrival, we couldn't find any sort of shelter and camping outdoors
at 6,750 feet is not pleasant. The government expedition allowed
us a berth in their temporary camp, and with a few Dyaks, we
began the construction of the first house in this area." The framework was made of saplings, the walls of bamboo, and the roof
of tree bark. Isingglass served as windowpanes to keep out the bit-
ing chill.

Next the Dyaks set to work on hewing out a canoe that was
urgently needed for transportation on Lake Paniai and the rivers
feeding into it. Because of the hearty appetites of the carriers, it
was difficult to lay in a sufficient reserve stock of food.

Writing to friends in August, he bewailed the fact that in the year
they had been on the field, he and his wife, Darlene, had been separated a total of seven months. "I have missed her greatly," he said,
"but we have done it gladly for Him and the gospel's sake." He
did not know then that he would not see his wife for almost another
six months!

Deibler had learned from the Kapaukus living about them that
deeper in the interior were other thousands of natives still unreached. This news he must have forwarded to his mentor in
Makassar, for Jaffray first mentioned the tribes of the inland areas
by name in a letter to Dr. A. C. Snead, Alliance foreign secretary,
in 1939; "There are the Monis, Danis, Uhundunis, and the vast and
populous Baliem Valley all of whom have never yet heard."

Deibler and Post finally sent word for their wives to join them.
They had hoped that the women could come directly to Enarotali
by airplane, but this proved impossible. Instead, they arrived at
Oeta on the government steamer *Albatros* February 10, 1940.
Walter Post reported: "It was not without some misgivings that I
contemplated taking Viola up that treacherous mountain path.
Wading through mud and mire, then picking one's way over

sharp limestone rocks, again climbing over large slippery boulders, or making a steep ascent up the mountain is no lady's job, believe me. It was not encouraging either to meet a returning road engineer in Oeta who had been assigned the task of ascertaining the cost of making a road to the Wissel Lakes, but had come back to Oeta after the first day. He said the trail was too difficult for him."

Before the trek got under way, Viola Post came down with an attack of the "five-day" fever. Just as she recovered, her husband contracted it. "The fever did not prevent our going up the river, though, and by the time we were ready for the trail, we were both okay again," he wrote.

The women proved equal to the grueling climb and made the trip in eight days! But the journey was not without incident. Traveling through rain for several hours the first day, they stopped to make camp in the midst of a tropical downpour. Soaked to the skin, they sought to construct a makeshift tent with a large piece of canvas. When they had set up their beds, the canvas began to leak and their bedding and clothing were drenched. The next day it continued to pour until midnight, and it was only then that they managed to get a little sleep. Fortunately, the next six days on the trail were pleasant and the ladies stood up to the assignment of crossing the fourteen mountain ranges between them and the lakes. The first two white women had reached central New Guinea.

The Kapaukus celebrated by serenading the women with yodeling and yelling, and then presented the newcomers with a pig. More than a hundred men and women milled about the yard of the new missionary station in their crude but genuine exhibition of welcome.

With their wives by their side, Deibler and Post pushed forward in their missionary program. Something like one thousand Kapaukus were listening eagerly to the gospel. But their time of service was to be brief, for Holland had fallen to the enemy in Europe and the Japanese war was spreading to the islands of southeast Asia. Then the Dutch government suddenly announced that it was closing

its post at Enarotali, and worse, it was discontinuing steamer service to the coast. The Deiblers left in September, 1940, returning
to Makassar to work in the Bible school even though the Japanese
troops did not arrive in New Guinea for another three years. Not
knowing when the enemy would come, Mrs. Post left for Australia
in 1941. It was a dark hour for the fledgling missionary endeavor
in New Guinea.

Then on the very day that the Japanese attacked Pearl Harbor,
Einar Mickelson, who had been serving in the East Indies, arrived
to join Walter Post and strengthen the beachhead at Enarotali. The
two stalwarts not only buoyed up the work among the Kapaukus,
but indefatigable Mickelson employed the hours of approaching
defeat by establishing a work among the Moni people in the Kemandora Valley—three days east of Enarotali. As the situation grew
more and more precarious, Post and Mickelson decided it was
foolhardy to remain in New Guinea any longer. They evacuated
their station at Enarotali just two days before the Japanese entered
the settlement. A band of sixteen Christian Kapaukus tearfully said
good-by to the departing missionaries.

When the Japanese troops swarmed into the Dutch East Indies,
they did not bother the missionaries at first. Then they killed F. C.
Jackson, an Alliance missionary pilot who had given aid to the
Dutch forces in Borneo. The reign of terror had begun. In short
order six Alliance missionaries were slain by the enemy soldiers.

The entire Makassar mission staff, including Dr. Jaffray and his
wife and the Deiblers, was moved to Benteng Tinggi, a health resort
a few miles away in the hills. There they remained unmolested until
March 13, 1942, when the Japanese arrested the men and interned
them in a police barracks in Makassar. The women were placed
under what might be called house arrest at the health resort, and,
for an unexplained reason, an exception was made to permit the
white-haired Jaffray to remain with the women for a year. Deibler,
sent later to the filthy, crowded concentration camp at Pare-Pare,
had to withstand Japanese brutality, rotten food, and the pain
of separation from the ones he loved. Disease broke out—malaria,

dysentery, beriberi, and hydrophobia. Russell Deibler fell mortally ill and joined his Maker on August 28, 1942.

Darlene, only three hours away by car, did not learn of his death until two months later when a Roman Catholic priest smuggled the news to her.

"The first night I thought I'd go crazy with grief, but God—how precious He has been to me," she wrote to her parents. "The heartache is still there but the terrible hurt has left me. Hardly a man from that camp where Russell was confined fails to tell me what a man of God he was—so kind and how much he was loved by all. I guess his lifework was finished and I know that his is the greater joy. Someday I shall see him again with my Saviour who has healed my broken heart."

During their imprisonment at Benteng Tinggi, Darlene had many hours with Dr. Jaffray, who spent his time writing or poring over his maps. She later recalled the unbowed faith of the old warrior:

"I remember again an afternoon in 1942 when I saw an old man dreaming dreams. Sitting in the corner of a little house in which we were imprisoned, Dr. Jaffray was intent in the study of a map of that great sweep of islands then known as the Netherlands East Indies. How often we've pored over that map and mentally checked off the cities and islands as they were invaded and fell . . . Singapore, Sumatra, Java, and Celebes. 'These, lassie,' he said as I knelt beside the chair, 'are the areas we must enter as soon as the war is over.'

"My thoughts were so full of the fears and anxieties, separations and tales of atrocities that had become such a part of our daily life. Suddenly I realized that to him they were but passing events that never altered the program of reaching the unreached, events that never marred the dream! His fingers traced a path through the Natuna and Anambas groups of islands, encircled central and southern Sumatra, passed over the haunts of the nomadic Punans in the hinterland of Borneo, caressed Bali with a prophecy that God would again reopen that door to the gospel, then moved on to Misool, the Isle of Demons, the Bird's Head of New Guinea, the Swart and Memberamo River Valleys, and at last coming to rest

over the Baliem Valley. 'This is our task and I can hear the sound
of a going in the tops of the mulberry trees, the noise of the marching feet of the mighty army of young men and women that God
is preparing for the occupation of these areas!' "

The band of prisoners kept alive on food smuggled to them by
three faithful natives, but for a period of six months the Japanese
never came near their place. Marauding native bandits took advantage of the situation. Darlene Deibler encountered one in the
hall at two o'clock one morning. "He proved to be a bigger coward
than I," she said, "for he ran. The bandits had cut away part
of the door with their long knives and had spent several hours in
the house, by the appearance of the place. After that we slept with
clubs and whistles under our pillows."

But the relative peace of Benteng Tinggi came to an end when
the Japanese moved the occupants five miles across the valley to a
prison camp at Molino. Five months later the women were transferred to Kampili, a huge camp thirty miles from Makassar, along
with sixteen hundred and fifteen other women. Dr. Jaffray and another Alliance missionary, W. E. Presswood, were sent north to
the mountain camp at Pare-Pare where Russell Deibler had died.
Allied airplanes subjected the camp to a fearful bombing in which
many were killed. Jaffray escaped death but Pare-Pare had been
destroyed. The prisoners were then herded deeper into the mountains and locked in buildings built for pigs. Presswood told about
the awful days:

"Shortly after our arrival there, dysentery broke out, and in the
next three months more than two-thirds of the six hundred men
took sick with this disease. Of this number over twenty-five died.
Food was short, sanitary conditions were beyond description. In
the midst of the dysentery epidemic we had constant air-raid
alarms. American planes flew over and around the camp daily,
bombing and machine-gunning the neighborhood. It was the rainy
season and the tropical downpour converted the small creek into
a mighty raging torrent during the night.

"Our camp life up to this time had been characterized by periods
of terrorism by the guards, when men were beaten senseless for the

least offense, revived by a pail of water, and then beaten again."

Once more the men were moved to a place Presswood described as worse than anything they yet had experienced. "Here our food consisted of a half pound of rice per day, with nothing to eat along with it. This proved too much for Dr. Jaffray. He weakened rapidly, like everyone else, but because of his age he could not hold out long."

Dr. Jaffray died on his filthy prison cot July 29, 1945, ironically enough two weeks before hostilities ceased and the prisoners were freed.

"One day it will all be finished," he had written in his 1941 report to the Alliance offices in New York, "and the weary feet, all scarred, bleeding and sore, will cross the last mountain and tread the last trail, reach the last tribe and win the last soul. Then He Himself will exclaim, 'Well done, good and faithful servant! How beautiful the feet that have brought good tidings and proclaimed salvation to perishing souls.' Then indeed it will be true that our Christ reigns over all the world, over every nation. Every knee shall bow and every tongue shall confess Him."

Jaffray concluded his report with a final exhortation to his fellow workers and a paean of praise: "Let us keep our eyes steadily upon the goal. . . . For when we hear the shout from the skies, all else will fade into utter insignificance. For the Lord shall descend—from heaven with a shout. Even so, come Lord Jesus."

Darlene Deibler was chosen by her Japanese captors as a leader of a huge bamboo shed at Kampili containing one hundred people of various nationalities. With her natural linguistic ability she had learned by this time to speak fairly fluently in Dutch and Malay and haltingly in Japanese, so she frequently acted as interpreter for the Japanese officials of the camp.

Then suddenly the Japanese secret police arrested her and threw her into the common prison at Makassar. She was accused of spying and going into the woods to contact the Allies on a hidden radio. Another woman missionary was beaten in an effort to gain evidence that Darlene was a spy. Next Darlene was placed in solitary confinement in a cell with no window. A small transom over

the door was her only source of light and air. She contracted
dysentery, tropical malaria, and beriberi, all at the same time. For
six weeks she was forced to exist on salt-free rice porridge. Failing
to obtain a confession, they threatened to behead her, then suddenly released her and sent her back to Kampili.

For a while she was restored to her position of shed leader, but
the fear that she might again fall into the hands of the secret police
preyed on her spirit. She felt her mind would snap. It was about this
time that Jaffray's daughter, Margaret—always the apple of his
eye—suffered a mental breakdown along with another woman
missionary in the camp.

"Never once, during those years of internment," Darlene wrote
home later, "did we have any contact with the outside world; no
news—good or bad; no Red Cross help."

The camp was pummeled again and again by Allied bombers.
When the alarm sounded, the prisoners had to leave the barracks
and head for the ditches until the all-clear sounded. For three
months bombs fell each day and each night. During the same period
a plague of mad dogs broke out and several prisoners were bitten
and died of rabies.

But more terror was to pour from the skies. There came a day
when five thousand incendiary bombs were showered on the camp
that covered a couple of acres. Everything went up in smoke, including the few remaining possessions. Fleeing to a bamboo grove,
the prisoners were forced at bayonet point to lie upon the ground
while the soldiers machine-gunned the airplanes.

The final days of imprisonment were spent in a camp a half mile
distant. Darlene had to crowd one hundred and sixteen people
into two rooms of a native hut thirty feet long and twelve feet
wide. After another month of bombings and an epidemic of
disease, peace came. Shaken by the horror of her experiences and
ill in mind and body, the young widow, her hair turned prematurely
gray, finally reached Seattle late in October. Tears of joy and sorrow
flowed freely as she rejoined her parents in Oakland, California.

From all appearances Darlene Deibler's usefulness was now
ended. Jaffray had died along with his courageous young lieuten-

ant—the man in whom he had placed his hopes for spiritual conquest. At such a moment the profane might ask: Did God mock these men with vision and hopes of winning lost tribes? A decade and more years would pass before the question would be answered gloriously in the negative. Throngs of the tribesmen for whom the two men had prayed would one day cast away their heathenish objects of worship and sing praise to the Lord of the universe, their Redeemer.

Darlene Deibler would yet be an important link in the work. Her years of suffering would prepare her for future witness. She would again experience days of fruitful, joyous service in New Guinea.

3

PRELUDE TO CONQUEST

As the Far Eastern phase of World War II developed, New Guinea —both Dutch and Australian segments—suffered along with the rest of the island world. The Japanese succeeded in gaining control of the northern and western parts of Dutch New Guinea, but the south coast communities remained free.

In 1944, General Douglas MacArthur battered his way into Hollandia, and set up his headquarters on nearby Lake Sentani. Soon the area around Hollandia was swarming with thousands of U.S. troops.

Earlier in his leapfrog campaign up the eastern New Guinea coast, MacArthur's chief aerial route for supplies lay over the Stanley Owen Range on the Australian side of the craggy island. When Hollandia was selected for his main base, it became imperative that a shorter air route be found between Dutch New Guinea and the supply base in Australia. Also, he wanted landing fields in the interior to use against the Japanese. With characteristic American drive, extensive aerial surveys were conducted over the hitherto uncharted terrain of the central highlands.

Probing back and forth through the towering peaks of the Oranje

Mountains, Major Myron J. Grimes of the Army Air Forces "re-discovered" the Grand Valley of the Baliem that had been forgotten in the eventful years since Archbold had found it. War correspondents George Lait and Harry E. Patterson promptly dubbed the hidden valley "Shangri-La" and the name added extra glamour and mystery. It became the subject of conversation first among air crews, then among the officers, GIs, and WACs who worked at headquarters. Because of the mounting curiosity the Army arranged for regular "indoctrination" flights in the big C-47s for military personnel on leave days.

It was such a flight on May 13, 1945, that crashed in the pass of the Oranje Mountains, causing the death of twenty-one soldiers and WACs. Again the Baliem Valley was back in the world's headlines. Public interest surged when it was reported that WAC Corporal Margaret Hastings, Lieutenant John S. McCollum, and Sergeant Kenneth Decker had survived the accident and were wandering around in the rugged mountains not far from the Baliem Valley. The Army parachuted medical corpsmen to treat the injuries of the trio, and made drops of food and clothing. It was decided that the only hope of rescuing the survivors was to send a glider into the valley and to use a towplane to launch it. A regular airplane had no place to land.

First, paratroopers led the party of three over the rough mountains to the valley where other paratroopers had prepared an airstrip from which the glider would be launched. It was an ingenious, risky, and very costly rescue, but it was successful. They finally reached Hollandia safely after spending seventeen days in the interior.

The story of New Guinea's "Shangri-La" and its Stone Age inhabitants stirred the imaginations of adventure-hungry magazine readers in the United States, but it only intensified the desire of missionaries to reach the tribe with the gospel. In the New York offices of the Christian and Missionary Alliance, Einar Mickelson and others from the East Indies field met with their denominational leaders and mapped out plans to re-enter New Guinea and re-establish their mission work. In the ponderous words of the minutes of that meeting dated December 5-6, 1945: "We approve the plan . . . to the effect that we count as our area of responsibility in New Guinea the Wissel Lakes region, the Kemandora Valley region, and the Dugandoga and Baliem Valley regions, thus reaching the Kapauku, the Moni, the Dani, and the Uhunduni tribes." The eager desire to reach the Baliem and the tribes of Dutch New Guinea had not been lost.

Mickelson returned to Makassar where he enlisted carriers, then proceeded to New Guinea. He arrived at the Wissel Lakes two full years before the government post was re-established at Enarotali. He had taken the precaution of including a battery-powered radio in his equipment, but during the air flight the battery was tipped over and the radio was rendered useless. This was to mean that for eight long months he would be entirely cut off from communication with the outside world. But he resignedly set about rebuilding the mission station that the Japanese had destroyed in their retreat. With help from friendly Kapaukus, he soon constructed a livable two-room bamboo house.

Mickelson had not been at Enarotali long before he learned from his Dyak workers, who had attended a local pig feast, that a band of Kapaukus were planning to attack the mission station and murder him and his whole party. With their distorted view of the world, the Kapaukus were convinced that Mickelson had been responsible for the Japanese invasion of their domain. This was no idle threat, he knew, for during the occupation, they had killed forty Japanese soldiers.

Looking out of his house, Mickelson saw that it was surrounded by scowling Kapaukus armed with spears and bows and arrows. He spent the night on his knees, praying that God would deliver him from the threatening mob. By dawn he found that the war party had slipped away during the night. There seemed to be no human explanation for this development, but Mickelson believed it was divine deliverance. In the ensuing years his life was similarly threatened on eight different occasions.

At the end of six months Mickelson's supplies of salt and other necessities were nearly depleted. With five carriers, he set out on the long trail to Oeta. Two of the Kapaukus bearing provisions for the trip deserted at the end of the first day. They apparently were afraid to continue over the long unused trail. Rumors then fed back to Enarotali that the entire party had been killed.

"It was not difficult to follow the old trail in the mountains," Mickelson wrote, "but when we began descending to lower altitudes, the path became less and less evident. As we neared the former base camp we found the trail had returned to the jungle. Through this dense growth we had to hack our way against many handicaps. It was seven-fifteen that night when we finally reached Orawaja. After our temporary shelter was completed, a tropical deluge of rain fell. We were glad that the trail was behind us."

The next day Mickelson and his three carriers built a raft on which they expected to float downstream to Oeta in two days.

"Thirty-five minutes after leaving Orawaja," Mickelson recorded, "our raft crashed into a partially submerged tree, and we were all swept into the flooded stream. Three of us, two Kapaukus and I, managed to grasp a branch of the tree, while the remaining two swam and reached what remained of the raft and supplies."

Mickelson helped one of the Kapaukus to a safe place on a limb, then looked for the second man, middle-aged Adama. Bubbles on the water helped Mickelson locate the native who was gamely still holding on to a tree limb though he was completely submerged. The missionary pulled him to safety.

"We were perched on the limbs of a large tree that had fallen into the water," said Mickelson, "but its roots still held fast to the shore, a hundred feet away. The trunk of the tree was submerged. . . . Though it may not have been impossible for two of us to reach shore by swimming, we knew the place was infested with crocodiles, and we didn't want to leave one native behind. We counted fifteen crocodile nests during our wanderings the following three days."

Adama suffered a deep gash on his leg that laid it bare to the bone. Mickelson was deeply touched as he bound up the man's wound. "I realized that this native not only was almost drowned but had suffered this severe injury because of me.

"For three days we wandered in the jungle headed for the coast.

We lived on tender shoots of palm trees and whatever else that we could find that was edible. The day before reaching safety, four of us fell sick. Our stomachs rebelled against the wild figs, berries, and fish we had been eating. We just lay in the mud too ill to move."

Finally the men gained enough strength to make another raft, and arrived at the coast the same day. It took another two days to reach Kokanao, administrative headquarters for the area, several miles to the east. There they bought rice, salt, and soap, but were unable to obtain badly needed clothing. The local official arranged for seventeen coastal carriers to assist Mickelson on the return journey. They traveled day after day through tropical rains until both men and supplies were completely soaked. It took most of one night for them to dry their clothing and foodstuff containers at the campfire. At dawn the next day, the party from the interior awoke to find that all their carriers had forsaken them. "Here we were in the heart of no man's land, without carriers," Mickelson said.

They spent two days constructing a shelter to store the supplies, but already the rice had begun to spoil. Again and again the men stumbled and fell on the slippery trail. Then on the second day Mickelson fell sprawling, ripping a gash across his nose. Lacking proper medical supplies, he calmly sat down and sewed up the wound with a needle and thread, then continued on his way.

Next day, the haggard company dragged into Enarotali, whispering prayers of thanksgiving.

By the spring of 1947 Mickelson had baptized his first Kapauku convert and was instructing a number of young men who would be the first students in the rudimentary Bible School. At the end of that year he was able to report that seventeen believers had been baptized, the nucleus of the first native church in the interior of Dutch New Guinea.

The work in the Wissel Lakes country was now well under way, but Mickelson still longed to reach the Baliem. Six years earlier he had made a difficult trek, in the company of a government official, Dr. J. V. DeBruijn, deep into the western interior, reaching the headwaters of the Ilaga River. By then most of the missionaries agreed that the only practicable way to get into the Baliem was by some kind of aircraft—probably an amphibian plane. Yet, lacking one, Mickelson and others thought it might be possible to reach the coveted valley by walking the mountain trails. Subsequent experiences showed the fallacy of this wishful thinking, but the dream of entering Cannibal Valley would not die.

Back in the United States a train of events was shaping up that would speed that happy day.

It began in 1941 in the library of Bob Jones College in Cleveland, Tennessee, where Gerald Rose, a husky student, was reading a copy of the *National Geographic Magazine* telling about Archbold's discovery of the Grand Valley.

"I had been under the impression for a long time," Jerry recalls, "that God wanted me to be a missionary but I couldn't settle on any field."

He had read scores of books about mission work around the world and was well acquainted with the biographies of great missionaries. But up to that time he felt he had received no divine guidance as to his future work overseas.

"That day in the library," Rose declares, "made an indelible impression on my heart. It was almost as though God spoke in an audible voice. These were the people and this was the place where I should serve!"

Eventually, he enrolled at Eastern Baptist Seminary in Philadelphia after hearing that a mission society, the Association of Baptists for World Evangelism, had been discussing Dutch New Guinea as a field. In due time he was accepted as a missionary candidate. While he continued his seminary studies, he went around to churches, showing a film that pictured the Alliance work in New Guinea. Included in one scene was a picture of Russell Deibler.

Frequently after a showing of the film, people would ask the seminary student, "Do you know Darlene Deibler?" This happened many times, for the young widow was a capable speaker in her own right and Christians from coast to coast had been stirred by her graphic accounts of three and a half years in a Japanese prison camp.

Jerry Rose estimates that he was asked the same question at least two hundred times, to which he was repetitiously forced to reply in the negative. Whereupon the usual comment was, "Well, you ought to know her."

The thought that he should be married before going to the mission field had often crossed Jerry's mind, but he began to wonder if now "the Lord was trying to show me something."

His travels took him to Detroit where he was employed for a time by an active Christian layman, a member of the Central Alliance Church. Darlene Deibler had been speaking in the area, but by the time Jerry learned about it from his employer, she had left for the West Coast. By now he had decided to throw caution to the winds and find out for himself what Darlene Deibler was like. Without further consultation, he flew to Seattle, only to learn that his quarry had just left for her parents' home in Oakland, California. Jerry followed.

When he reached the house in which Darlene Deibler and her family were living, he found no one at home. Jerry sat down on the front steps to wait.

The attractive young widow was not lacking in suitors, but she had put thoughts of marriage from her mind. Why she was willing to go out to dinner that night with a strange young man from the East, she cannot explain to this day. On their very first date, Jerry asked her to marry him. Bowled over by his candor and his complete assurance that this was God's will for them, she gave a sort of stunned consent. Later, when she tried to back out of the agreement, Jerry pleaded his cause for an hour in a long distance telephone call from the Midwest. This time his unorthodox courting won the day. They were married in Oakland April 4, 1948.

The Baptists had not received permission to enter New Guinea, so an arrangement was made whereby Jerry Rose was "loaned" to the Alliance work. Delayed for months by shipping strikes, the Roses finally sailed for the mission field early in 1949. They arrived at Biak, New Guinea's principal airport, and were able to board a Catalina flying boat bound for the Wissel Lakes.

Also aboard were Mr. and Mrs. Mickelson and their daughter,

Cynthia. Darlene Rose could not help but contrast this entry into the Wissel Lakes area with the rugged trek nine years before.

"Promptly at six o'clock yesterday morning," she wrote her friends at home, "the Catalina left the airport and turned its nose toward interior New Guinea. Fascinated, we watched the rivers, weary with their wanderings through the marshy lowlands, and then the majestic mountains loomed up in front of us. With what ease we rose above them and left the ranges one by one behind! It was not now a matter of footwork as it had been in 1940. The two men were up front with the plane crew. Mrs. Mickelson, Cynthia, four geese, and I occupied the blister. It was a wonderful place to sit, if you wanted to see where you were. Then suddenly I saw a familiar sight, the sun shimmering on Lake Paniai! At 7:45 A.M. the plane dropped onto its cool surface for a perfect landing. That which formerly meant days on an ill-defined trail, many hardships, and few supplies was accomplished in an hour and three-quarters in the air, and we had supplies to last us for many months."

The strange cycle of events had now made a full turn for Darlene. She was back in New Guinea ready to "do exploits for God."

It was not long before Jerry and Darlene Rose were busy learning the Kapauku language. In due time Darlene was proficient enough to teach school. Jerry's life was filled with treks into the interior, construction work, and finding ways to improve the local agriculture and to introduce farm animals that would provide the Kapaukus with better diets and a means of livelihood.

Darlene described a trip from Biak to the Wissel Lakes with one of the first loads of cattle that were flown into the area:

"A tinge of rose in the east heralded dawn's approach as we stepped from the jeep at Biak airport. Men were already crawling over the great body of the Catalina, making preparations for the flight to the Wissel Lakes. Jeeps seemed to arrive from all directions. To see the Roses off? Well, not exactly.

"Gus and Gertie, our two Hereford calves, and a Balinese heifer, yet without name, were the center of attraction. With no difficulty they were lifted into the tail of the plane and stood on the plywood platform that had been made for them. No ropes bound them, no sedatives were given. Through the warm-up, take-off, and flight, they hardly moved. The heifer thought this was just too unusual an experience to take standing up so she settled down on her haunches for the last ten minutes of the flight. After unloading the plane at Lake Paniai, the calves were flown to Lake Tigi. Now they are knee deep in grassland and fat as butter balls."

Exploratory trips into the uncharted trails of the interior were often grim adventures, but necessary evils, in the early days of the New Guinea operation. It took courage, great physical strength and stamina, and above all, a confidence that they were walking "in the shadow of the Almighty."

Jerry Rose was introduced to the trail two weeks after he arrived at Enarotali. A government expedition was about to leave for the Kemandora Valley and Rose and Kenneth Troutman, leader of the Wissel Lakes station, were permitted to join it. The party left Enarotali in boats, traveling a full day before they reached their first camping spot.

Four days more of hiking brought them to the Kemandora, the area in which Mickelson had opened work among the Moni tribe in 1942. The government expedition had its own interests, but Troutman and Rose were looking for a strategic center where they could establish a station and revive the Moni effort. The Kemandora, more fertile than the Wissel Lakes region, offered an abundant supply of food, an important factor since it would not be feasible to be supplied at that distance by carriers.

Homejo, the spot chosen for the new station, was located near salt wells that attracted trading parties of natives from deep in the interior. Relatively speaking, Homejo was just a step toward the eastern goals of the missionaries, but it was a step. Troutman, who would soon move with his family to Homejo, now headed back with Rose to Enarotali, having accomplished their mission.

In the summer and fall of 1950, Einar Mickelson pushed the frontier eastward even farther. Having met a group of Uhunduni tribesmen who had come to trade in the Kemandora in 1942, Mickelson had filed away the names of villages they had given him. Now he planned to visit them.

He made one trip with a Dutch agricultural expert, accompanied by carriers who bore provisions for a month's trek. But the journey was more rigorous than Mickelson estimated, and the month's food supply had to be stretched to keep them fed for forty days. But they did make some friendly contacts with Uhunduni villages. Later these thrusts into the interior would pay off.

Glistening snow-capped peaks, some of them over fifteen thousand feet, beckoned them on to become the first party to cross the mighty Nassau Range from north to south. But it was a perilous trip. Mickelson described it to friends.

"We traveled over possibly the worst trails I have seen, sometimes creeping along walls of gorges on stone ledges made slippery by moss and water spray. One night darkness had overtaken us before we had reached our destination. We were making our way along a gorge by feeling with our hands for the trail. Below us was a large mountain torrent filled with boulders. As we came to one dangerous section, I removed my shoes and inched my way over a slippery ledge aided by the light of a flickering torch which a native held for me."

Their shoes almost worn from their feet, their stomachs empty, and their bodies aching with fatigue, Mickelson and his companion reached home in safety.

Undaunted, Mickelson headed eastward again a month later, this time reaching the Ilaga River, some seven days from the Baliem. The privation and peril of this exploratory trek proved to be an even greater test of Mickelson's Viking character.

One night he made camp near a small Dani settlement nestled at the foot of a high mountain. A crowd of Danis came to escort him to their village. Mickelson sensed, though, that he was being led into a trap. The crafty natives offered him and Zaccheus Pakari, his Kapauku companion, two women for the night, in accordance with Dani custom.

In the singsong ceremony that follows, the men sit opposite the girls, chanting songs, swaying their bodies, and after a time gifts are exchanged. Then the man presents the girl with a yam on which a magic potion has been poured. Acceptance of the yam means the girl will be his partner for the night.

When Mickelson refused this form of hospitality, it became

more evident that the Danis had planned it to lure him from his camp so they could steal his provisions. He refused to leave his quarters. In the flickering rays of his camp light Mickelson could see more than a score of natives moving toward his tent. He was able to comprehend one ominous remark: "We will wait until he sleeps, then we will take his things." They came closer, but Mickelson sat up on his cot and began to write in his journal. The crowd continued to mill about his tent.

"Let's pray," the missionary shouted to Zaccheus. And forthwith Mickelson began to pray aloud as the baffled Danis stepped back. As the two men continued to pray, the group of natives began to break up. Finally only three men remained. They thought Mickelson had fallen asleep, when to their surprise he shouted at them in Moni, ordering them to get out. Whether the Danis understood another language, he did not know. But to his relief they left him for the night.

As he lay back on his cot, Mickelson could hear the sound of a singsong coming from the native village. He could tell by their voices that some of his carriers had yielded to temptation. Reviewing the experiences of the day, he decided that he would turn back. The trek to the Baliem Valley would have to come later.

The Danis had thought the party would continue through the uninhabited jungle to the east. Apparently, they had decided to set up an ambush when camp was made for the night. As the party started to ascend the narrow trail, the Danis showed their anger. One of them disgustedly hurled a sharpened tent pole after the departing group, missing Zaccheus by inches.

Commenting on the harrowing experience later, Mickelson said, "I was most afraid the Danis would steal my hiking shoes. This would have been a sentence of death, for no white man could make it back to civilization over that long, hard trail without shoes."

Einar Mickelson, pre-eminently a pioneer missionary with concerns for the spiritual welfare of primitive tribespeople, held a wide view of the missionary enterprise. His statesmanlike relations had won him the respect of the governing Dutch officials. Mickelson, along with Walter Post, had served as adviser to the Netherlands government-in-exile in Australia during the war years. His acceptance by the Dutch had started before World War II when he met DeBruijn, then an officer in charge of the government post at Enarotali. For a time before Japanese troops entered New Guinea, DeBruijn and Mickelson had shared the same quarters in the Kemandora Valley.

DeBruijn, a colorful guerrila fighter against the Japanese all during the war, had become the top-ranking expert on the native population of New Guinea. With a view toward conducting a government scientific expedition into the Baliem Valley, DeBruijn had gone to Holland to spend the better part of a year taking postgraduate work in anthropology at the University of Leiden. With encouragement from his friend, Mickelson obtained permission from Alliance officials to join DeBruijn at the university. If studying anthropology and delving into Dutch monographs would get him into the Baliem faster, Mickelson was for it. He also took the opportunity to meet with Dutch officials and acquaint them with his mission society's objectives in New Guinea.

As the leaders of the New Guinea operation plotted and planned to reach the Baliem Valley, the missionaries in the Wissel Lakes area carried on the day-by-day duties of life among the Kapaukus. From time to time the tribespeople seemed to make spiritual progress, especially some of the children. At other times the ugly patterns of the old heathen culture tried the patience and faith of the missionaries. Darlene Rose tells about one incident at Enarotali:

"After breakfast that morning, we went outside to put up clothesline poles. It did not occur to me that there was anything unusual about the fact that the school children had already gathered. Or that Tebaimabijuwua's mother and aunt were making a very early morning call.

"The Kapauku mother blurted out, 'Her older brother wants to sell Tebaimabijuwua!'

"I told them I did not think Christians should marry those who do not believe.

" 'It's better that she should finish school first,' said the mother.

"I heartily agreed. But I did not know that the brother had already sold the girl for a few cowrie shells, nor that she had run away during the night.

"At this point Big Brother came up the trail, watching me as I sewed covers for the children's schoolbooks. Another man was with him.

" 'That's the man who wants to marry Tebaimabijuwua,' the children said. He appeared to be three times the age of the little girl.

"I turned to Big Brother: 'He's too old for Tebaimabijuwua,' I said with rising anger. It was plain that the Kapauku's greed for cowrie shells overshadowed concern for his sister. They looked at one another, puzzled. Then I realized that the two men thought the girl was hiding in the house. 'Go, call her,' I said. They hurried from the house.

"By now it was eight o'clock and time for school to begin. During the chapel hour the children prayed earnestly for Tebaimabijuwua. While I was distributing their reading books, two of the little girls slipped out the back door of the church, and soon reappeared, looking very pleased with themselves. Tabaimabijuwua was with them. Frightened, she crawled under the lower part of the folding organ and the children crowded around to conceal her.

"At recess time Tebaimabijuwua, accompanied by another little girl named Peumabi, left the school, saying they were going to hide.

"School continued to one o'clock and I went back to the house for dinner. Just as we were sitting down to the table, Peumabi came running with some schoolboys:

" 'Mama, they've found her,' she cried.

"I ran to the door, asking, 'Where is she?' As I spoke I saw Big Brother and another man, armed with bows and arrows, forcing Tebaimabijuwua up the path toward the house. Then I saw that her hair was covered with spider webs and weeds, and that blood was streaming down her left shoulder and arm. She had been shot twice by her brother's arrows.

"Instead of passing by the house, as her brother had ordered, Tebaimabijuwa dashed through the open doorway. Her brother

Richard Lenehan

This was the missionaries' first view of "Cannibal Valley," an unexplored wilderness in the primitive heartland of Dutch New Guinea. An amphibian plane's daring landing on this treacherous stretch of the Baliem River marked the beginning of the Christian mission to Stone Age savages of the Dani tribe.

Plane travel is always perilous in the mountainous interior where air currents shift suddenly and clouds encircle the peaks. Al Lewis, pioneer missionary pilot flying supplies to missionary outposts, lost his life in a crash in narrow Baliem Pass. The plane below overturned on its first landing attempt at the new Homejo airstrip; curious Moni tribesmen (right) thought this was normal landing procedure. Missionaries William Cutts and Kenneth Troutman discuss the accident with Civil Aviation Director Hamers.

Alliance Witness

E. W. Ulrich

Kapauku tribesmen help load supplies into a longboat for the trip from the Obano airstrip across Lake Paniai to Enarotali, the first Christian and Missionary Alliance station in New Guinea. The planes of the Missionary Aviation Fellowship are the missionaries' only link with the outside world; there are no roads through the dense mountain forests separating the central highlands from the coastal swamps.

Lloyd Van Stone, a member of the first missionary landing party in the Baliem area (see Chapter 1), welcomes a band of Dani tribesmen to the Hetigima mission station.

Dani men sleep in round thatch-roofed huts (above); women, children, and pigs live together in nearby longhouses (below). Wooden fences surrounding the small settlements keep children and pigs from wandering away and help protect against enemy marauders.

E. W. Ulrich

New Guinea natives cross rivers and streams by swimming or paddling crude log rafts. Rapid waters are often spanned by rattan footbridges which sway dizzily above the swift current as a traveler inches his way across.

Tribesmen "shave" heavy beards by plucking out whiskers with bent twigs.

A constant pastime for Dani men, women, and children is picking the lice from one another's hair. Health standards are low among all tribes; natives suffering from hideous tropical diseases welcomed the "magic" of Western medicine introduced by missionaries.

Oswald F. Emery

Sweet potatoes, a staple of the Dani diet, grow in gardens surrounding the settlements. Men break up the rich earth with heavy wooden digging sticks (left); women do the planting, cultivating, harvesting. Native fruits and vegetables are bartered or sold for cowrie shells in primitive market places (above). Danis prepare roasting pits for a tribal pig feast (below).

Myron Bromley (lower left) and Jerry and Darlene Rose share a feast specially staged by the powerful Dani chief, Ukumhearik, in honor of Mrs. Rose's arrival as the first woman missionary in the Baliem Valley.

followed her and forced her out of the house with brute strength. He dropped his bow by his side, struggling with the crying child. Again she slipped away from him and fled inside the house, refusing to respond to his threats.

" 'Then I'll kill you!' he shouted. 'You can die!'

"And twice again he tried to shoot her. The little girl stood there without flinching. I knew she was determined that she would not marry the man who had bought her even if it meant death. Somehow I managed to get her brother out of the house. As he left, I asked the children to fetch Tebaimabijuwua's mother.

"Then I saw that a crowd of about thirty men, all armed with bows and arrows, were standing in front of the house. I rushed up to the prospective bridegroom and asked him if he thought it was right for the brother to shoot the child. He shrugged his shoulders. The other men giggled. One said flippantly, 'Kapaukus do it this way!' A wave of contempt swept through me. What a fine, chivalrous group of men!

" 'Well, I don't like it,' I said. 'I think it's bad.'

"Perhaps in self-defense, the wife-seeker said meekly, 'She can go to school after we marry.' I doubted it. He probably wanted to start a new garden. 'You tell her,' he said.

"I went back to where the child was standing just inside the door. There was a pool of blood at her feet about the size of a salad plate. I conveyed the message.

" 'But I won't marry him!' she said.

"At this I saw her mother coming up the trail and I went to meet her. 'Do you know your son shot Tebaimabijuwua?' I said. She didn't wait to reply. Grabbing up a piece of wood, she rushed at the youth with the ferocity of a mother bear robbed of her whelps. By a small margin, he escaped the blow intended for him. Such a flow of words I hope I never hear again. I tried to calm her but the intensity of her feelings permitted no control. Like a geyser they gushed out—all the hurt and injustices, the cruelties and woes of heathen womanhood. My heart ached for her, but the men were beginning to bristle.

"I sent for the chieftain of the village, then went down to the church to pray. As I dropped to my knees, I heard the words in my heart, 'Is there anything too hard for me?' I needed no further assurance. A schoolboy told me the chieftain had arrived, and I went out to meet him.

"The chieftain suggested that the couple be married and that they both attend school, since Big Brother had already accepted the cowrie shells. I saw that Tebaimabijuwua was crying.

"As I tried to comfort her, one of the young men taunted her. My heart rebelled against the injustice of it all. I could restrain the tears no longer, and I turned on the crowd, 'This is terrible,' I cried.

"The chieftain, normally a vacillating figurehead, suddenly came to life. 'There,' he said. 'Mama's crying because she loves and pities one of her schoolgirls. If she teaches them, she may say what they do.' Most of the men nodded assent; some hung their heads. It was as though the fear of the Lord had fallen upon them. One by one they began to slip away. Big Brother said something to the chieftain, vaulted the fence, and was gone.

" 'What did he say?' I asked.

" 'He said Tebaimabijuwua could have two or three months to think it over.'

"The Lord had overruled that which centuries of heathen practice had made customary and binding. I commended the child to the Lord in a brief prayer, dressed her wounds, and sat down to eat a cold meal.

"Some eight months later Tebaimabijuwua became the wife of one of our Christian boys."

The missionaries were slowly winning their way with the Kapaukus in the Wissel Lakes area. Work had been started among the Moni tribe in the Kemandora Valley. Mickelson had made some contacts with Uhundunis and Danis, but his deep desire to reach the Baliem Valley was not yet satisfied.

4

TREK TO THE VALLEY RIM

His unheated room in a Leiden rooming house in Holland did not cool Mickelson's ever-present missionary concern. One of his letters to New York contained a carefully worked-out program of entering the Baliem, using maps and a point-by-point outline of procedure. He lived for the day he could carry out his ideas.

Back in New Guinea the urge to reach the Baliem was equally strong in the hearts of Troutman and Rose. On a trek in the summer of 1951 they penetrated into the fabulous Ilaga Valley, in the very heart of western Dutch New Guinea. It was about halfway between Enarotali to the west and the Baliem Valley to the east. Surrounded by towering peaks, the floor of the valley was seven thousand five hundred feet above sea level. Troutman's journal portrays what they encountered on that significant expedition:

"The bivouac at Kogotapa is exactly halfway between Kumopa and Homejo and we were able to reach this place at 3:00 P.M. We had just finished setting up our camp when we had a real downpour of rain which lasted well into the night. This rain was a real test for the water repellent that I had put on the tents. To my disappointment it did not work. It takes a good tent to withstand water in the downfalls we have in the mountains."

On the seventh day out, he wrote:

"At Engeneng, two hours east of Zanespa, we stopped to rest and were met with the usual sight following a death in the family. Everyone was covered with mud and a young girl was suffering from infection where she had cut off her finger as a sign of sorrow."

Carrier problems developed on the ninth day:

"We could not leave Gelabagi because one of the carriers left us and one was sick. We gave medicine to the sick man and prayed for him.

"For a while it looked like our expedition had come to an end. . . . The local people refused to help us because a war was pending and they dared not leave. A few Danis said they would go, but they wanted us to pay them an ax in advance. This is the same as saying, 'Give me the ax and you will never see us again.' You never pay the people here before they do the work. . . . There was only one thing to do—rearrange our supplies. We left behind enough food for the return trip to Homejo and also our much cherished air mattresses. However, we felt that food was more important than such items of luxury. The rest of the trip we used the earth as a mattress."

On August 13, the twelfth day, the journal continued:

"Spent the day at Wanabigi resting and fixing up our things for the rest of the trip. We were also able to witness to these people of the Lord. In the afternoon they built a large fire and cooked an abundance of beans, squash, and green vegetables in a pit lined with hot stones. The result was very appetizing and we ate a good portion along with our Dani hosts. The question of our proceeding came up. . . . The Danis said that there were no people living in the entire region ten days ahead of us and we would all die. . . . We promised them no one would go hungry. Finally they said, 'We will proceed to the east tomorrow.'"

"August 14, thirteenth day—Today we climbed an elevation of 7,000 feet at the rattan bridge crossing the Kemaboe River to an elevation of 10,700 feet on the ridge between Ugumba and the central plateau. . . . We had a beautiful day after climbing for one and a half hours and were greeted with that sight of all sights, the snow-capped Carstensz. . . . We arrived at our camp at Imbuna-bundi at 5:00 P.M. One year before, Mickelson slept here."

Problems developed on the following day:

"Left Imbunabundi and stopped later to rest at Endatapa at an elevation of 10,400 feet. Descended to the small Neaboe River, then ascended to the plateau. This was a hard day, for the carriers were again in bad spirits. Many times during the day we heard them hissing, which meant something had gone wrong. Some were constantly saying, 'Mana ebaja? What are you looking for? Why must you come on such a trip as this? Indi-hitija. We will die.' We had a little idea of what Moses must have gone through in the wilderness. On one occasion we felt we had to punish a carrier for not obeying us, whereupon all of them threw down their loads and said, 'We are going home.' I said, 'It is fine. You may go, and we will die here.' Then they said, 'No, tuan, we will not leave you.' Franz Titaheluw, Indonesian guru [teacher] traveling with us, has developed an infection in his foot. . . . Camped at Kelalimi, elevation 11,200 feet."

Troutman records that August 19, the eighteenth day, they decided to hold a service for the people living in the valley where they expected to camp for a few days. More trouble:

"We were not in the valley long before we realized that we were in the midst of a cunning and scheming people. This was the Uhunduni tribal area. They wanted to get as much from us as possible before we reached the Danis. . . . In the village of Zosa the chief brought us a pig. In the spirit of friendship we gave him an ax and began to butcher the pig. We told the people, as best we could, our purpose in coming. We wanted them freed from the bonds of Satan and brought to the light of the gospel. However, their idea of friendship was not the same as ours, for when our carriers were about to eat their food, the chief stopped them, saying they could not eat until they first gave gifts to his wife who had raised the pig. This cost our carriers salt, beads, and shells.

Knowing they were strangers, they knew they must comply with the wishes of their host."

They had traveled for three weeks when they reached Elamaga, later to become the site of work among the western Dani tribe. Troutman described the friendly reception:

"When we arrived at this village we received a royal welcome. The chief said we were to stay in his house for the first day and night. Then we could camp and receive the rest of the people of the area. The chief had killed several pigs. Cutting strips of pork three feet long from the leg of the pig, he roasted them over the hot coals. When the meat was roasted, the chief cut it and presented the pieces to us as a token of friendship. . . . We made a cake with our biscuit mix to the amazement of our audience.

"When we discussed the subject of going on farther, in typical native style they talked to one another in shocked amazement and regret. 'Tuan,' they replied, 'we cannot go now as there is a war to the east.' So we dropped the matter and prepared to lie down for the night. We slept that night on the earth floor of the Dani house while our Moni carriers were sleeping on the floor above us. We lay in a shower of dirt from above all night long. . . . The Dani men's houses are round with a ground floor that permits four and a half feet of standing room. Above that is the coarse, woven floor upon which they sleep at night."

Troutman and Rose remained at the Elamaga camp for six days, trying to learn about the valley. They located a small plateau just north of Elamaga which they considered for an airplane landing strip.

"This is 7,500 feet above sea level," Troutman wrote, "and the airstrip site is only 2,000 feet long, which is inadequate. However, the spot is ideal for dropping supplies from the air. We believe that a rack could be arranged for picking up mail and empty parachutes. The valley at this point is at least five miles wide."

The missionaries tried again and again to prevail on their hosts to accompany them farther east. Promises were made, then withdrawn. The travelers decided the village elders were putting pressure on the younger men not to make the trip.

"The Ilaga is a great trading center between the Baliem and the valleys to the west," Troutman chronicles. "We think that they were afraid future trade might be affected by such a trip. These Danis have a reputation as traders. Our friends promised us that if we returned to the Ilaga again they would take us on to the east. The Elamaga chief promised to visit us in two months when he comes to Zai for salt."

Troutman and his companion decided they had better return to Enarotali. The trip home was largely uneventful except for the difficulties of walking over the trail.

"From Endatapa to the ridge where you descend to the Ugimba," Troutman wrote, "one encounters the worst terrain that I have ever seen. A type of fir tree grows here with matted roots that wind all over the place. These roots are slippery and covered with moss, and there are many treacherous holes between the roots. To slip into them is dangerous. It would be easy for a man to break his leg."

But the Christian and Missionary Alliance was not the only agency interested in the area.

By 1951 other mission societies were making survey trips to New Guinea. Sending missionaries to Cannibal Valley was now a possibility. Both Alliance missionaries on the field and officials of the home board felt they had first claim upon the area. Memoranda flew from field to headquarters and back again.

The missionaries, frustrated by the agonizing delay of getting an airplane, grumbled among themselves and accused the officials at home of stalling. Mickelson had already been questioned in New York and asked pointedly about his alleged threat to quit the mission and go off on his own to the Baliem. He denied the allegation, pledging his loyalty to the Alliance. But his letters revealed his impatience. He used every method of prodding the board into action, wheedling, reproaching, and pleading that the Alliance had a solemn directive from above to claim the Baliem.

Actually, Alliance officials were also eager to move ahead in New Guinea, but there were the constant demands for personnel and funds from more than twenty fields and the cost of supplying an airplane was great.

Missionaries by their very nature are men of action. Some of them are individualists who get things done in their own way, and smart under the discipline of working with a team. Thus the missionaries not only resented the directives from New York but at times found it difficult to work with their associates. Living under the restrictions of life on a station can try the best of men, and the Alliance workers were no exception.

Early in 1951 Troutman wrote Dr. Snead about the visit of Walter Erikson, of the Evangelical Alliance Mission in Chicago: "Erikson came to Enarotali with the idea that he could step off to the Baliem from here. Such a thing is absolutely impossible."

Erikson in time abandoned the plan to enter the Baliem, and later, while seeking out a mission field in the Bird's Head, with George Tritt, the two men were slain by their carriers. They became the first martyrs in Dutch New Guinea.

Other societies probing the Baliem opportunity were the Regions Beyond Missionary Union, the Unevangelized Fields Mission, and the Australian Baptists. Ultimately all of these organizations came to join the Christian and Missionary Alliance in evangelizing the New Guinea highlands, but in 1951 their plans to enter the coveted valley were regarded as competitive by many of the pioneering Alliance workers. The lure of the Baliem was great even though there were other areas with large unreached tribal populations.

The probing efforts of the Alliance missionaries east from the Wissel Lakes through the rugged, hostile areas of the central highlands finally were crowned with success in a sixty-seven-day trek undertaken by Jerry Rose.

Accompanied by Robert Meyer-Ranneft, Jr., a Dutch government official, a police inspector named Van der Pant, and Franz Titaheluw, Rose reached the heights of the Ibele Valley overlooking the Baliem Valley. The Dutch government had requested that the expedition not enter the valley proper, but a successful crossing of the central highlands had been made and the Alliance missionaries now knew for certain where the population concentrations of the tribes were centered. News of the successful expedition reached high officials at The Hague and the trek was heralded by the newspapers in Holland.

Rose, who had yearned to minister to the people of the Baliem since his college days, was exultant: "It was a thrill to be absolutely surrounded by Danis after being interested in them so long. They certainly are more advanced than the Kapaukus and the Monis, although for thievery and deviltry they can be compared to the latter as Chicago gangsters to small-time crooks."

When Rose and his companions had traveled as far eastward as the Ilaga Valley, they had difficulty in getting a guide to take them through to the Baliem. Finally they prevailed upon a mentally unbalanced old Dani to escort them.

"When we finally broke out of the jungle at 10,500 feet," Rose reported, "we were amazed to see the Carstensz peaks were four degrees *north* of us. We proceeded eastward for two days, crossing the top of the plateau at about 12,000 feet, and abruptly dropped to the largest of the tributaries that make up the West Baliem River. The next three days' walk to the east are the most miserable in history. It is swamp country filled with what I have named 'harpoon' grass, a stiff swamp grass with black needlelike tips that break off on contact. Wounds are infected within twenty-four hours. Each night I went over my body and dug them out and advised the others to do the same. They ignored my suggestion and within a week I was doctoring innumerable infections on arms and legs."

When the hikers reached the Habbema Lake area, they found larger sweet potato gardens than they had seen in any other part of New Guinea. "It took us one and a half hours to walk through one garden," Rose said.

"Our insane Dani guide was killed in this area, brutally, unmercifully—the result of an old war. We had paid him off and severed relationships with him—fortunately—before the murder. He was shot with arrows and then pierced several times with the long spears the Danis carry. These are wicked instruments, some ten feet long."

On one occasion the party took a wrong turn in the trail and spent four or five days retracing their steps to continue the trip eastward. Then they sighted Mt. Wilhelmina and were able to plot their location. They knew they were near Archbold's old camp.

"Next morning was crisp and clear, so clear that the tents were sheathed in ice, like a plastic coating," Rose described it. "We tore down the slope and started looking for Archbold's dump, crossing a small river flowing into the east end of the lake on a bridge made thirteen years earlier by the Dyaks, tied and still holding with good old U.S. manila rope."

Finding a tinfoil wrapper from a chocolate bar and thirteen empty carrying tins, they poked through Archbold's mountain camp. "Old shoes, bottles, and general debris were everywhere," Rose recorded. "Made camp immediately and Franz went duck hunting. Incidentally, we ate twenty-three ducks in the course of the trip. Some from the rivers, some from small ponds. The most delicious was the extremely rare salvadorina. Ornothologically, it is a rare bird, but boiled in salt water, then fried in butter, it is rarer gastronomically.

"It was bitter cold at the lake and I fixed heating and cooking stoves. There was a supply of benzine left by Archbold. From some of the five-gallon tins, I fashioned stoves. I put four inches of sand in the bottom of the tins, then soaked it with benzine. Nothing finer. . . . We left the lake and climbed to 11,150 feet plus. To the north and east we could see the Grand Valley. . . . Finally, we camped for four days just above Archbold's Ibele campsite. Another five hours' walk and we would have been in the Grand Valley, but that was forbidden."

By walking steadily, the party was able to make it back to the Wissel Lakes in twenty-one days. Tired, grimy, and bearded, Jerry Rose knocked at the door of his home, saying to his startled wife, "Lady, can you spare a dime for a cup of coffee?"

The goal of reaching the Baliem Valley now seemed nearer. Walking over the trails was not the means of entrance into the valley. It was impossible to get there from either the north or south coast. The peaceful invasion must come from the air.

An emergency illness, one of many that would plague Jerry Rose, took him and Darlene back to the United States. The trip home and the days in the hospital were not pleasant, but this proved to be a profitable time of waiting upon the Lord. It turned out that the illness was not as serious as the doctors in New Guinea had feared. In a few months, the Roses were en route to New Guinea. Darlene described their return to Enarotali:

"Our welcome home was everything to be desired. We were embraced, wept and laughed over. Even the homecoming festival was not lacking. As we walked up the trail from the landing pier, Marta, [one of the Kapauku schoolgirls], beaming and chuckling, whispered that they had found some bees for me.

"Next day Marta and three other girls came to the house, bearing a gray, cone-shaped affair. It was placed on the coals of the fire and turned from time to time to insure just the right done-ness. Lifting the cone from the fire, Marta broke open the individual cells and took out the rare delicacy.

"Like perfect hostesses, the girls ate the bees that had been almost ready to emerge from their cells, saving the legless larvae for me.

" 'That's one for Mama,' they yelled as each salmon-pink bee-in-the-making was brought forth.

"I couldn't tell you how many I ate. And the flavor? So delicious that it beggars description."

Eating strange foods in strange places was not new to Darlene Rose. This was only one of many such experiences, and in the months ahead there would be more.

5

HEAVENLY MANDATE
REVIEWED

In the summer of 1952 the missionaries of the Christian and Missionary Alliance serving in New Guinea met at Enarotali to decide strategy and plans for the year ahead. They were joined by Dr. A. C. Snead, Foreign Department secretary, from the headquarters office in New York. Each tribe of the central highlands—the Kapaukus, Monis, Uhundunis, and Danis—was thoroughly discussed. Already there were thriving works among the Kapaukus in the area around Enarotali, the first station, and at a second station on the shores of Lake Tigi, several miles south of Lake Paniai. At Homejo, William and Grace Cutts, who replaced the Troutmans, had been working on the Moni language and saw the first meager fruits of their evangelism. They had also been joined by two fledgling missionaries. One of these young men, Harold W. Catto, was later to become the chairman of the New Guinea field.

Seeking always to reach the last tribe for Jesus Christ, the committee voted to approach the Uhunduni and Dani tribes in the Ilaga Valley, nearly one hundred miles to the east, even though workers were not yet available for this area.

But the crowning decision of the gathering concerned the Danis living in the Baliem Valley: The group voted unanimously to enter the valley by airplane. It was agreed that a base should be established at Hollandia, the nearest and most feasible port of supply. Assigned to the preliminary work there were Einar Mickelson, Jerry and Darlene Rose, and Lloyd and Doris Van Stone.

Although the Baliem Valley was in the ominous-sounding "uncontrolled" area of the interior, the Dutch government granted the Alliance missionaries permission to enter Cannibal Valley, insisting only that a two-engined airplane be employed in the aerial advance. But the government officials warned the missionaries, "Understand, you're on your own!"

In addition to the absolute necessity for an airplane to transport and supply missionaries assigned to the Baliem, there was a mounting problem at the other end of New Guinea. The growing staff of missionaries had stepped up the need for foodstuffs and supplies quite beyond the capacity of the government planes that served the Wissel Lakes. Sometimes supplies delivered to Biak lay in the warehouse for three months before they were delivered. An airplane for the Baliem operation could also supply all the New Guinea mission stations.

The Roses were as excited as children when they arrived in Hollandia. In short order Jerry found that for less than seven thousand dollars he could purchase a prefabricated mess hall that had been used previously by the KLM airline as an overnight stop for passengers on round-the-world flights. The building, about one hundred feet long and forty feet wide, was transported by truck to a hillside location near the Sentani Airport, about twenty miles west of Hollandia. Later Rose supervised construction of a hangar at the airport.

The Roses worked like beavers to prepare living quarters for the missionaries, hangar and shop for the airplane, and all the facilities for an efficient missionary base. It was backbreaking toil, but Jerry and Darlene Rose knew that they were closer to the day when they could take the gospel to the people in the hidden valley.

"Ten years have passed down the corridor of time since that

afternoon in 1942," Darlene wrote to friends in America. "Had
Dr. Jaffray lived to see this day he would have understood the feeling of my heart that nothing—no, not even sweating over supply
drums in this hot, smelly place—is common or mundane, if it is a
part of the culmination of an old man's dream and a fulfillment of
a young man's vision—the opening of the area over which a finger
and a heart came to rest—the Baliem Valley."

Back in the United States and Canada, Alliance churches were
responding to the special appeals for funds to buy an amphibian for
New Guinea. Al Lewis felt that the Irish-made Sealand was well
adapted to the peculiar flying problems of such a primitive field. Not
all the missionaries agreed with his choice. However, Lewis' long
experience in aviation and his strong convictions on the type of aircraft needed influenced the decision to buy the Sealand. Certainly
in the first phase of advance only an aircraft that could land on
water was a feasible choice.

About this time Grady Parrott, president of the Missionary Aviation Fellowship which provided airplane service for societies in
various parts of the world, made an aerial survey of New Guinea
for the missions that had established work there. Walter Post, Russell Deibler's partner in opening the work at the Wissel Lakes,
joined Parrott on a survey of the Baliem Valley in a chartered
airplane.

Post's description of the event is worth repeating:

"We left Sentani airstrip, just outside of Hollandia, at 10:05 A.M.
in a twin-motored Beechcraft belonging to an Australian excavating
firm. Pilot Girault and Al Lewis were in the cockpit. The passengers
included Messrs. Mickelson, Rose, Van Stone, an Australian friend
named Ross Powers, and me.

"As we gained altitude we got a clearer view of Lake Sentani
with its many bays pointing like long fingers in all directions. The
day was cloudy and we experienced a few bumps as we climbed
through the fleecy white clouds around the lake. By 10:20 we were
flying at 7,700 feet and had already made good headway on our
course which was taking us in a southwesterly direction toward the
Baliem. We were well above the clouds and in the distance could

glimpse the jagged mountain peaks and ranges which present such a formidable barrier to overland travel to the Baliem. The clouds were beginning to break and through the holes we could see only dense jungles with very sparse and scattered human population.

"In another fifteen minutes we were over an expansive stretch of plateau known as the level lake country, a malaria-infested area which presents another serious obstacle to anyone who desires to penetrate this untrodden jungle. Just beyond this we could see the wide and winding Idenburg River, wide and deep enough for a seaplane to land on it most anywhere. We were flying at 10,500 feet, and not far ahead of us were peaks and ranges from 12,000 to 15,000 feet high. By now the passengers were jumping from side to side, so as to get a good view of the mountains from both sides of the plane. We had left the stretch of country through which the Idenburg flows and were flying over rough mountain terrain. Brother Lewis pointed out that the range on the right was 11,647 feet high, according to the map. On the left was another of about the same height, so that we were going through a pass, a kind of majestic entrance to the Baliem Valley. One of the fellows called me over to the other side to see smoke and some gardens—the first signs of life for some time.

"At 11:05 A.M., just an hour after we had left Sentani strip, we entered the Baliem Valley. Since our plane cruised at a speed of 170 to 180 miles per hour, it was not difficult to figure out the distance we had traveled.

"What a vista now stretched out before us! What a contrast to the rough, inhospitable mountain country just left behind! Though we were now flying at 12,500 feet, the peaks and ranges still towered above us. But below lay the beautiful Baliem Valley, a vast carpet of green stretching out toward the west as far as we could see, surrounded by an expansive network of rugged mountains, some of them with snow-capped peaks.

"At the entrance to the valley it is from twenty to thirty miles wide. This part is well populated. The river winds serpentlike through the valley, passing villages and making its way through the well-cultivated and well-drained gardens of sweet potato and taro.

Practically the whole valley is under cultivation. Side valleys branching out from the Baliem also have gardens and villages. All along we could see well-defined trails, indicating that there must be considerable travel in the area. We were now nearing the upper Baliem where the valley is much narrower but still well populated.

"At 11:30 we were still flying westward, leaving the Baliem and going toward Lake Habbema, which is five days' walking from the Baliem. The lake is about 10,000 feet high and there is no population around it. At 11:35 we were over the lake which appeared to be about two miles long with excellent approaches for landing and take-off for planes. We can still see the evidences of the Archbold expedition which made its base on the shore of the lake during its visit to this area in 1938. Part of a jetty and many old tin cans scattered around gave the exact location of their camp. . . .

"We then turned around and went back to the Baliem Valley via the Wamena Valley. We slowly descended to 1,500 feet, just above the valley floor, where it was possible to get a better and closer view of the villages, which have two types of houses, round beehive-like dwellings and long rectangular houses all of them made of thatch. Mr. Rose told us that on his recent trip they discovered that the round houses are for the men and the rectangular ones are for the women. We tried to count the villages as we went along and managed to spot two to three hundred of them. For a brief period we flew at treetop level, which of course frightened the natives, many of whom were hiding in their gardens or running away for safety. We could distinguish some people who appeared to be unusually tall—much larger in physique than the Kapaukus. We also passed beautiful fields of taro, a tuberlike plant much more nutritious than the sweet potato.

"Brother Lewis pointed out a fairly straight stretch of the river where he thought the Sealand could land with comparative safety. . . . He said that it was a better landing place than the one he has been using in Borneo. . . . Altogether we flew up and down the valley for about an hour. As we left we flew up one of the valleys branching off from the main valley and found quite a large village nestled at the foot of the mountain. We then continued to climb until we reached 10,500 feet, and finding the pass between the two ranges through which we had entered, we made our way back to Sentani by 1:00 P.M. . . . We came back with the conviction that we must not delay in getting the gospel to these people isolated there in the Baliem Valley."

Subsequently Jerry Rose, accompanied by his wife, Darlene, and the Van Stones, made another air survey of the interior. It was on that flight that they spotted the site at Pyramid Mountain that later would be such an important station. The pyramid-shaped hill rose sharply from the valley floor to guard the upper end of the Baliem. It was almost forty miles from Hetigima.

"As I looked down at the vast sweep of the valley floor dotted with villages and gardens, and beautifully terraced hillsides reaching up toward the rim of the mountains," Darlene wrote a friend, "my heart thrilled with the anticipation of our soon occupying the area. I was interested in the villages and gardens, but more than that I was eager to see the people. Most of them were in hiding but a few of the braver ones stood out in the open, watching the plane as we made our way up and down the valley. As these few came into view, I talked to them in my heart, 'You, old man standing there in the village compound, will have the opportunity of hearing the gospel. Like one of our Kapauku Christians, you'll be able to say when death is near that your family need not grieve. For since you have come to know the Savior lives, someday you will rise from your shallow grave on the mountain slope to meet Him and them in the air.'

"Today a shadow falls across that picture. The summer is past, the summer is ended. Winter has come and what of that old man, poor lost soul behind the ranges? Or that little girl who scampered up the river's edge to find a hiding place in the tall grass? 'You, little girl, will find a place in the hearts and home as did Ruth [another pupil] and Marta and so many other Kapauku children. You will not need to fear being sold into a marriage that offers little more than a heartache. You, too, will know the Christ and come to find refuge in the shadow of the Almighty.' But the months have slipped by and what of that little girl?"

Darlene Rose lamented over the fact that "the door had been shut . . . for the preaching of the gospel. The other doors to the valley, like gaping wounds, stand wide open and through them death and sorrow, sickness, fear, and superstition, have passed to stalk their victims the length and the breadth of the valley."

In the vale of despair and discouragement, the Roses were faced more personally with the specter of death. In difficult labor in Hollandia Hospital, Darlene Rose was fighting for her life. She remembered her thoughts later: "So this is the valley of the shadow of death and I'm not afraid, for Thou art with me." But the birth of their firstborn, Bruce, on December 14, 1953, brought joy that overshadowed all the surrounding difficulties.

Ironically, Jerry Rose was unable to enter the valley on the initial flight. Recurring seizures of pain had been troubling him as he was engaged in the building program at Sentani. Finally, when he could stand it no longer, he was forced to fly home on an emergency furlough. It was a bitter experience, but no doubt emergency surgery saved his life. It was a part of a strange pattern of debility. Not one of the missionaries escaped illness or physical injury. For a time, it seemed as though the entire project was doomed.

While they were waiting for the arrival of the Sealand, the missionaries at Sentani sought to charter a Qantas airline amphibian that would make a preliminary flight into the Baliem, landing on Lake Habbema. They hoped that an overland party could hike into the valley and check the proposed river landing site for the Sealand. Rose and the others felt that the trip was well justified to circumvent the peril of landing on a river with uncharted shoals, sandbars, and floating logs. First, the Dutch government halted the project until officials were assured that Qantas could supply rescue airplanes in an emergency. When the expedition was finally ready to take off, word came from New York that the trip should be canceled. Alliance leaders felt that the churches which had sacrificially supported the purchase of the Sealand would question the need for a preliminary charter flight into the Baliem. Perhaps they also feared that an advance flight would rob the Sealand of first honors in entering Cannibal Valley. In any case, the Qantas flight was never made.

Most stay-at-home Christians idealize life on the mission field. They forget that missionaries, committed to doing the Lord's will, are still human beings. They face, on the one hand, the problem of maintaining their proper standards of living in difficult foreign cultures, on the other hand, there is always the danger that the gadgets of civilization will completely block the impact of their witness upon people of much simpler ways of living. There was the question always of whether a missionary would get too busy with side projects like raising livestock or engaging in agriculture at the expense of learning the new language and culture and seeking by more direct means the advancement of the gospel.

On the whole, the large denominational missionary societies feel that full-orbed Christian witness includes concern for the physical welfare of the people. They devote themselves to sanitation and hygiene measures, methods of improving gardening, and all the other areas that deal with the social or personal welfare of the group. But from the beginning, Alliance leaders had felt that their principal emphasis should be upon evangelism which results in the establishment of an indigenous church. They had always guarded against any tendency toward institutionalized missionary efforts that might deflect the thrust of pure gospel advance.

Jerry Rose and Einar Mickelson were questioned about engaging in activities that their co-workers felt were not in line with the major purpose of their mission.

Memoranda were exchanged between New Guinea to New York on such mundane matters as the feasibility of missionaries purchasing electric generators, power washing machines, and some of the accepted comforts of American life. These differences of opinion were often sources of sharp misunderstandings, and there were times when the spiritual tone of the missionary community sagged. The question of where to draw the line on such activities will never be completely settled, and there is much to be said for the emphasis that the gospel is not only a verbalized message, but that which involves every facet of human conduct and concern.

In one letter to the home office Mickelson wrote: "Please bear in mind that we feel it would be nice to have lights and conveniences but no, no never, at the cost of hindering the gospel from reaching these unreached tribes."

As the missionaries waited on the brink of that first Baliem flight, they had to face the fears that unconsciously hid in their hearts. They knew that the Danis were cruel, murderous foes, with short tempers and swift spears. The men who had tramped over the trails of the highlands had experienced so many hardships and perils, they knew the forthcoming mission was fraught with dangers that would not be evident to a newcomer.

"At times it frightens me when I contemplate the heavy responsibility of tackling the Great Baliem River Valley and its thousands of unreached souls," Mickelson wrote to an Alliance official. "You don't know how much it comforts me to know you, too, are concerned and that you are seeking the guidance of the Lord. I wish it would be possible for you to come out here, so that you could never forget the vision that would unroll before your eyes, uncounted Danis living their fear-and-devil-dominated lives totally ignorant of the fountain that was open for their cleansing."

Rose felt that when the Sealand reached New Guinea the demands for transportation and supplies in the Wissel Lakes would receive top priority. Thus, he feared, the Baliem project would be pushed well into the new year. And he couldn't forget the perils of the first landing on the Baliem River. "A Dutch pilot who flew over the area recently reported that the river is full of debris and a landing at that point would be dangerous," he wrote.

"Pray for us," he continued, "that in these waiting days the Holy Spirit will prepare the hearts of the Dani people for the coming of the gospel."

Rose and Mickelson lived chiefly for the day of entering the Baliem. They had suffered innumerable physical hardships, and risked their lives for this major goal. But the long communication line with New York was frustrating and discouraging. To the missionaries chafing under restraint in New Guinea, the actions of the board seemed interminably slow.

Word had gone from the field to New York that another mis-

sionary society was about to enter the Baliem. The men at headquarters would not be stampeded.

"I have already written you concerning . . . another society wanting to get into the Baliem," William F. Smalley, then area Secretary
of the Alliance, wrote Walter Post, who by this time had become
the board representative for New Guinea. "This is very disturbing
to us, because when we made our plans it was with the thought that
unless we got in, nobody would be going in. It was for that reason
that we were prepared to spend the enormous amounts of money
that seemed to be involved, in order that we might get the gospel
to these needy souls. Now, however, if it becomes a race between
us and another society, I am afraid our people would lose interest."

To this Post eventually replied,

"Will you pardon me when I say that we as a mission should go
forward with faith and a deep sense of conviction. The Lord laid
this area on the heart of Brother Jaffray. While we were occupying the Wissel Lakes, the Baliem was ever before us as the next
objective. Let us not then deviate from this call, not permit circumstances to fill our minds with doubt and hesitation, thus neu-
tralizing our efforts and robbing us of the consciousness of going
forward in the center of His will.

"I deeply feel, and I am sure you brethren share that with me,
that we should not be impelled to occupy the field from a sense
of competition with another mission. But as we examine our original call, I do not think we are moved by unworthy motives. I
believe that no one now questions the call of our Brother Jaffray
into the various fields in Indonesia, including the Wissel Lakes and
the Baliem Valley."

Post's reply to Smalley was deeply appreciated and the re-exami-
nation of motives convinced leaders at home and on the field that
they had a mandate from heaven to "invade" the Baliem.

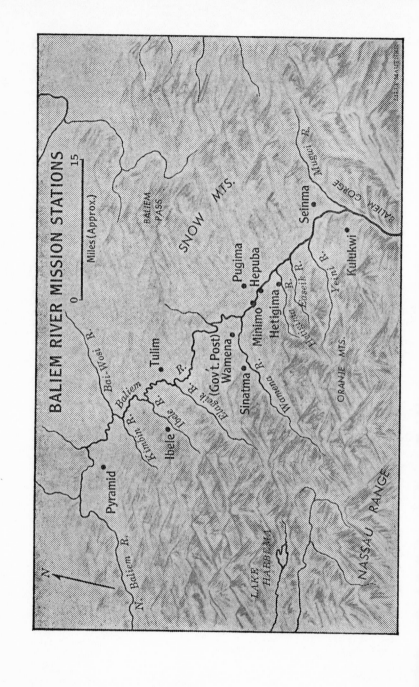

BALIEM RIVER MISSION STATIONS

6

A FEAST AND A FUNERAL

Left alone in the Baliem Valley, Van Stone and Bromley had plenty to keep them busy. While they knew that the low-water level of the Baliem River meant the Sealand could not land for an indefinite period, they were not completely isolated. They were able to communicate regularly via two-way radio with the coastal base at Sentani, and from time to time the Sealand came over to make drops of supplies.

Bromley, a bachelor, was more interested in getting to know the Dani people and to "break down" the language than he was in his personal appearance. He went about in an old khaki army jacket to which his toothbrush was attached with a long metal chain. His toothbrush was stuffed into an upper jacket pocket which was stained by dried-up rivulets of toothpaste. Most of the time he was unshaven, and wore an old battered campaign hat. His tent was furnished with an unmade canvas cot surrounded by books, papers, medicines, canned goods, a tape recorder, and miscellany.

But he tackled the complicated Dani language with scientific care and soon had recorded many tapes of words and phrases that fell from the lips of the natives. Then he would listen to the recordings, laboriously writing down each word and phrase in phonetic characters.

Before arriving on the field, he had taken the time to master Dutch so that he could read the only extant scientific works on the New Guinea tribes. He devoted himself to learning more about the strange Dani culture.

World War II soldiers had brought back reports that the Danis were giants. Other earlier scholarly studies had indicated that Dani men averaged about five feet in height. Bromley discovered that neither of these reports was true. The Danis, taller than any of the other tribes of the central highlands, average about five feet six inches, with some reaching a height of six feet. In spite of their diet that consists chiefly of sweet potatoes, the Danis are strong, muscular specimens of healthy manhood. Like the other tribes of New Guinea, they are complete strangers to any type of intoxicants, and are not afflicted with venereal disease, the scourge of some of the coastal tribes. Both men and older women puff on tobacco "cheroots," the smoke being drawn from the side rather than the end.

Even though anthropologists have no explanation for their origins, the Danis, as well as other tribes of the interior, are classified as Melanesians with Negroid features and dark-brown skins. The men wear virtually no clothing except hairnets, necklaces of cowrie and other broader, platelike shells. Most striking to the outside are their tubelike yellow gourds, sometimes as long as two feet which contrast against their brown skins. They create a bizarre overemphasis of nakedness. If anything happens to his gourd, the Dani is thoroughly embarrassed. Loincloths worn by other tribes or even the clothing worn by white men are immodest by Dani standards. Often the men "shave" or trim their beards, or remove unwanted body hair by plucking it out by the roots with crude tweezers made of a broken twig.

The men, rather than the women, wear elaborate headdresses and other forms of adornment. Besides the pig grease smeared over their bodies, the men, using charcoal or red or white clay, carefully create varying designs on their faces. The headdress, beads, and other adornment are more in evidence when the men are dressed for battle or festive occasions.

Dani girls, until they are given in marriage, wear grass skirts such as are found throughout the Pacific islands. When a man purchases a new wife, the women of the bridegroom's village "drape" the bride with a married woman's fiber skirt that is worn precariously below the abdomen and held in place by huge callouses that develop on the sides of the thighs. A long net hangs from the head to cover her back to a point well below the buttocks, which are always carefully covered even though the breasts are exposed. In their own way, Dani women are quite as modest as women of more sophisticated cultures.

While the Danis are classified as primitive Stone Age people, their rather highly developed system of agriculture and their engineering abilities in constructing elaborate rattan bridges place them several notches above other nomadic tribes.

The Danis live in villages, not in family units, but in U-shaped courtyards about which their straw-thatched houses are grouped. The men and boys (after they are six or eight years old) live in round houses that look like enormous thatched beehives. The women live with their children in long thatched houses in which the pigs are also kept. The polygynous Danis have houses for each wife and her respective broods, and each wife has a designated garden plot in which she grows sweet potatoes, taro, and spinach.

The men prepare the soil for the gardens, digging the ground with long pointed sticks two or three inches in diameter and above five or six feet in length. Once the soil is broken or "plowed," the women take over the planting, cultivating, and harvesting.

The men's round houses are made of crudely split wooden stakes, topped by a heavy straw thatch that protects the occupants from the sun and torrential tropical downpours. A narrow doorway which can be closed with a slatlike door provides the only light. Straw is scattered over the earthern floor and there is no furniture. In a center pit a continuous fire burns, assuring heat during chilly nights and a place to light cigarettes or roast potatoes when the mood seizes. About four feet above the ground a floor of saplings provides sleeping space for the men and boys. The only other articles are the family or village fetishes and charms preserved on racks. There are no knives or forks or cooking vessels, just round gourds which contain drinking water. Bows and arrows are kept close at hand for instant action.

The women's houses are similar. Access is gained through narrow slatted doorways into bare houses much cruder than civilized man would provide for farm animals. In the center a fire burns. Often rocks are heated here and then placed in an adjoining pit in which layers of native spinach and potatoes are laid when the menu calls for steamed sweet potatoes. There are no regular meal hours. Hunger seems to dictate the time for munching on the tasty sweet potatoes and slurping down the steamed spinach.

Dani babies are not weaned until they are four or five years old, and during the long lactation period a man does not sleep with that wife. Undoubtedly, this practice as well as the high mortality rate of men killed in battle has developed polygyny. Wives, like pigs, become the property of the men, and a Dani's status is determined by the number of his wives and pigs as well as his prowess in battle.

These were some of the first things Bromley discovered about Dani life. In later years he would become an authority on Dani culture and language. These were days of introduction.

The Baliem Valley missionaries soon found that the greatest device for developing friendship was Western medicine. Many of the Danis suffered from yaws, a disfiguring disease which, like leprosy, eats away the flesh of faces and bodies.

Using a hypodermic needle, the "shiny thorn," the missionaries soon were able to clear up stubborn cases of yaws with miraculous results. Before long the fame of the missionary "magic" had reached the ears of tribespeople all over the valley. The missionaries were happy to employ their knowledge of first aid to allay the suffering of the Danis. Beyond that they hoped that medical treatment would be an important step in introducing the natives to the Great Physician who could heal deeper spiritual needs.

By the end of September, 1954, Bromley was giving simple

gospel messages to the people, presenting the strange story of the
life and death of a man called Jesus Christ. Thus the ministry of
physical and spiritual healing proceeded hand in hand.

Lloyd Van Stone began construction of a permanent station at
Hetigima, nearly four miles below Minimo on the opposite bank of
the Baliem. He chose a site on sloping ground well back from the
river in a beautiful grove of casuarina trees.

The relative peace of the valley was broken on November 4 when
the airplane dropped a number of drums and boxes of supplies,
thereby attracting a good-sized throng of Danis. Suddenly a war
party of armed men from the Pugima area upstream rushed into
the camp, attacking the Minimo Danis with bows and arrows and
spears. In a matter of minutes two local natives had been killed
and three seriously wounded.

The campers, especially the Kapauku helpers, were completely
unnerved by the attack. When the amphibian arrived the following
day for the first time since the previous June, it brought in Jerry
Rose, who had returned from furlough, and evacuated all of the
frightened Kapaukus except faithful Elisa and Ruth, and the Biaker,
Adrian.

Describing Jerry Rose's arrival in the Baliem, Darlene wrote
from Sentani to friends at home:

"Just one hour and twenty minutes after we said good-by to
Jerry, I heard the voice of the pilot, Mr. Ulrich, say over the
radio, 'I have my floats down for making a run on the river pre-
paratory to landing.' Silence. Then after some moments we heard,
'Landed at 09:30.' I knew that after more than thirteen years of
waiting and praying, Jerry had at last arrived in the place to which
the Lord had called him. I felt a sob rise in my throat, not that
Jerry had left us but that Bruce and I could not have been along.

"This was the same morning that he had left and I knew already
that he had arrived. No two months' trekking over trails, no carriers to provide food for, no struggles to find a guide to take
one to the next watershed, no fear that they might be leading you
away from the 'big water,' no streams to ford, no leeches, no blis-

ters, no ulcers, no glasses broken in a fall—just one hour and twenty minutes sitting in the comfortable seat of a plane and he was there. . . . Thank you, Lord, for the plane, the pilot, the mechanic, and the radios.

"Bruce, the present man of the house, and I hold forth in the storehouse here at Sentani. We have cleaned four rooms at the far end for living quarters. Yesterday afternoon as I sat with Bruce in the living room, I thought, 'Now this is what they mean by belonging to the animal kingdom.' A mud dauber flew in and out with red clay for the nest it was building. I watched with interest until I discovered the building lot was a corner of my folding organ, and down came clay house, choice worms, spiders and all. Myriads of ants crawled on the rafters above. . . . A house lizard jumped from one bookshelf to another. We don't discourage them for they kill insects, including mosquitoes.

"The rooms are not screened, but Jerry put up a framework around our bed and closed it in with screening. That's where Bruce goes at bedtime, and usually not too long thereafter I yield the battlefield to the mosquitoes and join him.

"To date our kill on snakes: two death adders just outside the building, two six-inch red snakes—species unknown—in the house. I have never been squeamish about creatures, so we have learned to live and let live.

"Bruce, now eleven months, speaks four languages—eleven words in English, one in Dutch, two in Malay, and the fourth is a language all his own. I trust he will be adding Dani to his growing vocabulary.

"How I praise the Lord that we are back on the field. This week I should be able to finish the artwork on a primer in the Kapauku language, then I'll have more time to spend on the language of the lower Baliem. Pray that the Lord will enable us to master the language. A missionary's work can never be satisfactory with just a smattering of a foreign tongue. During these waiting days, I often think of the verse in Proverbs: 'Hope deferred maketh the heart sick: but when the desire cometh, it is a tree of life. Jerry has moved into the second half of the verse, but we are still in part 'a.' "

Meanwhile Jerry was getting settled in the Baliem. His diary tells of his first days there: "Wednesday morning, Minimo Camp— It was a real joy to come in. All the way this song kept ringing in my heart, 'There'll be peace in the valley for me.' And indeed a quiet hush and sense of His peace and presence are mine. I haven't seen any natives yet. The folks in this end of the valley do not know the word 'Dani.' We are going to move the camp today or tomorrow upriver. . . .

"I need a mosquito net. Last night the mosquitos nearly ate my ears off.

"Wednesday night—This morning after writing you we had devotions, then the plane came in and we unloaded it. In the afternoon Myron, Lloyd, and I went upriver for about two and a half hours in the outboard motorboat. With the 16 h.p. motor wide open, there were places where we were barely able to move forward. . . . We went into one village and saw the people. They are about the same type as those in the upper Ibele. . . . They are dirty as they can be, but the children are cute and lovable.

"About five o'clock I went downstream to Hetigima where Lloyd lives. On shore we climbed up the bank until we reached the place where Lloyd is building. It is a beautiful spot about fifteen minutes from the river. His house is all framed in and he is putting on the aluminum roof. . . . We did the forty-five minute trip back upstream by moonlight and it was really beautiful. When we reached camp, Myron had supper ready, including blueberry muffins made from a mix.

"It is amazing how much Myron has done on the language. It is a kick to watch him speak to the natives. He wrinkles his nose and uses his hands, but he really rattles it off. . . .

"There are hundreds of ducks on the river—the kind we had at the Lakes and two other varieties. The natives all talk about how big I am and want to feel my arms and legs. And the red bandana handkerchief! I'm sure I could use a thousand of them for trade if I had them. You have never seen such excitement as when I pull out my bandana and blow my nose.

"It's 10:15 and I am dead tired. Tramping around at this altitude takes getting used to. I'm longing for you and darling Bruce to come in."

Jerry Rose had brought with him an outboard motor that made abandonment of the Minimo camp a possibility. Equipped with a motor-powered boat, the missionaries no longer would have to remain at the mosquito-infested Minimo battleground. After surveys had been conducted, Jerry Rose decided to build his house near the village of Hepuba. This was on the opposite side of the river perhaps a half mile below Minimo and about three miles above Hetigima, Van Stone's new station.

It was in this interval that Van Stone and Rose located an airstrip site more than halfway up the valley near the confluence with the Wamena River. A month later when a government party headed by Dr. J. V. DeBruijn arrived to make a week-long survey, the missionaries showed them the Wamena site, which was later to become the first government station and major airstrip in the valley.

By this time the Danis were getting used to white men, but the arrival of Darlene Rose, first white woman to enter Cannibal Valley, stirred up more excitement than any previous event. Hundreds of Dani women gathered to welcome her. As the boat moved down the Baliem toward the Roses' new station at Hepuba, crowds of Dani men and women shouted, "Mama, Mama," the title they had learned from Elisa and Ruth Gobai, who in earlier years had lived with the Roses at the Wissel Lakes.

At Hepuba the Dani women poured into the camp. Myron Bromley estimated that more natives visited them on that single day than the missionary party had encountered in all of the previous months. The women ran their mutilated fingers through Darlene's hair, and pinched and rubbed her skin in their curiosity. "Am I being examined or tenderized?" she asked her husband.

Then it was that Ukumhearik, the Dani chief of the area, joined the circle. A brown-skinned native of about medium height, with his frizzy hair done up in the usual fiber net, Ukumhearik warmly greeted Jerry and Darlene Rose, Myron Bromley, Lloyd Van Stone, and the government men. He immediately announced that the Danis had prepared a pig feast celebrating Darlene's arrival.

There was nothing about Ukumhearik's appearance that bespoke the chief, except for a huge, flat white shell that rested across his chest. Nor was there anything in his manner to indicate that here was the most potent adversary the missionaries were to encounter in their struggle to evangelize the Baliem Valley.

He seemed genuinely to like the newcomers. Soft-spoken and unobstrusive, he squatted on his haunches, native-fashion, and with a blade of grass between his teeth, began a friendly, relaxed conversation.

It was only through the whispered comments of other Danis that the missionaries learned of Ukumhearik's true stature.

In spite of his unimpressive appearance, the Danis said, Ukumhearik was a potentate who exercised the power of life and death over about ten thousand tribesmen. He was the most powerful chief in the Baliem Valley, and no doubt in all New Guinea.

Gradually, the missionaries began to understand that the unimpressive little man was Mr. Big of the Baliem Valley. In American terms he would have been the poor boy from across the tracks who was now president of seventeen corporations and board member of forty-three.

He was, in effect, a self-made man. He had attained his position of eminence through achievements which bring status under primitive culture. He had proved his virility by killing scores of his foes. He was the possessor of twenty-two wives and several droves of fat pigs. And no doubt he had many strings of cowrie shells tucked away for safekeeping.

Not until many later experiences did the missionaries come to realize that they had in Ukumhearik a foe who would do all he could to frustrate their efforts.

He remained unshakably opposed to the bringing of the gospel message, knowing that it would threaten the very bastions of his power, everything that made him the respected chief that he was—warfare, polygamy, and pagan cruelty.

It was out of sheer fear of Ukumhearik that many Danis refused to embrace Christianity. Time and again they tearfully admitted to the missionaries that they would love to have their hearts treated by Jesus but dared not risk the chief's wrath.

Yet Ukumhearik continued to cloak his antagonism with apparent fondness for the missionaries. He showed appreciation for their medicines. He was fascinated by their gadgets. He was impressed by their airplanes and radios.

Darlene was now introduced to the leading men who stood in front of Ukumhearik's house, shaking hands with them one by one until she reached the final man, a wizened elder. Instead of shaking her hand, he reached out and drew the astonished woman into an embrace, enfolding her against his grease-smeared body. After a series of hugs Darlene managed to break his clinch and step back to the protection of her husband.

"I don't know if I like this or not," she confided to Jerry.

"That old fellow is as blind as a bat," Jerry said with a wry smile. "He probably thought he was hugging another man."

Ukumhearik invited Darlene to the place of honor, a grass spot in the courtyard where he was already seated. Then Jerry and Myron were told where they should sit. Now, in ceremonial fashion, the Danis carried in a good-sized pig which was held fore and aft by two men, while a third shot an arrow through its vitals. Next they singed off the bristles and slit open the animal's stomach. The men, using sharp bamboo knives, removed the ribs to roast them over the coals directly, while the rest of the pork was cut up and placed in the cooking pit for steaming.

Ukumhearik, sitting directly in front of Darlene, first tidied himself up, removing the filth that had gathered between his toes. He looked up momentarily to notice that Darlene had discarded a rib bone after eating the roasted meat. Clucking disapproval, Ukumhearik picked up the discarded rib bone, and with a long fingernail, removed the rest of the flesh and membrane that still clung to it. This tender morsel he rolled on his thigh. Then he picked up a bone discarded by Bromley and repeated the performance. Now it was a sizable bit of meat. Before Darlene knew what was happening, Ukumhearik had popped the dainty morsel into her mouth. Without protest, she ate the meat, graciously thanking her host for his kindness.

One of the government men, who had accompanied the missionaries to the pig feast, bent down to whisper something to Myron Bromley, then left the courtyard in a hurry. Later he confronted Darlene Rose.

"Oh, Mrs. Rose," he protested. "How could you do that?"

"Do what?" she asked innocently.

"Eat that dirty, dirty meat," he said, "out from under that dirty nail and off that dirty leg. You ate it!"

"Mr. Van Damen," Darlene laughed, "I don't know what you've been thinking, but I have some idea of what's been happening to your stomach."

Then Myron said, "Darlene, how could you eat that pork?"

"Well, Myron," she said, "I saw you take a similar morsel from Ukumhearik and you ate it."

"That's what you think," he said, as he pulled the meat from his pocket.

Darlene later said that she had never been bothered by a sensitive stomach, something that had served her in good stead during the years she had been forced to eat dog livers taken from the garbage cans in the Japanese concentration camp and later when she worked among the Kapaukus.

By this time Ukumhearik had another dainty section of steamed pork for his guest of honor. It was the fatty portion from the pig's abdomen, lined with the animal's teats. Obediently she ate the pork, describing it as "mealy and chewy" to the gaping missionaries and government men.

Now Ukumhearik was offering Darlene a bundle of pig intestines wrapped in sweet potatoes, but it began to rain. He said, "Why not wrap this up and take it home with you to eat later?"

Ukumhearik now announced that he was adopting Darlene Rose into his clan. Henceforth she was his "daughter."

"Paseh, father," Darlene replied, acknowledging the honor. Ukumhearik, about Darlene's age, looked startled. He mumbled something to Bromley.

"He wants you to call him *'Nerok,'* a fellow clansman of the same age level," Bromley explained.

"Nerok," said Darlene obediently, and Ukumhearik beamed his pleasure.

The ceremony was over but it was the beginning of a long association between the missionaries and the powerful Ukumhearik.

It was not long after this that Jerry Rose attended the funeral for Watagon, a Dani youth who had endeared himself to the Roses during their stay at Hepuba. Watagon had carried baby Bruce Rose on his shoulders and fondled him like a brother. "Watagon," Jerry Rose said, "was one of those people to whom one is drawn instinctively. I was terribly shocked when I heard that he had been killed in battle. They knew I was his friend and they had come to invite me to the funeral.

"I hiked from Hepuba to Watagon's village, about forty-five minutes' walk down the trail. Ukumhearik was standing outside, and I inquired if it was all right for me to attend the funeral ceremony. I didn't want to break any taboos or impose myself upon the family in their grief. Ukumhearik assured me that I was welcome and escorted me into the village enclosure, a triangular-shaped courtyard.

"By the time I arrived one hundred and fifty to two hundred people had already crowded themselves into the enclosure. Even before I had reached the village, I heard them chanting. Now it was louder. Seated at the narrow angle of the V-shaped courtyard were the women and children. They carried the first part of the chanted melody, then the older men and boys at the opposite end of the yard picked up the tune and chanted what seemed to be a counterpart. The chanting continued throughout the funeral, and with one exception, the singers never missed a beat.

"Blood was streaming down the heads and shoulders and backs of the mourners. I wondered what had happened. I knew of the practice of chopping off fingers and slicing off pieces of ear, but this did not explain the blood over their bodies. Then I noticed that as the mourners climbed over the stile into the courtyard, they walked over to a pile of huge rocks, picked one up, and joined the chanting.

"As they marched, almost in step with the music, they beat their heads until the blood gushed out, and covered their bodies, as they walked toward the funeral pyre. Each person stood by the pyre and for a time seemed to lead the chanting, then melted back into the crowd.

"Meanwhile a man was chopping wood that was being neatly stacked to provide a resting place later for the corpse to be cremated. The pyre, when completed, measured about seven or eight feet long, four feet wide, and four feet high. The logs were carefully arranged to provide a good draft so that the body would be completely consumed by the flames.

"Watagon was a very popular young man and the crowd at the ceremony must have numbered five or six hundred. . . . Now the chanting stopped abruptly. I saw no signal. I heard no order. Suddenly it was so quiet you could have heard a leaf fall from a tree. Just as quickly the chant picked up again, this time in a faster tempo. They were carrying Watagon's body to the funeral pyre. They laid him on his side with his hands folded under his head as though he were asleep, his legs bent to fit properly on the pyre. Then other logs were carefully laid about him until the body was scarcely visible. Next they brought his bow and arrows which had been broken as an insult by the enemy, and laid the weapons on the funeral pyre along with the dead warrior's feather headdress, his neckband of shells, and other personal belongings. Then a flaming torch of wood ignited the pyre. The chant continued.

"The stench of the burning body was terrible, but I stayed to watch the entire proceeding. I felt the loss of Watagon who had been my good friend, and I wept. . . ."

After the embers cooled, some elderly men took some of the dead man's bones. One of them slipped out to the woods and brought back a seedling. Mixing the bones with oil, they planted the seedling in a little fenced enclosure at the side of the village. This was their memorial to the boy who had died in battle.

"I rose to go, but I heard someone call my name. It was Wooledomo, Watagon's older brother. He came toward me, crying out, 'Can you help me? Can you help me?' I am convinced that he was not asking for shells or material gifts; he wanted something more. At that time I had no command of the language. How I longed to quote the words of Christ, 'Let not your heart be troubled; ye believe in God, believe also in me.'

"But Wooledomo, with the pig fat on his face and the blood matting his hair, threw his arms about me, laid his head upon my shoulder, and sobbed as though his heart would break. All I could do was to put my arms about him and sob with him, sharing with him in his grief. How I longed to tell him of the One who had died to put away death forever for all who believe on His Name."

In subsequent days the missionaries learned more about the grisly customs of the Danis, especially the practice of cutting off fingers to express mourning. Usually women and girls followed this practice, using a stone ax to chop off a finger after striking the "crazy bone" as a crude anesthetic to numb the arm. Yet the victims often fainted and the wounds became badly infected. Again and again the missionaries were called upon to treat the wounds, maybe weeks after the funeral. The boys, who need their fingers for pulling the bowstring and throwing their spears, submit instead to having the upper portions of their ears sliced off.

The Danis couldn't understand why the missionaries' fingers and ears were intact. "Didn't you love your father and mother?" they often asked.

On one occasion Lloyd Van Stone heard a sharp cry at a funeral. A man had fainted as he chopped off his fingers with a steel ax. Then, in their confusion, the Danis excitely brought the four fingers and placed them in Van Stone's hand.

There seem to be differing accounts of what happens to the fingers and ears that are chopped off. Sometimes the fingers are thrown on the funeral pyre or placed in the men's houses on the rack above the fire, but Darlene Rose tells of cannibalistic aspects of the brutal custom.

On one occasion when Darlene had just dressed the ears of about fifteen little boys and the stumps of the fingers of several girls, she seized the opportunity to talk to them about the subject. In previous attempts the Dani children, like their elders, had denied that their part of the tribe ate human flesh. This time she tried another tack:

"Just how do you decide who eats those bits of ears?" she asked the children.

"Oh," they said, "they are passed out to the mourning relatives sitting around the funeral pyre."

"Whose ears are cut?"

"They are relatives'. The boys are relatives of the man who has died. Sometimes it's an important man, not a relative. Sometimes the boys have their ears cut off at a feast maybe one or two years after a man has died. Then the older men of the clan slice off the boys' ears and roast them on the funeral pyre. Different ones eat the ears."

"The fingers—who eats those?"

"Oh, we usually don't eat the fingers. They are put on the drying rack above the fire in the middle of the round house," one boy explained.

Then another boy spoke up: "They are eaten sometimes. I even saw a man in our village at Tulim who ate both the fingers and the ears of the young boys. He said he didn't bother to cook them or roast them. He just ate them raw."

"How terrible to eat them raw like that," another boy said. "Just like eating a crunchy raw potato. Just think of the 'crunch, crunch' it would make in your mouth!"

The first real setback in the missionaries' relations with the Dani people began in March, 1955, when an epidemic of measles broke out in the tribe. Diseases like measles often kill off large segments of a primitive group. Isolated tribes seem to have no immunity against the contagious diseases that are so common in civilized lands.

For some reason the Danis became suspicious of the aluminum

sheeting used in constructing homes. The natives were also fearful of the influence exerted by the steel drums used to transport all sorts of missionary equipment and supplies. The missionaries would find their houses painted with pig's blood, employed as a protection against evil spirits. Taboos were placed upon the mission stations, and neither women nor children could visit the homes of the white men. Fortunately, the strained relations disappeared when no death occurred from the epidemic.

Then came the fateful day of April 28, 1955. To the Baliem missionaries it began like any other day, except that it was a bit cloudy. Also, Jerry Rose and Lloyd Van Stone were entertaining Dick Lenehan, Sealand engineer-mechanic, who had come to the valley for a few days' rest. He and Al Lewis had just spent several weeks on a major overhaul of the Sealand motors and the pilot had urged Dick to take some time off.

Rose and Van Stone had left their families at Hepuba while they and Dick Lenehan traveled upriver in their motorboat to the landing site to await the expected arrival of the Sealand. After some time had elapsed, the three men came to the conclusion that bad weather on the other side of the mountains had forced Al Lewis to remain at Sentani. They decided it would be a good day to visit an area, located up the Aike, one of the side streams that enters the Baliem above Minimo.

Chugging up the Aike in the motorboat, the men were forced to dodge low-hanging tree branches. They enjoyed the scenery as they proceeded up the winding river. When they realized the water was getting too shallow, they stopped the boat. Just ahead they saw a native village. Jerry Rose remained with the boat, while his companions climbed an embankment leading up the settlement. They called out greetings, but the villagers fled in obvious fright. A few began to peer from behind trees; then some of the bolder ones cautiously came forward and gingerly shook the hands of the missionaries.

Knowing the advantage of medical treatment in the winning of friends quickly, Van Stone began to give penicillin injections to the Danis who were suffering from yaws. The natives had already heard about the benefits of this drug. The atmosphere of the village grew friendlier. Everything seemed to be going well. Then suddenly, an elderly man came running up the trail, yelling and brandishing a spear that he pointed with both hands at the two missionaries. The missionaries sought to quiet him, but he would not be placated. Instead, another Dani rushed to a nearby house and came back with a spear to side with the older man. Within moments the quiet village became a howling mob.

Van Stone drew his pistol and fired it over the heads of the Danis. The report of the gun confused the natives enough to permit Van Stone and Lenehan to race for the boat. As they ran, they were followed by a hail of spears. Van Stone swerved just in time to avoid being hit by one that buried itself in the center of the trail right where he had been running. Arrows began to rain upon the fleeing missionaries. The three men fired their weapons into the air again. Jerry Rose started the motorboat. Racing along either side of the stream, Van Stone and Lenehan eased the boat over a protruding log, then jumped into the craft. As it sped down the narrow, twisting stream, they feared every minute they would be killed in an ambush. The boat kept going until they reached the Baliem and crossed to the other side of the big river.

By this time Lloyd Van Stone discovered that an annoying "branch" that was hindering his leg movements actually was an arrow that had entered his left leg above the knee. In the confusion up the stream he had broken off the arrow, but the arrowhead had remained firmly inbedded in his leg. On the bank of the Baliem the three missionaries took time out to offer a prayer of thanksgiving that their lives had been spared. Then they boarded the boat again and chugged downstream to Hepuba to join the ladies and children.

Darlene tells about the arrival of the men on that fateful day:

" 'Why, Lloyd's limping!' I exclaimed. 'He must have been hurt.' My heart was in my mouth, for I knew they had arrived much earlier than we had expected them.

"Lloyd called out, 'Walk quietly to the house as though nothing had happened, and close the windows.' Doris grabbed my hand.

Both of us were trembling. We walked into the house and I started making coffee. Lloyd went into the bedroom while Bruce and I walked to get some water, trying to act as natural as possible before the natives. Then Doris came out and told me Lloyd had an arrow in his knee.

"Burney started to cry. 'Darlene, please talk to him,' Doris said. I grabbed Burney's finger that had just been burned on our boiler, as the natives watched intently.

"Burney, we'll act as though it was your finger that is causing the trouble. These people mustn't know your father was shot.'

"I slipped off the bandage from the boy's finger. A big blister had already formed.

" 'What is it?' the curious natives asked.

" 'He burned his finger in the fire,' I replied.

" '*Eigwo!* What a pity!" the natives exclaimed as they examined Burney's finger closely. We walked in the house and I dressed his injury again.

"The coffee was percolating as I went outside to greet Dick Lenehan and Jerry who were coming up the trail. They seemed relaxed, laughing as they talked, walking toward the house. The natives now turned their attention, monkeylike, to the ducks Jerry was carrying.

"I heated hot water for Jerry as soon as he had removed his trail boots. Then he began to scrub his hands. Using a cotton swab dipped in alcohol, he prepared the flesh on Lloyd's leg for four incisions that were necessary to reach the head of the arrow. When Jerry pulled the arrow from the wound with a sterilized pair of pliers, it was at least two inches long."

After administering a shot of penicillin to Van Stone, Jerry Rose and Dick Lenehan prepared to leave for Hetigima. They wanted to be near the radio at Hetigima when the broadcast from Sentani would be heard the next morning.

However, as they were going out the door, some of the natives began to yell, "Plane, plane!"

Darlene remembers the events well:

"We ran outside. Dick immediately could tell by the sound of the motors that it wasn't our plane. Then we saw that it was a Dutch Navy Catalina. A training flight, we all thought. The plane followed the course of the river, back up and down again. When it appeared over us a second time, it swooped over the house and dropped something.

"Lloyd saw how tense Dick was and it dawned upon him what was passing through the mind of the airplane mechanic: Something had happened to our plane!

"Jerry and some of the natives ran into the woods to find the object that had been dropped. Then the Catalina flew low over us a third time, dropping a message that landed in a tree in front of the house. When it had been retrieved, we read the cryptic note: 'Contact Hollandia at once.' Jerry and Dick left on a run for Hetigima and the radio.

"It seemed forever until a message reached us from Hetigima. Jerry and Dick finally heard the voice of Mary Lewis, the pilot's wife, and Myron Bromley, trying to contact Al Lewis by radio. Our battery was down, so the people at Sentani were unable to get a message from the Baliem. Later, we learned it had buoyed them up with false hopes. They had thought that no word from the valley radio meant that Al had landed on the Baliem River and was staying overnight."

Van Stone slept in the tent and Doris and Darlene slept in the house. It was a long dreadful night, with all of the adults tossing restlessly, and trying to figure out what had happened to the airplane and its skilled pilot. Their hearts went out to Mary Lewis who they knew would be waiting by the radio at Sentani.

What would be the future of the work in the Baliem Valley if the airplane and its pilot were lost? Would the missionaries be evacuated? What would be the attitude of the natives if the missionaries were marooned in the valley? Would the men be able to stay if the women and children were forced to leave? Could the Missionary Aviation Fellowship airplane that served other societies land at Hetigima?

It was a night of unanswered questions and tense anxiety. Only next day did the Baliem workers learn that Al Lewis, heading the

Sealand toward the Baliem Valley, had reported his last position over the Idenburg River at 9:23 A.M. There was just one more fragmentary report.

Al Lewis, a few days earlier, had suffered an injury to his eye when his hand slipped while cranking the propeller. He developed a black eye. This gave meaning to a cryptic message he spoke into the airplane microphone a short time after he had given his position over the Idenburg. Dave Steiger, MAF pilot flying over the western end of New Guinea, heard Lewis say, "It's as black here as my left eye." Dark clouds apparently had closed in on him as he sought to pilot the Sealand through the treacherous Pass Valley. But it was a month later before missionaries and pilots were able to learn what had happened.

At Sentani Mary Lewis and Myron Bromley, who had gone to Hollandia for dental work, called on the radio incessantly, hoping against hope that contact might be made with the airplane. Lewis had been eager to make as many trips as he could into the Baliem with supplies, since the water level of the Baliem was dropping again. Thus, even though the weather at Lake Sentani had been cloudy and threatening, he had decided to fly into the valley after receiving word that the sky was fairly clear in the Baliem.

Unaccompanied, he had taken off from the Sentani airstrip at 8:40 A.M. He indicated that the flight was proceeding according to plan when he called in from the Idenburg, saying then that everything was normal except that a light rain was falling. A few minutes later, Steiger heard what proved to be his last message.

In spite of adverse weather conditions the Netherlands government that afternoon sent out a Navy Catalina to start an aerial search that continued for the next five days. Charles Mellis, MAF pilot, quickly changed from wheels on his Piper Pacer to pontoons, then flew into the Baliem to pick up Dick Lenehan, who joined him in the search for the missing craft.

Even after the Dutch government called off its search, MAF pilots continued to fly back and forth across the high ridges, seeking to locate the amphibian that had disappeared without a trace. The aerial hunt was complicated by persistent rumors that an airplanes had been seen flying over Lake Sentani about 11:00 A.M. on April 28. A party af searchers dragged the lake for two days in the vicinity of an oil slick near the spot where rumors had placed the plane.

Kenneth Troutman, board representative, had flown in from Enarotali to direct the search, and had conferred with government officials, MAF pilots, and Richard Lenehan in the vain rescue efforts. Finally he chartered an Australian airplane to comb the mountains. It was not until May 28, exactly a month after the Sealand had last been seen, that Troutman, flying over the rugged Pass Valley, accompanied by Lenehan and two Dutch civil aviation officials, had spotted the wreckage of the Alliance airplane. It was lying on the high rugged slopes of the north side of a cliff guarding the Pass Valley. Ironically, Lewis had crashed not far from the site of the accident that had taken the lives of twenty-one soldiers and WACs.

Intense studies of the terrain were made from the air and government maps were examined closely to determine whether an overland search party could reach the crash site, but the Dutch government finally ruled that they had neither the men nor the equipment for such an undertaking. The gallant missionaries and sympathetic government officials did not know it then, but four years were to intervene before a land party would reach the site.

Lewis' death and the loss of the airplane was a severe blow to the band of missionaries in the Baliem. They well knew how dependent they were on the airplane for survival. It was a dark period that was brightened only by the emergency flights and food drops provided by the pilots of the Missionary Aviation Fellowship. As a precautionary measure, the wives and children of the Baliem missionaries were evacuated from the valley.

In New York City, Alliance officials decided to take another look at the New Guinea aviation program. They considered a number of factors that had changed since the flying operation had been launched a year earlier. While it had been mandatory that the initial flights into the mountainous interior of New Guinea be made in an airplane that could land on water, surveys had revealed that very satisfactory landing strips could be built at Hetigima, Wamena in the central valley, and near Pyramid Mountain in the upper part of the valley.

In the western part of the highlands there were airstrip sites at Obano, opposite Enarotali on the other side of Lake Paniai, Lake Tigi, and Homejo. Furthermore, impressed by the experience of the MAF fliers, who used Piper Pacers and similar single-engine airplanes, Dutch authorities were inclined to relax the ruling that only twin-engined airplanes could make flights into the rugged interior. Finally, a year's experience with the Sealand had demonstrated that successful flights into the valley depended on the water level of the Baliem River. This was a great limitation to the missionary program that required year-round dependable flight service.

After much discussion, Alliance leaders decided that the society would purchase two single-engined Cessna 180 airplanes. In the interval between April and September, 1955, the Baliem and other stations were served by MAF airplane. First airstrip in the Baliem Valley was the one that had been rushed to completion by July 16 at Hetigima. Other strips were constructed later at stations in the western end of New Guinea.

In the years ahead the airplane would continue to aid the missionaries. Other brave pilots would fly over the ranges to maintain the aerial lifeline, but the name of Al Lewis was written in heaven as the pilot who initiated the missionary flight program in New Guinea. In a very real sense Pilot Lewis had become Martyr Lewis, a faithful witness who laid down his life in bringing the gospel to the tribespeople of Dutch New Guinea.

7

HURDLES TO A CULTURE

"Death, death, death! When will it cease? Or when at least will it be illuminated by the Light of Life that transcends its tragedy? The year ends with a week of death from war and disease and feuding. We pray that God will soon let new life be born in men's hearts here. I try to help our friends with pliers [to remove arrow tips]. I try to help them with pills. But I am kicked in the face with the suddenness of death. We sometimes dream that the work could progress were there not the fightings and feuds—only to sit with mud-smeared mourners around the pyres of new victims. We dream of great achievement—only to be shaken by inexplicable personal failure."

These were the anguished words of Myron Bromley as he came into daily contact with the harsh, crude brutality of savage culture. He was more deeply convinced than ever that divine, redemptive help was the only answer.

Turning from the sordid scenes from which his sensitive soul recoiled, he concluded,

"No, the answer is not in us nor in our efforts, nor in our culture; it is in Christ, who waits to see if we will believe Him, if we will let Him accomplish His purpose during the year. God helping me, no, God living through me, I shall see His triumph this coming twelve months."

There were all kinds of hurdles and obstructions that hindered missionary advance in the Baliem Valley but none loomed so large as the towering wall of language difference. Reduced to its simplest elements, the job of proclaiming the gospel is one of effective communication. Ever since the confusion of tongues at Babel, the servants of the Lord in all generations first have had to make themselves understood. Christian witness involves total life impact, but this does not negate the fact that thoughts are conveyed principally by words—words that must be comprehensible to the listener.

In the beginning the missionaries had to rely on gestures to convey their thoughts. Attempts to speak the native language confused the Danis, who responded by shouting into their ears as though they were deaf.

Painfully, the missionaries, and especially Myron Bromley with his knowledge of linguistics, began to compile lists of words and expressions in the slow, tedious job of language analysis. In their isolation from the rest of the world, the Danis had little appreciation of the sore trials the missionaries were experiencing in trying to understand and make themselves understood.

"The language helpers have been a bit of a problem," Bromley noted in a letter to his mother. "Many of the young folks have been reluctant to share their language and the older folks, who try their best to help, have been unable to comprehend what I want. But some have been really helpful. One is an impressive headman we have dubbed Redbeard because of the strawberry blond streak in the middle of his bushy whiskers. His name is Wenekali. He has consistently worked for us, bringing us garden produce and freshly killed pork. He gets restless when I try to work with him for long periods of time, but he is excellent at giving me normal conversational idioms.

"All have been more helpful than the fellow with whom I tried to check the dialect the day of our last preliminary contact trip.

To my dismay I discovered after twenty minutes of disconcerting work that he said an 'l' where everyone else made an 'n' sound because of some mouth deformity. Well, that's still not as bad as Eugene Nida's story of the new missionary who ran into a stutterer as the only willing informant."

Bromley described his first attempts at preaching the gospel at a mountain village where he had been invited for the first time. After giving several injections for yaws, he sat down in the men's courtyard and tried to tell them about Christ.

"It was one of the most discouraging experiences I've had," he recounted. "I used pictures from a scripture calendar and tried my best to say all I could as simply and intelligently as possible. But the natives looked as if I were talking in Latin about the price of corn in Asia. . . . Yet in some places in the Pugima Valley where I have talked to folk in a village for the first time, I have been greeted with a series of intelligent questions. Indeed, this is the work of His Spirit and if He does not open men's minds and hearts, our task is helpless. Perhaps the Lord wanted to remind me that this message is not something to be casually huckstered but a redemptive cry of good news to be passionately shared in His Spirit's power."

It was almost a year before Bromley was able to write a technical paper entitled "The Phonetic Structure of the Language of the Lower Grand Baliem Valley." By then he knew that the Dani language of the lower valley contained seventeen consonants and seven vowels. At first he could recognize only five vowels. Then one day he discovered that there were two "high-front double-E-like vowels and two high-back-W- or double-O-like vowels." These seemingly insignificant discoveries constituted a major breakthrough and cleared up a number of problems relating to the sound structure of the strange tribal tongue.

Bromley worked away at his tedious task. In the first three months of 1955, he concentrated on problems of pitch, stress, and length of vowels, but, he wrote a friend, "the grammar is still in the diaper stage."

Pictures of life in the valley were graphically related by Bromley in a letter sent to his mother in Meadville, Pennsylvania:

"Nahulukak, my best little language informant from this area, took me on a Cook's tour of our gardens, pointing out the spot where some of the Dani pigs had eaten some of our sweet potatoes. He showed me the section where the soybeans were growing. The people are crazy about soybeans. We are hoping we can introduce them here. Any increase in their protein diet would be helpful to the people. So for his work, Nahulukak got a handful of soy beans and tops from our spinach plants.

"He's an intriguing kid . . . an excellent informant as long as he can keep still. That's not long because he's all boy. Nakulukak is one of the few Danis who jump me on my pronunciation and grammar. He just bluntly says, 'That's terrible.' He does not give up riding me until I get rid of the mistake. . . . He's the boy who told me one day when I skipped shaving that my 'garden needed weeding.' "

"I've tried to talk about John 3:16," he told his mother in another letter, dated August 7, 1955, "but I'm sure I made a lot of blunders, for I didn't go over the verse ahead of time with anyone. You can imagine how faulty my interpretation must have been, since we have no adequate terms for 'God,' 'believe,' or 'everlasting life.' I talk about 'Jesus' father' because we know as yet of no belief of these people that would furnish a good term for 'God.' They know of the ghosts of their dead, of noise-making, heart-stealing spirits of the lowland peoples that cause people to lose their minds. They speak of the sun and moon as husband and wife and they think of the rain as a person. Also they talk about a tiny man up in the sky called Hulisogom, but they are vague about the origin of earth. So far I have not discovered that they have a creation story.

"For the word 'believe' I get along with the term that means 'hear' or 'understand.' I can say 'I think he's telling the truth,' but that's something different from Biblical faith.

"As for everlasting life, I can say that we will remain alive, but that is not Jesus' or John's idea. Or I can say our skin and bones and our meat and blood will die but our souls will live, but this is not the Biblical idea either. How to say that God creates in us a new kind of life that will be ours right now and forever is something I don't know yet.

"When I try to explain the whole concept of Jesus' dying for us, I say that he died in our interest that we may remain alive . . . but the whole central concept of the atonement is beyond the grasp of our language. Probably this is because we don't really know how to talk about sin. I usually use the expression 'bad acting,' but that's quite different from the true concept of sin. One could talk about breaking taboos, but that's exactly the idea we don't want to use, since we are so uncertain about the meaning of *wesa,* or taboo, in the thought and culture of these people. Acts that are so obviously sinful to us are items of cultural praise—killing, cruelty to enemies, hatred, pride, jealousy, disdain of the weak and the inferior.

"This afternoon I did my best to talk straight to a little boy I strongly suspect of stealing a file from me, but he pleaded innocence persistently. We surely have not suffered greatly from thievery but the problem is increasing. . . . Their pattern of treatment is to beat the culprit, kill a pig, or steal something of his. . . . We almost never know certainly who does the stealing, and I've only heard one person confess to doing something wrong."

During his first year or two in the Baliem, Bromley spent as much time giving first aid and medical treatments as he devoted to language study. He described his experiences in letters home:

"The little boy that is staying with us told me his grandfather was ill. I finally trudged up the mountain trail to the old man's village. I found that it was situated just beyond Pugima where two women, victims of a sneak attack in their gardens by our villagers, were being cremated. When I reached the home of old Ohali (Home Firewood), I discovered that he was a very sick man. He seemed to be suffering from some sort of malaria, so I gave him medicine. But he was too near death. A few days later I went to his funeral. On my way up to the village, I could see the smoke rising from the hill beyond Minimo. It was a victory signal at

Pugima, marking the favorable outcome in a skirmish that day. Two of the men from our village were trapped and killed. . . . The fighting party came back without the bodies, but next day the enemies carried them to the top of the ridge. Our people went up to get them, carrying the corpses right by our station. One of the men's bodies was perforated with spear wounds. Both of these young men had worked for us and I knew them well."

Sensitive to human suffering, the linguist never could understand the incessant cruelty of heathen life. He told his mother about the spearing of a young Dani:

"A young friend of ours named Lanite stole and ate a pig belonging to an important man in Pobietma. Later I saw the irate owner of the stolen pig walking down the trail behind our property. He was carrying a huge pig (apparently one taken as a reimbursement for his lost property), and behind him another man was carrying a second pig (extra reimbursement). . . . Ukumhearik gave the word that Lanite should not get off so lightly, so two young warriors were dispatched by the chief to punish Lanite. They caught him in his garden and speared him twice.

"When I went up to see him the next day, Lanite looked bad, but not as feeble as one would expect a fellow to be who had two spears thrust clear through him. I washed the wounds, sprinkled them with sulpha powder, gave him a shot of penicillin, and then prayed with him. When I saw him again two days later I found that he had made amazing improvement. By some miracle the spears must have missed his intestines. His only remaining problem seems to be that the spear wound in the front abdominal wall has caused a sort of rupture."

On another occasion Bromley tried vainly to save the life of a man who had been wounded in one of the interminable feuds. The missionary, summoned to the injured man's village, found the victim with a six-inch portion of a spear imbedded in his back. The natives had tried to remove the section of spear with dirty needles and even tried pulling it out with their teeth. When Bromley arrived the man was already unconscious and burning up with fever. With a sterilized pair of pliers Bromley pulled out the spear that had apparently been wedged between two vertebrae. But the shock of the extraction was too much for the injured man. Bromley learned next day that he had died.

Every moment he could spare from his medical ministrations he continued to devote to his linguistic task.

Bromley found that in the forty-mile length of the valley there were probably three major dialects. Dialect A could understand B, B could understand C, but A could not understand C and vice versa.

Some experts on the language of primitive peoples once maintained that the simpler and least advanced peoples spoke simple dialects, but Bromley discovered that the Stone Age Danis used one possessing strange patterns of syntax and complicated verb forms. He learned that in the highly complicated language structure a single verb might have two thousand different forms. By the use of auxiliaries added to a basic verb stem a Dani is able to express a wide variety of meaning.

In his attempts to get acquainted with the people Bromley often joined them in the singing of their folk songs even when he did not understand the words. He found later that he had been singing ribald songs dealing with intimate sexual matters—a subject hardly suited to the spiritual standards of the Christian worker.

The enormous job of language reduction is only the first step in the formidable linguistic problem. All the time he was becoming more familiar with the language, Bromley was engaged in teaching his colleagues to understand and speak the native tongue, since no real missionary work could be accomplished until the workers could converse fairly fluently. Since Dani is not a written language, it was necessary to develop an orthography so that the Danis could learn to read their own tongue. Teaching the Danis to read and write was to come later, along with the job of translating the Bible and other materials into Dani. The Church of Christ in central New Guinea one day would need the Holy Scriptures as its authority and source of strength.

Myron Bromley's knowledge of the language advanced. He was enabled to probe deeper into the complex culture of the Danis, learning the meaning of Solomon's comment, "The tender mercies of the wicked are cruel."

Selekarogo, an amiable-looking Dani living near the mission station at Hepuba, stole a pig and butchered it. When the animal's owner, a tribesman living in the hillside village on the opposite side of the Baliem, discovered his loss, he sought retribution. Normally, the matter would have been settled by the thief's returning a pig for the one stolen, or the owner might seize a pig from the thief in revenge.

When the raiding party set out to follow the second course they were repulsed with casualties. Selekarogo thrust his spear through a boy accompanying the raiders, killing him instantly, and then seriously wounded a young warrior.

Myron Bromley climbed the hill to give medical treatment to the injured warrior. As the missionary looked out upon the valley he could see a column of smoke rising from the village where Selekarogo lived. It was then that Bromley learned that the body of the boy who had been killed was being roasted—the first cannibalistic act that had occurred since the missionaries had entered the valley. "Those twisting columns of smoke," Bromley said, "symbolized to me strands of wicked cruelty braided into Baliem life."

The killing might have ended there but Ukumhearik, chief in Selekarogo's village, would not let the matter rest. He announced that the avenging raiders from the enemy village had taken a pig that belonged to him. Ukumhearik dispatched Yameke, his brother and one of his important aides, to kill the headman of the enemy hillside village. Yameke, who was very friendly to Bromley, had that very day been helping the missionary sew the torn fly of a tent. He left this task to carry out his murderous mission. In another skirmish, a second headman from the hillside village was wounded. But this was not the end.

The widowed mother of the boy killed in the raid could bear no further grief. Only a short time before her hubsand had been killed in battle. With the boy's death, only she and a baby daughter survived. Grief-stricken, she rushed down to the river, drowning herself and her baby girl.

The price for the stolen pig could now be reckoned: two men had been seriously wounded and four other persons were dead.

Far from enjoying a peaceful, idyllic life that many feel is only spoiled by missionary "intrusion," the Stone Age Danis lived constantly in the shadow of fear and death. Even tiny children could be heard to say again and again, "That's *wesa* [taboo]; aren't you afraid?"

Wesa and *ajuk* (fear) were woven into the warp and woof of the Dani social structure. Almost anything one might discuss was *wesa:* the sun and the moon; large trees and rocks; the consecrated lineage fetishes and charms; the magic pigs; the initiation rites for boys.

Exalted also in the Dani culture was the place of the pig. It was not just a domestic animal raised for its meat; men often prized their pigs above their wives. The pig's place in Dani culture and economy is explained by Jerry Rose:

"It's a vicious circle. You can start anywhere you want: The more pigs a man has, the more cowrie shells he can get. The more shells he possesses, the more wives he can buy. The more wives he owns, the more sweet potato gardens can be cultivated; the more sweet potatoes, the more pigs he can feed, the more cowrie shells, the more wives. Thus, the circle includes greed for cowrie shells, plural marriage, and pigs."

Christianity strikes at the core of Dani culture, disrupting the old patterns. A Christian Dani could hardly survive in the old cultural pattern.

"A Christian Dani with only one wife," Rose pointed out, "would virtually take a vow of poverty for the rest of his life. He would have no prestige in the eyes of his people, who are most impressed by cowrie shells, wives, and pigs."

Looking down upon the apparently peaceful valley from the air, one sees clumps of native houses. Tree-lined hills guard the

serenity of the lovely hidden valley. This is the outward picture.
But behind it lurks fear, superstition, and death.

Villages are grouped according to kinship structure. Clans are
made up of exogamous moieties, that is, portions of the tribe into
which other portions may not marry. The important blood line is
patrilineal, stemming from the importance of the father. Thus a
Dani is primarily concerned with knowing to which moiety he
belongs. It is *wesa* for one to marry into his own moiety, compar-
able to incest in Western society.

The moieties are linked into confederacies which are maintained
throughout the centuries and determine the battle lines for the
warfare that is conducted on a cyclic basis. Fighting is not only a
Dani's normal recreation, but his way of demonstrating his virility
and courage. A man who does not engage in battle, they say, will
lose his powers and may even go blind.

In time Myron Bromley was able to piece together the Dani
version of the story of creation. One of his Dani friends described
it this way:

"There was always earth, or, if not, it just came of itself. We
do not know. But a long time ago the very first people came out
of the water that splashed down the mountain on the other side
of the valley. There were lots of them, both men and women. It's
quite natural that they appeared here, for one can easily see that
this is very near the center of the earth. Here the sky is high and
the pillars that hold it up are nowhere visible.

"Those first people came clan by clan, each clan carrying something. The Aso [mythical being] brought sweet potatoes. Lokobal
[another mythical personality] brought the water of the Baliem
and pigs. One clan furnished tobacco and stones. Others brought
taro, fire, mosquitoes, flies, and sores, and the braided vine rope
with which the pigs are tied. After the first pig feast, one pigtail
fled in fright to the top of the mountains to become the tall pan-
danus tree with its meaty, nutlike fruit.

"So, furnished with everything, the people spread, clan paired
with clan. . . . Only later did attacks prompt war that separated
the people into enemy groups. That is what they say."

Up to this time Myron Bromley had not married. One of the Alliance officials had confided to Bromley's mother that he should now do so. When this word reached New Guinea it met with considerable resistance from the young linguist.

"I know that bacherlorhood can get to be a habit," he wrote the leader, "and I've asked God to deliver me from obstinancy in this matter. However, one factor has rather strongly turned me from this possibility—so many other folks have felt God's direction. Somehow I feel God is gentleman enough to talk to me about my life before He speaks, or at least while He speaks, to others about me, if I am willing to hear."

Subsequent events removed the need for concern about Bromley's unmarried state.

8

CANNIBAL FEAST

Marooned since Al Lewis' death, Lloyd Van Stone and Jerry Rose tackled the crucial job of building a landing strip for small airplanes at Hetigima in the lower end of Baliem Valley. By this time they were convinced that they must look to land planes rather than to amphibians for year-round air service. Thus they would be undisturbed by the vagaries of the river.

After some experimenting, they chose a long sloping location on the hillside just south of the Van Stones' station. The construction operation was a sizable engineering feat that had to be accomplished without the aid of modern equipment.

Fortunately, the Danis came out in large numbers and proved to be willing workers under the direction of the two missionaries. The whole area first had to be cleared, trees felled and removed, stone fences and abandoned gardens leveled. Using both stone and steel axes, the Danis whacked away, and with their crude digging sticks, used normally to plow their gardens, they removed the smaller hummocks of earth. This became fill for the lower spots.

The project, which began on May 20, 1955, was completed less

120

than two months later. On July 16 Charles Mellis, MAF pilot, landed his Pacer on the new fourteen-hundred-foot airstrip, the first of a network of all-weather fields that would serve the Baliem Valley.

The establishment of air transportation in the Baliem meant not only that wives and children could return from the coast. It meant that the work of the Lord could proceed more effectively.

Three weeks before the first airplane landed, Hutsunek, eleven-year-old brother of Chief Ukumhearik, fell from a tree and was badly injured. Hutsunek, who lived in the family village of Pobietma less than a mile away, sent for the missionaries, believing they could relieve his suffering.

Van Stone found him lying in a dark corner in his mother's long grass house. Since his leg was twisted in a strange position, it was obvious that it had been broken. Blood was also flowing from his mouth and ears. Van Stone called for additional help, and soon was joined by Rose and Bromley. The three missionaries set the boy's leg and sewed up his torn lip.

But the following morning when Van Stone visited Hutsunek, he found that the family had removed the splint. The missionary carried Hutsunek to the mission station and the leg was reset. Van Stone kept him in his home.

A few days later the boy, languishing on his cot, said,

"Tuan Peton [Stone], I'm going to die."

Van Stone scarcely comprehended what the boy was saying.

Hutsunek repeated, "I'm going to die." Preoccupied with other matters, the missionary left the boy alone as he went out briefly. He returned a few minutes later to find Hutsunek lying on his side face down. Turning the boy over, he was convinced he was near death. A native blurted out, "Tuan, he's dead."

Myron Bromley was summoned and the two missionaries worked over the sick boy, then prayed for him. Van Stone sat by Hutsunek's bedside most of the night. By early morning the lad seemed to be breathing normally again.

But Hutsunek was an unruly patient. Five days later Van Stone was awakened by what he thought was the noise of the ever-present rats. He arose to find that Hutsunek was trying to get the door open so he could return to his own home. Hutsunek, a member of the "royal" household, sullenly refused to talk. Next morning after Van Stone had reported the matter to Hutsunek's mother, she reprimanded the lad and told him he must obey the missionary. Again his leg had to be reset.

For a week Hutsunek again seemed on the way to recovery, then one night he fell from the cot on which he was sleeping. On the very next day the MAF airplane made the initial landing at Hetigima. The missionaries quickly decided that they would have Hutsunek transported to the hospital in Hollandia. So it was that the airplane's well-timed appearance probably saved the life of the chief's brother.

Proper medical treatment and nursing care at the hospital quickly restored Hutsunek to health. His return to the valley was a cause for great rejoicing. Ukumhearik was plainly pleased even though he still continued to resist the spiritual ministry offered by the white men.

Airplane service was badly needed for other reasons, too. Growth of the missionary force in the Wissel Lakes region had created a far greater demand for transport and supplies than the existing government aircraft could provide. At first the Alliance workers in that area hoped they could construct an airstrip adjacent to Enarotali, headquarters of the Kapauku work. But they were then advised that the ground around Enarotali was too boggy to support a field.

The missionaries finally located a natural landing strip on the flat land adjacent to a lovely cove of Lake Paniai, about five miles due west of Enarotali. Even though this meant a five-mile ferry trip across the lake to bring in supplies and baggage, it was a great relief to the missionary operation.

By now the Alliance's own airplane, a Cessna 180, had resumed the service maintained temporarily by MAF. Heading the restored aviation program was Ed Ulrich, Al Lewis' co-pilot. He was ably helped by William Paul, a new pilot, and Dick Lenehan, who continued to serve as mechanic.

Air transportation took on greater importance in 1956 as the missionary program was expanded throughout all of New Guinea. In addition to the solid work that was developing in the Wissel Lakes area, missionary teams fanned out from Enarotali to the long coveted Ilaga Valley with its teeming populations of Danis and Uhundunis. The Ilaga soon would be the pivotal link spiritually as well as geographically between the Wissel Lakes and the Baliem.

In the same year the Alliance dispatched six new missionary couples into the Baliem Valley. They would build and occupy a network of permanent stations and airstrips that would make it possible for them to reach the principal population concentrations of the valley.

Other missionary societies by now were becoming active.

The Unevangelized Fields Mission, which had long studied the opportunities of Dutch New Guinea, first established a station at Sengge, about fifty miles south of Hollandia. Then a UFM exploration party made an overland trek from the Baliem Valley to Archbold Lake, high in the mountains to the north, after being flown to the Baliem River landing site by the Alliance airplane. Finding the population sparse in the immediate vicinity of Archbold Lake, the UFM missionaries established an airstrip and station at Bokodini on the Habblifoeri River.

Australian Baptists, after conferring with the other missionary societies and the Dutch government, entered the North Baliem area to the west of the Grand Valley. The Regions Beyond Missionary Union sent a survey party into the Swart Valley, to the west of Bokodini and northwest of the main valley of the Baliem. The Evangelical Alliance Mission had already established work in the Bird's Head at New Guinea's extreme western tip. Subsequently this mission sent workers into the desolate swamp country of the south coast where Michael Rockefeller later was lost.

Comity discussions between the evangelical missionary groups had resulted in amicable arrangements of the territories each would occupy in virtually all of the interior. As befitted their calling, the various groups would work together to further the gospel.

Co-operation of the missionary societies was best symbolized by the construction of a new airstrip at Pyramid Mountain which soon would become the largest station in the Baliem.

Decision of the Australian Baptists and Alliance missionaries to join together in the construction of the airfield at Pyramid was prompted by two considerations: By combining forces, Einar Mickelson and Lloyd Van Stone felt there would be mutual protection against an attack from the natives of the region who they knew were hostile. To the Baptists the airstrip would be an intermediate point for airplanes flying to their mission territory.

The mission groups agreed in advance that they would approach the new Pyramid site from two directions and would meet there on August 1. Accordingly, a party of five Australians, accompanied by seven carriers, decided to hike overland from the new Unevangelized Fields Mission at Bokodini, several miles north of the Baliem Valley, to Pyramid.

Meanwhile, five Alliance missionaries, including Mickelson, Van Stone, and Bromley, and two of the new missionaries, planned to travel at least half of the route from Hetigima to Pyramid up the Baliem River in a sixteen-foot outboard boat. The new missionaries were Edward Maxey, who served as an assistant pastor in Dr. A. W. Tozer's church in Chicago, and Henry Young, a sturdily built former lumberman from British Columbia.

As the boat bearing the Alliance party chugged upstream, the missionaries sought to show friendship to natives they encountered enroute by tossing them gifts of cowrie shells. Curious Danis were quick to accept these gifts.

Only one incident suggested Dani hostility. At the confluence of the Ibele River, halfway to their destination, the Alliance group discovered that some natives had placed a huge log near the riverbank and then stacked a huge pile of dry grass behind it. As the boat approached the log, the Danis ignited the grass. It seemed to the missionaries more like a native prank than an act of hostility.

That night the Alliance missionaries camped several miles above the Ibele. They slept soundly under a tarpaulin. Any earlier apprehension seemed unjustified. Next morning they marched overland to Pyramid, making their rendezvous with the Baptists at the end of the second day.

The following day the members of the two mission groups, aided by native workers, began to clear the land for the airstrip. In less than a month they had leveled off the new landing field. Now there were airstrips at both ends of the Baliem Valley and before long Hetigima would be linked to others spotted at intervals clear across western Dutch New Guinea. Just to the west of Pyramid was the stream which flowed into the Baliem River. On this tributary, which was called the North Baliem, although it flowed from west to east, the Australian Baptists built a station to be known as Tiom.

Back in the Grand Valley of the Baliem the other new missionaries were assigned to various stations, according to the time of their arrival. Since the Van Stones had departed on furlough, Tom and Frances Bozeman were sent to Hetigima. Bozeman, nearly six feet tall, with brown eyes and hair, was a smiling intense extrovert with a pleasant Southern accent. His wife was a pretty blue-eyed blonde whose speech indicated her Florida birthplace. They had two small daughters, Rosalind and Esther. The Hepuba station, which had been the Roses' home, was consolidated with Hetigima. Bromley moved to the Bozeman station, making his home in a nearby gudang (storehouse).

It was not long before the Bozemans were describing their new impressions to friends back in the States:

"The children are getting used to the Danis. When we go on trail, the natives carry Rosalind and Esther on their shoulders. Nearly every time the girls fall asleep before we reach home. The Danis just can't pronounce our name. The nearest they come to it is 'Boatman.' The other night we heard a weird chant coming from the back of the house. The Danis were repeating 'Tuan Boatman' again and again. We finally went to the door, holding our breath. They just wanted to give us a huge sweet potato."

New Guinea just wasn't like Florida. "In the States when we wanted to relax," the Bozemans wrote friends, "we drove down town to the Dairy Queen for some ice cream. Now, we go down to Elisa and Ruth's and watch a pig killing.

"The Danis are great. We just love every one of them, even though they have pig fat and soot smeared on their bodies. We find it easy to put our arms around them and hug their smelly necks. This may sound funny to you but the Danis are very likable and they've already formed a big place in our hearts."

Within a few months Tom Bozeman had demonstrated that he was missionary material. He made remarkable progress in speaking the language, and his warm, easy manner won him the loyalty of the Danis living in the vicinity.

Probably Bozeman's most significant achievement was gaining the friendship of Ukumhearik, the powerful chief. Ukumhearik showed more deference to Bozeman than to any of the other white men stationed in the valley. But Bozeman was also aware that the wily headman's smiles did not change his deep-seated aversion to the gospel message.

Bozeman and Ed Maxey, who later would open a new mid-valley station at Tulim, worked together on a number of mission projects. They tramped over the stony trails, visited native villages, and slaved to learn the tricky native tongue. They also shared in an experience that no missionary had witnessed first-hand: the gruesome sight of natives consuming the body of a slain foe.

There were many reports of cannibalism but none of the missionaries had witnessed it. Danis had told Myron Bromley of victory celebrations after battles that ended in a feast on human flesh; he had even seen the smoke of the macabre victory fires.

Tom Bozeman tells the story:

"The Danis around Hetigima told me that there was hardly a person in our area that had not tasted human flesh at one time or another. Yet, it's funny when you talk to the Danis on our side of the Baliem. They say, 'Oh, no, we don't eat people; they do it on the other side of the river.' But when you question the residents of the opposite side of the valley, they deny the charge and accuse the Danis in our area.

"The Danis were always involved in battles and men were being wounded and killed so often, it had become a part of our lives. I remember the Sunday afternoon, though, when some of the villagers living near us dropped by our station after a big battle.

"I asked them how the battle had gone. They replied, 'Great! We killed a fellow, speared him right through the heart. He dropped dead and the enemy left him where he fell as they retreated. So we grabbed his body and hid it. Tomorrow we're going to have a big feast. We want you to come and see it.'

"None of us were really interested in seeing anyone eaten, but we thought we should verify the story. Next morning Ed and I went down to the Baliem River and crossed to the other side on a little Dani raft. People were already gathering on the other side of the river. There was the witch doctor and families—fathers, mothers, boys and girls. Before long hundreds of Danis had gathered for the feast. We walked with them for what must have been an hour's hike to the side of a hill where the big event was to take place.

"Already the dark-skinned natives, all painted up and dressed in their finest feathers and beads, were racing back and forth in a victory dance. They just run back and forth, the men in one group and the women in another. Sometimes they change the back-and-forth pattern and dance around in circles.

" 'Well,' I said to my Dani friends. 'You're going to have a cannibal feast, but where's the body?'

"Several little boys took me by the hand and led me over to the side of the hill.

" 'Here he is,' they cried, watching to see how the white man would react.

"Sure enough, there was a man's dead body under a layer of grass, where the corpse had been concealed since the previous day's battle.

"I could see the Danis were working themselves into a frenzy. They hardly had time for Ed and me to treat their battle wounds and to give them shots of penicillin.

"It was ten o'clock in the morning and it was getting awfully hot. You can imagine the state of that corpse lying there in the hot sunshine.

"The dance continued until everyone who was expected to be present had arrived.

" 'Let's go and cut a pole,' one Dani yelled.

"We were about a mile and a half from the edge of enemy territory in a no-man's land where the battles are always fought. On the knoll of the hill above I could see that a crowd of the enemy had gathered to watch the proceedings. They had been told that their foes were going to eat the body of their kinsman. They were watching, fearfully waiting for the awful ceremony to begin.

"A group of the victors came running with an eight-foot wooden pole and some dried banana fiber. Using the fiber as rope, the Danis tied the corpse to the pole. Then four strong young warriors hoisted the pole to their shoulders and carried the body, pierced with fifteen or more spear wounds, across the battle ground to a place closer to the mourners on the ridge of the hill. Crossing the fields, the carriers had to knock down fences as they struggled with their heavy burden. It was a nasty sight as they carried the bloody corpse for almost an hour's walk to conduct the feast in full view of the enemy gallery.

"Up on the hillside, black with people, the crowd was milling about, crying, weeping, and shouting.

" 'Give us back our body,' they cried. They wanted to have an honorable cremation for their dead warrior and they hated the shame of this terrible spectacle—the most stinging insult in Dani culture.

" 'We're going to eat him,' the victorious crowd below shouted in derision.

"Finally, the carriers dropped their burden on the ground and the banana fibers were untied. The Danis had brought the body as close as they dared, close enough for the defeated group to see, but not near enough to prompt a counterattack.

"Ed and I pressed close. Then we saw scores of women, rushing en masse toward the body. Many of them were armed with digging

Chief Ukumhearik, a smiling but deadly foe of Christianity, holds life-and-death sway over more than 10,000 Danis in the region near Hetigima. Outwardly friendly to missionaries, he fears and fights the threat of the gospel to the old order which permits him to keep 22 wives and to wage savage and unlimited warfare against traditional enemies.

E. W. Ulrich

Dani warriors smear pig grease on their hair and bodies, and rub soot into their faces before battles or tribal ceremonies. Boar tusks, beads and fetishes, cowrie shells, and war bonnets are frequent adornment. Combat weapons include 15-foot spears, bows and arrows, and stone-headed battle-axes.

E. W. Ulrich

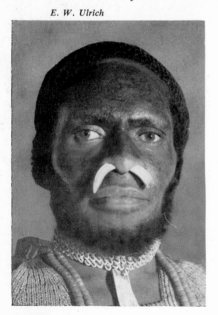

Oswald F. Emery

This Dani chief (right), whose cowrie-shell necklace shows his power and prestige, is famed for the hundreds he has killed in hand-to-hand combat.

Richard Lenehan

Massed on a hilltop, Dani warriors begin their savage charge toward the foe; returning from the attack (below), the victors bear captured spears of fallen enemies.

Richard Lenehan

Dani cannibals strap the body of an enemy battle victim to a carrying pole; missionaries Tom Bozeman and Edward Maxey witnessed with horror the cannibal feast which followed (see Chapter 8). As the message of the Christian gospel is heard, cannibalism and tribal warfare are dying out.

Oswald F. Emery

A group of Danis prepare a funeral pyre for the body of a small child. Corpses are always cremated by the Uhunduni, Kapauku, and Dani tribes; Monis, however, "bury" the corpse in a tree where it is consumed by birds of prey and by tropical rain and heat. Malnutrition, sudden sweeping epidemics, and savage battles contribute to the high death rate in all tribes.

Dani women show their grief over the death of a relative by smearing themselves with clay. More gruesome signs of mourning are the clipped ears and chopped fingers of children (below).

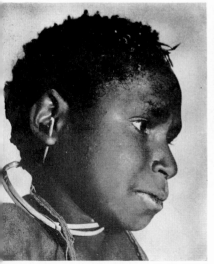

E. W. Ulrich

E. W. Ulrich

A band of Kapauku warriors attacking Obano killed two children and an Indonesian pastor and his wife, burned the church and manse (above), and ripped apart the missionary airplane (below). This savage uprising by a hostile minority faction in the generally friendly Kapauku tribe nearly severed the aerial lifeline of mission work in the Wissel Lakes area.

sticks, the wooden poles that are used to break up the ground when they prepare their gardens.

"As I was standing by the victim's body, the women came in groups of about twenty to rotate in a circle about the corpse. In a torrent of worked-up rage, they began to jump up and down on the corpse, jabbing it with digging sticks, and stomping upon the man with their feet. Some of them were thinking, no doubt, about the battles in which their own loved ones had been killed. Now they were venting their wrath on the lifeless body underfoot: for an hour or more the women continued to dance and shriek their insults upon the slain foe.

"While the pandemonium continued, some of the men had been building a fire near the body. As the women stopped their yelling and frenzied actions, I saw a man advancing with a knife.

"It was a knife they had made from one of our long spikes. It had been pounded until it was flat and then it was sharpened to a keen edge. The men started to remove a toe from the corpse. But the knife was not the proper tool, so he went for his ax. I was standing by taking pictures.

"Now another Dani came up with some bamboo knives. These knives, by the way, are as sharp as any steel blade known to civilized man. The man with the bamboo knife began to cut the meat from the dead man's calves. I became nauseated. I saw Ed Maxey, his face green, run to the edge of the crowd."

The two missionaries, sickened and depressed by the awful rite of Cannibal Valley, returned to their homes. They wanted to blot from their minds the ugly things they had witnessed.

Yet it was at the cannibal feast that Tom Bozeman first met Hilittu, a slender, bright-eyed Dani boy who had participated in the awful ceremony. There was something about Hilittu that attracted Bozeman. The missionary learned that the youth's father had been killed in battle and that his mother had died of some illness. As an orphan he had been drifting about without a permanent home, living with brothers and uncles. The Dani lad told Bozeman that he would like to work for him, so he became the houseboy at the mission.

Up to that time the Danis around Hetigima had listened to the gospel sullenly or apathetically. Others seemed to sense the significance of the Christian message and the demands it would make on their lives. They spurned the message, taking their cue from their leaders, especially Chief Ukumhearik, who wielded the greatest negative influence.

But Hilittu listened to Bozeman as he conducted gospel services for the Danis each Sunday evening at the mission station. Bozeman prayed privately for Hilittu and longed to see him turn from the evil spirits of his ancestors to the open arms of Jesus Christ. It was not long before Hilittu began to ask sharp questions.

"People here say that when you die your spirit goes down to where the ghosts live beneath the earth," he would say. "What about this? When I die, what's going to happen?"

The boy had seen one of the Dani men expire while Bozeman was attempting to treat him for an illness.

"I don't want the fire," the dying man cried out. "I'm burning."

Whether the man was suffering from fever or talking irrationally in his agony, no one could say, but the incident made a strong impression on Hilittu, who had seen so much violence and death.

With serious brown eyes, Hilittu would look up at Tom Bozeman and say, "You have been talking about heaven and hell. I just don't understand all of this."

Bozeman tried to explain that the important issue was that Christ had made a way for men to have fellowship with God by forgiving them of their sins and giving them new life. Through Christ's death and resurrection a way had been made for all men to live without fear of death and hell. Hilittu knew that his people existed in a constant bondage of fear, and he longed for a better life. He continued to ask questions until one day he suddenly told the Bozemans that he wanted Jesus to "treat" his heart. Bozeman urged the boy to seek forgiveness.

"O Jesus," Hilittu prayed, "I want you to treat my heart. I want you to take away all the bad things I've done. I've eaten people. I've stolen things. I've lied."

From that day forward Hilittu never seemed to hear enough

about Jesus. He began to pray for his enemies, even those who had killed his father. He told Bozeman, "I'm not going to fight anymore. And I'm through with my fetishes."

Soon his own relatives and the people in his village noticed the difference in his way of life. He had thrown away his magic charms. He no longer joined the others in warfare. Instead he was known to be praying regularly, and he no longer worked on Sundays. He did not preach, but his quiet Christian witness soon was known throughout the entire lower Baliem Valley.

Bozeman's investigations into cannibalism check with the findings of Myron Bromley. The Danis do not consume human flesh primarily to satisfy their hunger, although they have some pleasure in eating it. It tastes like pork, they say. Their chief reason for cannibalism is to show contempt for their foes.

The missionaries who on this occasion witnessed cannibalism vowed that they must never again attend such rites. Both of them, as well as other missionaries, have had opportunities to see repeat performances but they have steadfastly avoided them.

Hilittu's conversion and the Christlike character of his life contrasted sharply with the horrors of cannibalism. Bozeman and Maxey resolved that they would redouble their efforts to preach the gospel to the Danis. They wanted more than ever to deliver the people from their depraved culture. Indeed, they looked forward to a day when many Danis would lay down their weapons of warfare and Christ's peace would reign in the valley.

9

SEED ON STONY GROUND

The hidden valleys of Dutch New Guinea yielded reluctantly to the claims of Christ's gospel.

It was true that the small spark lighted in the Wissel Lakes area in western New Guinea now had been fanned into a steady flame. Kapaukus were turning to Christ in increasing numbers.

Also, the long-awaited entrance into the Baliem Valley, far to the east, had been made. A few proud Dani warriors were beginning to listen to the strange story of a Man who came from heaven to die that they might live.

But progress with the Moni tribe was discouraging. The missionaries working with these people did not have a great success story to relate. Among them were a dedicated couple who had been struggling at Homejo station, three or four days' hard hiking east of Enarotali in the Kemandora Valley, William Cutts and his wife Grace. They made a marvelous missionary team.

Grace Cutts was the life of the station at Homejo. She was a buxom, dark-haired, outgoing person. Her eyes were brown and merry and her laugh rang out frequently. Daughter of a Jewish father and a Gentile mother, she had come to the mission field from Binghamton, New York. Most of the time she was properly attired in bluejeans that seem to strain a bit as she moved about the mission station. She waited on her guests and shouted out Moni instructions to her houseboys without pausing for breath.

Gracie, as everyone called her, roamed the slopes around Homejo at any time of the day or night, calling on Moni families, playing with their children, nursing them through their illnesses.

The trail that drained the strength of strong men was nothing to her. She trudged up and down the winding paths like a sure-footed mountain goat. Often when she came to a steep descent, she would slide down the hillside on the back of her jeans, whooping with joy as she went.

Her great heart constantly went out to the needy Moni children. She finally undertook to rear two of them, one of whom was hopelessly feeble-minded. Missionary officials, however, advised her that it would be better to place the native children with their own people. Later the couple adopted two American children while they were home on furlough.

In contrast to his robust wife, Bill Cutts was a wiry, lean man with thinning blond hair and a quiet scholarly manner. Because of physical handicaps, Cutts had some difficulty convincing Alliance leaders that he was qualified for the mission field. But he was finally sent off with their blessing even though at least one physician had refused to give him medical clearance. In the years that followed, his superiors never regretted the exception they had made. He proved to be a superb linguist and one of the hardest working missionaries on the rugged New Guinea field.

In the latter part of 1955 Louis L. King, newly appointed Alliance area secretary for the Far East, made a visit to New Guinea. First on his schedule, so he told the Missionaries at Enarotali, was a visit to Bill and Gracie Cutts. Since the Homejo airstrip had not yet been opened, that would mean he would have to travel by boat for the first part of his journey, then go the rest of the way on foot.

His account of the trip from Enarotali reveals what traveling from one station to another meant before airplanes reduced days of walking to minutes of flying. After spending Thanksgiving Day with the workers at Enarotali, King set off the next morning for Homejo. This is how he described the experience:

"Friday just after sunup, clad in a borrowed helmut, a borrowed shirt, borrowed hobnail boots, and wearing two pairs of borrowed woolen socks held up by pieces of borrowed surgical gauze, I walked with Mr. Troutman (the field chairman) and our Kapauku carriers to the boat on Lake Paniai. Eight missionaries stood on the pier to take pictures of this strange man from New York or to express regret for the blisters, aches, and fatigue he would surely experience during the week ahead.

"The five-hour motorboat trip across the cold, gray, mournful lake and up the river took us past many dugout canoes with fires burning in them. These were to keep the Kapauku women warm as they fished for shrimp. We also passed the place where only a few months before the natives had formed a battle line in a desperate effort to rid the area of all white people, including the missionaries.

"A little beyond, we left the boat, and plunged into a mysterious territory which until our missionaries arrived in 1939 was unknown, unmapped, unexplored, and untouched by the white man. This is the private domain of the Kapauku and Moni peoples, and is still the outer limits of New Guinea's frontier civilization. Indeed, upon leaving Enarotali five hours before, we had been immediately cut off from all civilized people and would see none until we reached Homejo three days later. Beyond Homejo more than a month's hike would be required to reach our mission settlement in the Baliem Valley. We were therefore shut up with black-skinned, fuzzy-haired men of pigmy size, each of whom carried a bow and a plentiful supply of arrows.

"Our eight carriers were bearded and wore no clothing excepting the usual gourd, and a boar's tusk through the nose. They were short, yet exhibited strength and stamina, though their diet consisted only of sweet potatoes and the leaves of wild plants. Each of them carried approximately forty-five pounds on his shoulder or back—food and clothing for use on the trail and supplies for the missionaries whom we would visit.

"Starting overland, we slogged along in swamps, goose-stepping from one tuft of grass to the next; sometimes we slipped and sank to our hips in the mud and slime. Emerging from the grassy swamp we entered a water-sogged forest and forged ahead by stepping on the gnarled roots of bushes and trees. One false step might mean a muddy bath and a sprained ankle or worse. At rare intervals we passed near to small villages, but for the most part there was no sight or sound of human life, nothing but extreme loneliness, and the harsh, tortuous trail which at times was so indistinct it required the constant vigilance of our guide to direct us. Even the atmosphere was weird and foreboding under the shade of the tall trees.

"Late in the afternoon when camp was made we ate supper, consisting of fried cabbage and boiled rice, held a gospel service for the carriers, and went to bed shortly after sunset. Despite our extra clothing we shivered all night.

"The second day's hike was a killer. We had to cross two mountain passes, each over seven thousand feet high. Unlike the Baliem Valley, this is wooded country, and many giant trees had fallen across the trail and we had to climb over them. There were places where the ascent was so steep we pulled ourselves upward by tree roots as if climbing a ladder. The descent in places was so abrupt and hazardous it defies description.

"In the valley between the mountains we threaded our way through much water, climbed over rocks and logs, and walked in the deep, rushing torrents of the river which had to be crossed and recrossed unnumbered times. Sometimes as I walked along I was so hot I actually steamed; the perspiration falling from my face and hands was a continual surprise to the carriers since they do not sweat so freely. But as soon as I stopped to rest I shivered from the mountain cold. It was at this juncture I developed 'New Guinea knee' [a stiffness of the joints]. Thereafter every step was painful.

"When a halt was called for the night my energy was gone; one knee would hardly function and fatigue was intense. I lay on the ground in my wet clothing, covered by a jacket and tarpaulin for the better part of an hour before being sufficiently revived to be able to change them. That night we sang gospel hymns around the blazing campfire. I was still not too warm; the chilling blast penetrated my windbreaker, woolen sweater, and flannel shirt. The carriers were cold too. By the light from the fire I could see the gooseflesh on their bodies.

"On the third day, after a five-hour trek, we came out of the dense forest at a great altitude and looked down on Homejo. The land before us was mostly bare of trees and rocky of surface, with rolling, uninviting hills covered with coarse grass and spotted with occasional Moni villages. Away in the distance, in a valley pinched between great towering mountains, stood the mission houses. What a welcome sight, even though one full hour of walking and climbing lay ahead of us!

"The missionaries, Rev. and Mrs. W. A. Cutts, had seen us at a great distance, and shouting greetings, came up the trail to greet us. Soon they escorted us to their home where we enjoyed good food, pleasant fellowship, and restful, warm beds.

"We spent a day and a half preaching to the recent converts, inspecting the airstrip upon which construction had begun, and consulting with the workers concerning their problems. On the return trip we were accompanied over the long weary trail by the Homejo missionaries and twenty carriers.

"As we crossed Lake Paniai on the last lap of the trip we were plagued with torrential rain driven by a stiff, cold wind. Leaving Mr. Troutman to handle the outboard motor, I covered myself completely with a tarpaulin. Presently my Kapauku carrier slid under too. Soon he was asleep, his naked body lying peacefully against me for the remaining three hours of the trip."

Bill and Gracie Cutts had been assigned to Homejo in 1950 when Kenneth Troutman and his wife went home on furlough. The missionary work among the Monis had been started by Einar Mickelson before World War II. When the missionaries re-entered New Guinea, first the headquarters at Enarotali was reopened, then the Troutmans were assigned to Homejo to revive the Moni work.

It took five long days on that first trip for Bill and Gracie Cutts to hike from Enarotali to Homejo. As the sun was setting on the fifth day, their future home was visible on the hill just ahead of them on the trail. Tired as they were, they quickened their steps. They were eager to see the place where they would live for the next few years.

It was a two-story house of rough-hewn local timber that Troutman had laboriously constructed with his own hands. Crude boards served as the siding for the lower half; the upstairs walls were of canvas. But to the weary, footsore couple, it was a mansion. Excitedly, Gracie ran from room to room, examining every part of her new home.

In time the missionaries found that the old building had its shortcomings. There were huge cracks between the floor planks. The openings were so wide that when articles were dropped accidentally on the second floor, Bill or Gracie had to crawl under the house to find them.

Soon Gracie Cutts had set the long-vacated mission home in order. It offered spartan comfort and it was clean; but it was hardly luxurious.

Before long Cutts was reducing the difficult language to writing, preparing primers and translating portions of Scripture into Moni. But the lazy natives showed little appreciation.

When Gracie Cutts, with characteristic enthusiasm, announced that permission had been granted for them to construct an airstrip at Homejo, to her dismay Monis shrugged their shoulders with indifference. They refused to help with the onerous work of clearing the stony ground of the proposed mountaintop airfield. The hard, hot job of leveling the ground fell to Bill Cutts and a few Kapaukus he was able to bring in from the Wissel Lakes.

Cutts preached faithfully to the Monis, but they were unresponsive. For a while they came out to the Sunday morning services, listening halfheartedly to the message. But at the slightest excuse they stayed home.

When a whooping cough epidemic broke out in the tribe, the Monis blamed the missionaries. There was much grumbling. They began to threaten to kill the white couple. It was a period of tension and fear. Only a sturdy pair such as Bill and Gracie could have stood up under the constant danger of death. They had come to Homejo with high expectations of blessing and spiritual success, but their love and compassionate service brought a thankless response.

It was not easy to discover why the Monis were so belligerent. Mostly, their antagonism seemed to stem from ignorance and superstition. They resented the new patterns of life that they thought would result from accepting the message of the missionaries. They were not willing to pay the price of discipleship.

It was a dark hour for the self-sacrificing couple. The undisciplined native children refused to come to school. Their parents would not attend church services. Attendance fell off to almost nothing. Things reached such a stage that the missionaries faced the possibility of closing the station at Homejo.

But after some weeks the tension lifted. Church attendance suddenly shot up to two hundred and three hundred each Sunday. About one hundred pupils appeared at school. The spurt of new attendance was as difficult to understand as the earlier antagonism. The natives seemed to think they would gain somehow by attending church services.

In spite of this mysterious resurgence, Bill and Gracie Cutts still had little to show for their hard toil. Once again their congregation dwindled, but never did the attendance fall to the previous low. The missionaries continued steadfastly at their task. After nine years they had gathered a congregation of thirty baptized believers and organized a Moni church with two native elders. That was all.

Not unlike many people in other parts of the world, the Monis cared little for spiritual matters. On the other hand, they always enjoyed attending pig feasts and funerals.

Their ways of life were inextricably bound up with their economy. Homejo, on the main trail between the Wissel Lakes and the Baliem Valley, was known throughout the mountains of New Guinea because of its salt wells. The Monis prepare salt by dropping porous vines down into the briny water of the wells. Then the salt-laden vines are pulled up, dried, and burned. The salty ashes next are tamped into molds that are made by digging slender cylindrical holes in the ground and lining them with leaves. Then the molds of salt are removed along with their covering of leaves. These salt molds are dried over the fire to become one of the most important trading items in interior New Guinea. The trader Monis take some of the salt over the trail to the west and sell it to the Kapaukus for cowrie shells. With the shells they then travel east, sometimes to the Ilaga Valley and farther, to buy pigs from the Danis.

The Monis live in clusters of houses, with round ones for the men and long ones for the women—a house for each wife with her children and pigs. Sometimes a man's two wives live at either end of a long house—a sort of primitive duplex. But each wife has her own pigs to care for and her own gardens to cultivate. By having separate garden plots for each wife, a husband can compare the production and thereby determine who is the most industrious. The laggards are scolded and sometimes beaten.

When a man dies, especially a headman or prominent tribesman, the Moni culture demands that his favorite wife accompany him on the trip into the next world. Members of his family gather for a council and decide which of the surviving widows shall join the husband in death. There is nothing the hapless victim can do to avoid execution, even though she sometimes seeks to hide from her killers. Sometimes one relative will serve as the cold-blooded executioner, shooting the widow down with arrows. Other times the killing is done by several members of the family. In these corporate executions, according to Cutts, the Monis will pull the twelve-inch points from their arrows, then stab the woman at close range.

Then she is buried with her husband. Actually "buried" isn't the right word, for the Monis dispose of their dead usually by placing the corpse in a tree. They build a sort of tree house which is covered with bark. Then the body is left there to be destroyed by birds of prey, the wind, and the rain. Often all that can be seen after a while are the bleached bones that remain there until they fall to the ground.

Frequently, the body of an important man is kept in his home for many days until all his property is disposed of. Bill Cutts recalls visiting the home of a chief who had died. In the house filled with the stench of the decaying corpse, the wives and other relatives sat about scraping the skin of the body that was propped near the fire. By drying the body, scraping the skin, and wiping the excretions with grass and weeds, the corpse was given a form of crude embalming.

Women may be killed by the clan for other reasons, too. If, for example, a woman is found guilty of adultery, she is slain and her body is thrown into the nearest river.

Like other highland tribes during periods of mourning, the Monis smear their bodies with mud and cry for many days. Women and even small children, in their grief, will take a sharp rock or an ax and slash off their fingers to demonstrate the depth of their sorrow.

If twins are born to a family, normally the second is killed because it is regarded as the offspring of the devil. One couple followed custom and left the second twin outside of the house, partially covered with dirt. But the mother had to listen to her infant crying throughout the night. Toward morning she could stand it no longer; she brought the child back into the house and saved its life. This couple was one of the few pagan families in the Homejo area to rear a set of twins.

Monis consult witches, who are known as bat girls because of their reputed ability to commune with bats for directions to perform black magic. If someone is ill, the family may ask the bat girl to name the person responsible for the malady. This person then must die. For a fee of cowrie shells the witch communes with the evil spirits ostensibly embodied in bats. The bat girls are consulted about other matters too. Often the size of the fee gives the questioner the answer he really wants. Frequently the bat girl chooses as the victim some widow, or perhaps an elderly wife too old to work profitably in the garden. Or a woman victim might be accused of putting worms into her husband's food. The worms he has allegedly consumed cast a spell on him, so that he becomes unsuccessful in shell trading, his gardens fail, and his pigs die. Thus the magic finger points to the innocent victim and the villagers join together to execute her by filling her body with arrows. Then the corpse is tied to a pole and tossed into the river.

The pig feast with its erotic dances tends to perpetuate the abuses of the old tribal culture. Generally, the date coincides with the ripening of the taro roots, since they are served with the steamed pork. The feast occurs at regular intervals, usually every two or three years, and lasting for several weeks.

First the pig feast dance house is constructed. The Moni men cut down saplings that are used to frame the building. They are also used for the important function of providing for a springy floor for the dancing. While the house has a roof of tree bark, the sides are usually left open.

When the event is held, the men and women mingle in the monotonous rhythm of the dance, which consists of nothing but jumping up and down on the floor for hours on end. The dancers shout and sing, and the strong odor of unwashed greasy bodies fills the atmosphere.

Related to dance-house custom are the singsongs which bring young men and women together for a night of courtship that usually is climaxed by unbridled sensuality. The young men line up on one side of the house, the women on the other. They sit facing one another as they chant and sway through the night hours. Small gifts are passed from the young men to the women and then from the women to the men. Occasionally, couples slip off during the ceremony after prearranged signals that follow the exchange of gifts. The songs they sing are suggestive and erotic.

When the dance and the singsongs are concluded, great numbers of pigs are killed and then cut up into sections which are sold for cowrie shells. After the buying period of the first day, the remainder of the pork is distributed on the second day to widows, orphans, and other needy people. Thus the tribal group takes care of its basic social obligations. No one need be hungry.

A Moni woman is nothing but chattel. A little girl is carried around on her father's shoulders with apparent filial affection. But by the time she reaches the age of ten or eleven, she seems automatically to become the property of her older brothers and uncles, who have the right to sell her to the highest bidder within proper clan boundaries. More than likely a girl of such tender years is purchased by an older man, such as a chief, who already has three or four wives. Younger men might desire her, but it is usually the older, more prosperous men who can afford the bid-up price for young girls. The younger fellows have to take older widows or less desirable mates. It is a cruel arrangement.

A child-bride is thus taken from the loving atmosphere of her own home into the strange surroundings of a family where she is subjected to the hatred and jealousy of the other wives. Polygamy may be an accepted custom in the culture, but several women married to one man live in a veritable hell. Since the husband has complete control over his wife, he can beat her senseless if he so desires. That is his business and no one intervenes. Not a voice is raised even if a man were to kill his wife. It happens far too often.

Gracie Cutts often had Moni women come to her with their faces beaten to a pulp. The wretched women would seek medical aid from the missionaries, then returned to their homes to bear children, cook meals, cultivate their gardens, and care for the pigs. These animals are so important to the native families that when a sow dies, her litter will be wet nursed by the wives of the owner. It is not uncommon to find a woman nursing a child in one arm and holding a piglet in the other. One can understand why the suicide rate is high amog Moni women.

Marriage settlements are usually made after a couple has lived together, not before. This had led to a deeply entrenched practice of trial marriage. When a young man sees a woman he likes, he will often take her forcefully. They live together as man and wife even though the union is not recognized as official until the marriage settlement has been made. Sometimes the deal is not concluded until after the birth of the first child.

A trial marriage is frequently dissolved for any one of various reasons. Sometimes the young man tires of the arrangement and just decides he will not ask for a marriage settlement. More frequently the young man's family is unable to raise the amount demanded by the young woman's brothers or uncles. In such instances she is forced to enter into another trial marriage until a man is found who can pay the number of cowrie shells demanded.

In pagan Moni society there is little or no reproach to either the young woman or man if the trial marriage does not become permanent. But it creates real problems for Christians.

Bill and Gracie Cutts found that some of the Christian youths of their area sought to marry, but because of the limited resources of their families, they lost, not one prospective wife to higher bidders, but several in succession. Thus they remained without mates because the deep-rooted cultural patterns hindered progress toward a Christian concept of marriage.

The story of a Christian youth named Dugu Dugu Bega and a Christian girl, Boma Jumba, epitomizes the problem.

Dugu Dugu, a lad of sixteen, became interested in thirteen-year-old Boma while they were attending the mission school. Seeking to handle the matter correctly, Dugu Dugu asked Gracie Cutts to serve as his intermediary to learn whether Boma would have him. The girl returned Dugu Dugu's love, so he took her as his bride to his father's home and set up housekeeping.

Boma, an orphan, had been living with her older sister and a brother-in-law named Taome, who were also believers. Indeed it was through their influence that Boma had become a Christian.

Dugu Dugu would have willingly waited for his bride until the marriage settlement was completed, but that was not the way of the tribe.

Boma's sister and brother-in-law were happy about the love affair and readily gave their blessing to the union, but Boma's eldest brother had other ideas. He felt he could get a better price by selling her to another man. Custom granted him the right to bargain, even though he had not helped in any way to rear his sister. Thus, on a certain day he came and forcibly took Boma from Dugu Dugu. Boma ran away, but was captured again. The missionaries witnessed the sad physical struggle. Boma's sister was tearfully trying to hold on to Boma; her brother was pulling her along the ground in the other direction. Taome, the good brother-in-law, was shouting against this injustice, while his aged mother attempted to beat off the offender. Then friends of Boma's brother rushed into the fray. Other villagers began to snatch the bows and arrows from the contestants on both sides to prevent bloodshed.

As the argument grew hotter, poor Boma was dropped to the ground, where she sat utterly exhausted from the tug of war. She was the picture of dejection. But finally her brother had his way and dragged her off to his house.

Even though it is never the responsibility of the bride's family to help provide for the marriage settlement, Taome began to champion the cause of Dugu Dugu, his fellow Christian. Up to this time, Taome had a natural craving for earthly goods, but the plight of Boma and Dugu Dugu moved his heart. He presented a valuable indo shell, a rare type of cowrie, to Boma's brother, who promptly spurned it. Instead, the brother began to bargain with a visiting chief who was seeking a bride for his son.

The chief had come to the Homejo mission station to be treated for a centipede bite. While he was being cared for by the missionaries, he showed a deep interest in the gospel. Bill Cutts told his patient that a follower of the Lord would not take away a man's wife to give her to his son. The chief agreed, and the missionaries learned that he told his son not to expect family aid in buying Boma.

Later Taome and Dugu Dugu visited the mission station. It was evident from their manner that they had good news. Taome squatted down and pulled a pouch from his carrying sack. Out of that he took another pouch, and out of that another, until he came to an old white indo cowrie shell with a huge crack that had been filled with beeswax. In Western terms it was not beautiful, but it was very attractive and valuable to the Monis who are impressed by the age and history of cowrie shells. Thus shells that are handed down from generation to generation become smoother and whiter, and what is more important, more valuable in the process.

Taome had learned that Boma's brother had a change of heart; that he liked the indo shell better than the one the chief had offered him. Taome, in providing the payment, was acting solely out of Christian grace. Bill Cutts was deeply moved as he saw this attitude that seemed to reflect the Lord's command "that ye love one another, as I have loved you."

In order to show their regard for Dugu Dugu, Bill and Gracie Cutts turned all the cowrie shells they possessed over to the youth, then prayed with him and Taome. The official settlement was yet to come.

A week later Dugu Dugu excitedly announced to the missionaries, "They are laying out the shells now." Bill and Gracie accompanied him to his village three-quarters of a mile away. They found a gathering of parties to the agreement sitting in a circle in a clearing surrounded by tall reeds. In the center was a piece of old cloth.

The Monis greeted them in soft tones that contrasted with their normal noisy ways. The mood underlined the seriousness of the ceremony. It was a closed meeting in which only those who had given shells could participate. The Monis, including members of Dugu Dugu's family, made room for Bill and Gracie to sit in the circle.

Taome's prized indo shell was lying in the center of the cloth with two hundred other shells arranged in groups of ten and twenty. Not counting the indo, the shells were equivalent in value to twenty-five large pigs. No one could assess the value of Taome's shell, which was the only one he had ever acquired. When the missionaries' contribution was mentioned, the emotional Monis acknowledged the gift with quiet tears. Everyone was impressed by the wealth heaped there on one piece of colth.

It still was the privilege of Boma's brother to reject the payment, huge though it was. The crowd waited tensely. At this point he strode into the clearing, looked around at the group, and proceeded carefully to examine the array of shells. A spokesman quietly described the value of each shell by recounting its history. The indo shell proved to be the deciding factor. The brother picked it up with the other shells, thereby indicating the deal was closed.

While the purchase price was high and sacrificially collected, the marriage settlement for two Christian young people made spiritual history in the tribe. Later Taome and his wife and the newlyweds, Dugu Dugu and Boma, dedicated their lives for Christian service and left for Enarotali to attend the Bible school.

The time came when Bill and Gracie Cutts were due for a furlough. It was 1959 and they had spent nine years at Homejo. In casting up the balance sheet, they found little to show for their years of faithful witness. Moni converts could be counted in the dozens rather than in the hundreds. Yet among them was a young man named Simon, who became a capable Bible teacher and preacher. He would be heard from again.

The missionaries would go home for a breather, but they were determined to resume their work with renewed zeal. They did not know that on their return to the field they would experience the blessing of their lives—but at a new station.

10

UPRISING AT OBANO

Of the four major tribes of Dutch New Guinea, the Danis, the Monis, the Kapaukus, and the Uhundunis, only the last-named had yet to be reached. This strange people had retreated to the most isolated valleys on either side of the high Nassau Range which forms the lofty spine of the country. The Uhundunis, defeated in the constant warfare between the tribes, had developed a hangdog mentality.

In their earlier hikes into the interior Mickelson, Troutman, and Rose had fairly well determined the boundaries of the Uhunduni settlements, and they had shared the concern of the Alliance mission to reach them for Christ. Yet transporting and providing supplies to future missionaries in the Ilaga Valley, in the very heart of the rugged land between the Wissel Lakes to the west and the Baliem Valley at the east, posed real problems. Distance made overland supply lines unfeasible.

There were two developments that speeded the entrance of Uhunduni territory: first, the missionaries now realized that there was no hidden valley or peak that could not be reached by the

single-engined light airplane; and, second, the Lord seemingly had
placed a burden for the tribe upon a couple who were equal to
the task. They were a tall, rangy Westerner, Donald Gibbons, and
his wife, Alice, a lithe, dark-haired girl.

The young couple, not too long out of Simpson Bible Institute of
Seattle, had been content to go to the field that their leaders picked
for them. In 1953 when they found themselves in Dutch New
Guinea, they were first stationed among the Kapaukus. They applied themselves to the language and began to serve faithfully.

While Donald and Alice Gibbons were at Enarotali, they were
introduced to another young couple who were also new on the
field, Gordon and Peggy Larson. Of Swedish ancestry, Larson had
been brought up in Jamestown, New York. He had met his blonde
wife, a Kentuckian, when both were stationed in wartime Washing-
ton. While there the Larsons had received a missionary call. This
had directed Larson to training at Asbury Theological Seminary.
Later he took graduate work in linguistics and anthropology at the
University of Michigan.

The Larsons had not been in New Guinea long before they were
sent to take over the Moni work at Homejo while Bill and Gracie
Cutts were home on furlough. Their selection proved to be an
important link in reaching the Uhundunis.

While he was at Homejo, Larson met a group of Uhundunis who
had come to the salt wells on a trading mission. He talked with
them through an interpreter and learned where they lived. When
he later described this contact with Gibbons, a spark was ignited
in the latter's heart. The two friends discussed the possibility of
visiting the distant Uhunduni settlements. In due time the mission's
field committee appointed Larson and Gibbons to conduct a survey
of the Ilaga Valley where many of the Uhundunis were known to
live. It was confidently hoped that the expedition would result
eventually in opening work among the tribe.

Accompanied by eight Kapauku and eight Moni carriers, the
two missionaries left Enarotali in June, 1954, and hiked eastward
for fourteen long days. They found the difficulties of the trail to
be all that earlier survey teams had reported. Travel was slow

and arduous. Following native trails meant taking the topography as it came: the boggy swamps with sticky mud, the gloomy forests with long scraggy roots that tripped up the most wary, and the stony mountain pathways that tore thick hiking boots.

The party wound a long file through the tortuous mountain passes, the carriers grunting and sweating in the heat of the tropical sun. As they reached the bleak unpopulated plateau that seemed to stretch dully in the distance, members of the caravan felt the chill of the high altitudes. The naked Kapaukus and Monis complained. There were days when the men were forced to walk an entire day in the pelting rain.

Then one morning they came to the crest of the mountains bordering the north side of the Ilaga Valley. From this outlook Gibbons and Larson gazed, excited as boys over reaching their goal. Across from them was the southern rim of the valley made by the snow-covered peaks of the Nassau Range. Dotted in the valley were scores of native settlements from which the smoke ascended in beckoning spirals. This was the Ilaga, crossroads of the central highlands where native traders from the east and west met. One day it would be the cradle of a spiritual movement that would spread into all the valleys of the interior.

The population of the Ilaga was made up of two groups: one-fourth Uhundunis, the rest western Danis, the dominant tribe, who had migrated there from the Baliem. The latter had relatives in all the intervening territory. Relations generally between the two tribes in the Ilaga were good, chiefly because of intermarriage. But the Danis had been constantly engaged in a recurring cycle of warfare with traditional clan enemies among their tribe to the east and north.

Gibbons and Larson pushed on with their pace quickened by anticipation.

They were trudging through the lower Ilaga Valley followed by a group of singing natives when they had their first alarming experience. The motley crowd trailing them was made up of Danis, Uhundunis, and a few members of the Ndauwa tribe, who were apparently impressed by their first sight of white men. Friendly tribesmen had warned the missionaries about the dangers of the trail. But they had heard this so often that they shrugged it off and continued on their way. One night some of their supplies were stolen. This was the only inkling that they might be in peril.

Following the course of the Ilaga River downstream, the missionaries asked the band of followers where the bridge was located. They were told it was farther downstream. When the expedition arrived at the location that had been described, the natives admitted there was no bridge. Gibbons, Larson, and their carriers finally were able to cross the river by improvising one. By three o'clock in the afternoon they knew they were facing an attack. A Dani rushed one of the Kapauku carriers and snatched his load of supplies. The missionary party then formed a single file with Larson at the head and Gibbons at the rear.

They came into a clearing and found themselves surrounded by a raiding party of a hundred or more natives. The spokesman of the group shouted, "Give us your cowrie shells."

The carriers for the missionary party were trembling with fear. The Kapaukus began to turn over their shells to the raiders without a shred of resistance. But even this tribute did not satisfy the enemy. Suddenly a Dani warrior drew his bow and shot an arrow through the shoulder of a Kapauku carrier. The twang of the bowstring and the scream of the injured carrier charged the atmosphere with tension.

"Wadirunga!" shouted one of the Kapaukus, meaning, "There's no point in resisting further!"

Now the raiders closed in, seizing one carrying tin after another. In a moment all of the expedition's equipment was strewn about the ground. Sleeping bags, medicine, and food went scattering. During the attack Larson sought desperately to retrieve what he could. Gibbons hustled off with one of the Kapauku carriers and two tins of rescued provisions. Larson was tempted to throw one Dani's carrying net into the river, but stopped himself. It would only mean further retaliation. The missionaries finally broke away from their antagonists. They realized that they were deep in hostile territory, and fifteen days from home.

The missionary party took shelter under a huge rock that jutted out to form a roof. They built a fire and took inventory of the things they had saved: three tin blickeys containing food, trading items, and Gibbons' sleeping bag. To their amazement Gibbons and Larson found that if they used the food and trading objects sparingly, they could travel for another two weeks!

Before retiring, Larson heard Andobome, a Moni carrier, pray, "Lord, they've treated us badly. Just send those people to hell."

Simon, the Moni preacher, offered a rebuke to that kind of praying. "We've got to show them love," he countered.

That night the rushing Ilaga River lulled the men to sleep. The stone overhead was for them "a rock in a weary land."

Next day the travelers found the residents of the area in which they had been assaulted extremely friendly and sympathetic. They made it plain that they did not share the attitudes of the attackers. Larson and Gibbons spent two days with the natives of the lower Ilaga, then they gathered their men together to move on toward home. They planned to return by way of the Beoga, a small conical valley lying to the north of the Ilaga proper behind a high range of mountains. Gibbons particularly wanted to go there because of its large Uhunduni population.

After a hard day of hiking up and over the rugged pass into the Beoga, the missionaries were received with warm hospitality by the Beoga Uhundunis. Immediately the natives wanted to kill pigs and hold a big feast in their honor. Gibbons and Larson were deeply affected by this warm response, but they knew they must push on. They told their native hosts that the expedition was returning to the Wissel Lakes area but would come back later.

However, they did remain long enough to conduct a gospel service. Nearly three hundred Uhundunis of the Beoga Valley for the first time drank in the story of God's redeeming love. Simon, the Moni convert, preached in Moni and the local Uhunduni chief, a bi-lingual, interpreted for him. It was a stirring sight to watch the faces of the eager Uhundunis. They were fascinated by the message of eternal life. At every mention of the resurrection and heaven, the Uhundunis shouted, "Yes, yes!" Later the missionaries were to learn the significance of this friendly reaction. It had greater importance than they realized then.

The survey of the Ilaga and Beoga Valleys proved to be another milestone in the advance of the evangel. Larson and Gibbons were now convinced that an airstrip could be constructed in the Ilaga to serve one or more mission stations. The Beoga Valley, because of the topography, would be more difficult to reach except by over-land trek from the Ilaga. A Beoga airstrip appeared to be out of the question. Ed Ulrich, who had checked the site from the air, said he had "the feeling of looking down inside an ice cream cone."

The party returned to Enarotali safe and sound, but two years would intervene before Don Gibbons realized his desire of es-tablishing a station among the Uhundunis.

Some time after this Gibbons took a trip into the Uhunduni ter-ritory south of Carstensz Peak, high point of the Nassau Range. However, in twenty-nine days of walking Gibbons wore out four pairs of sturdy hobnailed boots. When he finally reached the section south of the high mountain range, he discovered that Roman Cath-olic missionaries had preceded him. He was greeted by Uhundunis who made the sign of the cross even before they would take a drink of water, and they already could chant the "Ave Maria." He re-turned to Enarotali to continue his work among the Kapaukus, meanwhile dreaming and praying that he might serve his beloved Uhundunis.

Wars raged in the Ilaga Valley from shortly after the 1954 visit by the two missionaries for a period of nearly two years. It obvi-ously was not the propitious time to enter the area and establish missionary work. But early in 1956, Gelaane, a Dani chieftain from the Ilaga, visited Homejo and urged the missionaries to return there. Word had also been received that peace had come to the valley. Soon afterward Kenneth Troutman, in his role of field chair-man, was flown by pilot Ulrich on an aerial survey of the Ilaga and Beoga Valleys. Reappointed to the Uhunduni tribe, Larson and Gibbons set off again in August, 1956, for the Ilaga, de-termined to stay until they had built an airstrip and established stations.

The expeditionary force had other problems on this trip. It was almost impossible to enlist carriers either from among the Kapaukus or the Monis. Finally they rounded up enough men to take them several days' walk beyond Homejo, but when the carriers reached the head of the Kemandora Valley, they realized that they would have to travel five straight days over an uninhabited plateau at an altitude of eleven thousand feet or more. The carriers threw down their loads and refused to go farther. The Dani tribesmen living in the vicinity also were unwilling.

Larson and Gibbons held a consultation. They decided that Gibbons should return to Homejo to recruit other carriers. Larson would stay on along with his three remaining Moni carriers. He set up camp near a Dani mountain village called Ugwimba. It was cold and desolate on the high windy plateau.

No sooner had Gibbons left than Larson came down with a high fever. Tossing about on his cot in a crude lean-to of wooden fence slabs and a plastic tent fly, Larson sought to call for help on his radio. He found that his hand-cranked radio had gone dead. For days Larson lay ill, with only his carriers and the strangers of Ugwimba to nurse him. Separated from his friends and weakened by the fever, he remained helpless in his tent for three weeks.

This was the low point in Gordon Larson's missionary experience. Brooding over his lot, he became more and more discouraged. Had he failed to understand God's leading? If the Ilaga was to be reached, why was he obliged to pass through this dark hour? Did the Lord want him to return to Homejo? Like Abraham, "an horror of great darkness fell upon him."

But in this Gethsemane Larson turned to his New Testament. He read again the Lord's promise in Hebrews 13:5: "I will never leave thee, nor forsake thee." It was like an audible voice from above.

Larson poured out his doubts and discouragement in soul-agonizing prayer. He had reached a crisis: Should he remain where he was or seek to return to his home?

The next day he received the answer. While he was engaged in his devotions after lunch, he waited quietly before the Lord in prayer. It was a strange experience, he recounted afterward, for he suddenly was swept with a great sense of assurance that he was to continue his journey. He knew for a certainty that the Ilaga Valley would be opened. His depression had ended. Later he learned that his companion, Don Gibbons, had been passing through a similar experience at Homejo. He, too, had found confidence that they would reach their goal.

From that time forth, Larson said he felt that nothing could deter him. "I would have stayed on, no matter what I had to put up with."

At the end of three weeks Gibbons rejoined Larson at Ugwimba, and they prepared to resume their journey to the Ilaga. But the Danis that they had employed as carriers balked. The missionaries finally said they would go on alone and would obtain Moni or Uhunduni carriers in the Dugandoga Valley that lay ahead. This threat goaded the reluctant carriers into continuing with them. The party reached the Ilaga Valley in September.

When they arrived at the first native village they were met by a band of Danis. The warriors, armed with spears, were all dancing in a circle. It was a double-pronged affair. In one sense, it was a welcome party, but the cautious natives were also scrutinizing the missionaries to see that their intentions were peaceful. At the request of the Danis, Gibbons fired his shotgun at a piece of wood to demonstrate the power of the weapon. Then they asked Larson to take their pictures with his camera. They believed that the camera somehow could record their inmost feelings, and, in this case, prove to the missionaries that they had not been involved in the attack upon them two years before. From this point on the missionaries were received warmly in the Ilaga Valley.

After dickering they were able to purchase an airstrip site on the north slope of the valley for five steel axes!

The missionaries discovered that they had been too optimistic about the time it would take to construct the landing strip. Instead of an estimated three or four weeks, they spent seven difficult months on the formidable task. Both Gibbons and Larson had had assurance from the Lord that they would establish work in the

Ilaga, but they had failed to read the heavenly communication fully. Larson later admitted that the backbreaking job was one of the hardest trials of his life.

The terrain that had looked so good during the aerial survey was found to be entirely too soft and mucky for an airstrip. This meant that they had to remove a three-foot layer of muddy topsoil for the entire length of the strip, which at first was fifteen hundred feet. Next they were instructed by radio that the strip would have to be eighteen hundred feet in length. That meant tearing away a sizable knoll, which might not have been necessary if the proper length had been given when the site was first chosen. The belated decision also made it necessary to fill in a deep gully. There was wry consolation in the knowledge that the earth from the knoll would serve to fill the gully.

The people of the Ilaga proved to be most responsive and willing to help. At times Larson and Gibbons had a crew of one thousand men. All of the earth removal had to be done with wooden digging sticks and shovels. There were no bulldozers, steam rollers, or other heavy equipment.

The missionaries, separated all these months from their families, who were back in the Wissel Lakes area, lived in two small, bark-covered gudangs. It was a dreary experience, with nothing but work, work, work.

The only interruptions occurred when the torrential rains fell, keeping them from the job. But the rains filled them with dismay because they threatened to wash away the airfield.

On one such occasion Gibbons and Larson were sitting in their gudang chatting. Gibbons' spirits were particularly low.

"Gordon," he said, "I'm beginning to think we ought to ditch this site and go somewhere else."

"Oh, surely not," Larson said, seeking to comfort his friend. "It's just the rainy season. It will soon dry out and everything will be fine."

Infected by Larson's optimism, Gibbons left Larson's shack in high spirits. He returned to his own gudang, whistling.

But Gibbons' comments preyed on Larson's mind. He felt the

crushing burden of the project. He began to have fierce doubts about his own prediction.

One of the joys that came to them were the drops of supplies from the missionary airplane. They also welcomed the daily conversations on their portable short-wave radio with their families at the Wissel Lakes. This not only warmed their hearts, but it brought them better rapport with the tribesmen. When the natives heard the voices of women coming over the radio, they were satisfied that the strange box was not a part of some strange spirit worship.

For a time Gibbons was confined to his bed with infectious hepatitis. He fretted over the several weeks of enforced idleness when so much still remained to be done.

Finally, after seven months, the construction work ended, and in February, 1957, when the first airplane came in for a landing, Don Gibbons and Gordon Larson were joined by their wives and children. The building of the Ilaga strip became the keystone of an unseen arch that before long would be revealed.

From the standpoint of air communication, it now meant that any interior mission station in Dutch New Guinea would not be more than thirty minutes away from a neighbor. Traveling time from Nabire, a new supply port on the coast west of Enarotali, to Obana, was thirty minutes; Obana to Homejo, twenty minutes; Homejo to Ilaga, thirty minutes; Ilaga to Baliem, thirty minutes.

Ed Ulrich, the pilot who had taken over the flying of the Alliance airplanes after Al Lewis met his death, was a regular visitor at the new airstrip site. He could not land, but he dropped all the supplies to Larson and Gibbons and talked to them by radio.

This competent airman had flown a half-million miles as a wartime and missionary pilot, but he regarded the one hundred and fifty thousand miles he had flown in New Guinea as a service for Christ that had brought him his greatest satisfaction.

From the time he had accompanied Al Lewis on the long ferry trip with the new Sealand from Belfast, Ireland, to Hollandia, Dutch New Guinea, Ed Ulrich had been actively involved in every missionary advance made possible by airplane service. He recalled the epochal flight when the first party of missionaries had landed in the Baliem Valley and the occupation of mysterious Cannibal Valley was begun. When the waters of the Baliem River receded and prevented the pilots from landing on its surface, Ulrich had parachuted supplies in fifty-five-gallon drums to maintain the slender missionary life line. He had even dropped a gasoline-operated battery charger and an automobile-type storage battery filled with acid. When the missionaries in Homejo were cut off from their overland supply route because of native uprisings, Ulrich had brought succour with the plane. On one occasion he dropped off a live kitten as a Christmas present for one of the missionary children at Homejo.

With the purchase of the Cessna to replace the tragic loss of the Sealand, Ulrich, aided by Dick Lenehan, the mechanic, had instituted regular service to all of the new airstrips, beginning a new day for missionary work in New Guinea. In his first year of flying the Cessna, Ulrich had traveled seventy-five thousand air miles—three times the distance around the world.

Operating an aerial supply line for missionaries was full of strain and danger. The pilot had to be ever aware of the rapidly changing weather pattern. There was the peril of clouds that rested almost constantly over many valleys, as well as the strong winds that developed by midday and made landings impossible. Traveling from Sentani to the Wissel Lakes meant flying over four hundred miles of unsurveyed jungle swamps and mountains without a single emergency landing spot.

The small mission station airstrips of the interior were located in hazardous places—one strip had been constructed on the side of a mountain with a nine per cent grade, another had for its approach a gaping fifteen-hundred-foot gorge. On one occasion as Ulrich was just about to land at a difficult mountain strip, three wild pigs darted across the runway. Only by "giving it the gun" quickly was he able to nose the airplane up again and avoid a possible fatal accident.

When Ulrich learned that Bill Cutts had completed the badly needed airstrip at Homejo, at the end of September, 1956, he was eager to establish air service to these worthy missionaries. Ulrich picked up a Mr. Hamers, of the Dutch Civil Aviation Service, and set off to fly into Homejo for the first time. With the confidence of years of flying experience, Ulrich let the Cessna down gently. But in landing, it struck a soft spot on the runway and flipped over on its back. Fortunately, both Ulrich and Hamers escaped injury, but it appeared for a time that the Cessna was a total loss.

Fortunately, a second Cessna, which had been on order for many months, had just been delivered at the air base at Sentani. The Alliance air service, halted by the Homejo crash, would continue.

Ulrich hiked out to Enarotali and flew by commercial airplane to Sentani. He arrived just in time to test the new Cessna. Thus he was prepared for the arrival of Robert Chrisman, newly appointed Far Eastern secretary, who had come to New Guinea for an extensive survey of the field. After he visited the missionaries in the Baliem, Ulrich flew his important passenger to the airstrip at Obano, on Lake Paniai.

At a ceremony in which Chrisman took part, the new craft was dedicated at Obano on November 3, 1956. Among those also participating were Kenneth Troutman, the board representative for New Guinea; Ed Ulrich; Walter Post, veteran missionary; and an Indonesian pastor, R. Lesnusa, and his wife, who served the struggling Kapauku church at Obano. The audience consisted of five Indonesian teachers and eleven missionaries, including Miss Elze Stringer, a Dutch teacher who directed the mission school at the Obano outpost. Following the service, Chrisman and the other missionaries went in boats to Enarotali. They wanted to spend the night there and attend church the following day, Sunday.

The next noon while the missionaries were enjoying their Sunday dinner, they were interrupted by a Kapauku teacher. He reported that someone at Obano, five miles across Lake Paniai, was flashing a mirror as a distress signal. When the missionaries rushed from the house, they could see clouds of smoke billowing above Obano.

Soon word came that the Indonesian missionary family living there had been murdered, and the mission chapel, pastor's house, and school building had been burned to the ground. The new missionary airplane, in service only two weeks, had been destroyed. Everything that Elze Stringer owned, except the clothes she wore, was either stolen or burned in the fire.

The mission station had felt the brunt of a Kapauku uprising that vented its fury on the lonely Obano station, symbol of the white man's invasion.

As the story was reconstructed, Pastor Lesnusa had conducted the Sunday morning service at his tiny chapel. He was just finishing dinner when he heard a commotion in the nearby house of a Biak carpenter. He went out to investigate and was warned by some schoolboys, "Tuan, there is trouble; go home immediately."

As they spoke, armed Kapauku warriors burst forth from the tall grass and began to shoot their arrows at the Indonesian. A schoolboy tried to shield the pastor, but by the time Lesnusa had reached his home, he was fatally wounded.

The attacking Kapaukus pursued him, breaking down the doors of the house with their axes. Mrs. Lesnusa pleaded, "If you want our things, take them, but don't kill us." The marauders replied by killing her and two ten-year-old children who were staying with the Lesnusas, Martha Rumaseb and Robert Paksoal. They were the children of two other Indonesian staff workers. A Kapauku girl who was in the house escaped through a window.

The commotion that Lesnusa had heard involved the struggle between a carpenter, who lived on the grounds, and two Kapaukus who were caught in the act of stealing guns that had been left in the house. The firearms belonged to two native policemen who had left the building to prepare their noon meal.

One of the policemen, a Kapauku, escaped, but the other, a Biak, raced across the compound with an ax in his hand. Several of the school children tried to form a protective cordon about him, but the frenzied warriors broke up the crowd by pricking the children with the arrowheads, then filled the policeman's body with arrows. The carpenter was unhurt.

Days before the outbreak the missionaries and Dutch authorities had been hearing rumors that the Kapaukus planned to drive all foreigners—Dutch, Americans, and Indonesians—out of their country. Lesnusa had had assurances from Watikitaka, one of the local village leaders at Obano, that there was nothing to fear. He had also said that he and his people would protect the personnel of the school if anything did happen.

Some of the missionaries attending the dedication service had sensed an eerie quietness at Obano. When their boats arrived from Enarotali, they had found few of the local Kapaukus hanging around, and not a single native canoe was anchored in the bay. Lesnusa, when questioned, had said he felt there was no cause for alarm.

After they had murdered their victims at Obano, the crazed mob proceeded to demolish all the property. They burned several buildings to the ground, then hacked the mission airplane to pieces with their axes. The instruments from the dashboard were scattered along the runway, the aluminum was chopped from the fuselage, and even some of the cylinders were chipped from the engine.

Elated by their success, the Kapaukus proceeded to stir up other villages to join in their uprising. They cut a finger from Lesnusa's already mutilated body and sent it around to all the villages around Lake Paniai. One of the policeman's fingers was sent to villages in the Lake Tigi district. Only three other villages responded to the call, but the missionary family and other foreigners in the Wissel Lakes area were deeply concerned. Large numbers of Kapaukus were reported in the hills above the main mission base at Enarotali.

When Chrisman learned about the danger, he ordered all the missionaries of the area to gather in the compound at Enarotali. He decided that Bill and Gracie Cutts were too far off to be in immediate danger. Don Gibbons and Gordon Larson, fifteen days away in the Ilaga, were forced to sweat it out as they realized the wide gap between them and their imperiled families.

For several days the missionaries huddled together in the big missionary house at Enarotali. Then one day they saw squadrons of Dutch soldiers being landed from government airplanes. The troops had been sent in to restore order forcibly.

They immediately began to lob mortar shells into the thickets around the lakes where the wily Kapaukus were hiding out. But in spite of their superior weapons, the soldiers had little success in combating the rebellious natives. The Kapauku warriors from their protective cover jeered and mocked the troops trying to flush their quarry from the thickets. But the Dutch persisted in tracking down the rebels one by one. They were forced to kill the diehards who refused to surrender.

It was difficult to account for the sudden outburst. The best explanation was that the superstitious natives were stirred first by the epidemic that was killing off their valued pigs. This disaster, they reasoned, was an expression of the displeasure of the evil spirits because the foreigners had been allowed to remain in the area. Also, the older Kapaukus felt that the changing culture patterns following the coming of civilization weakened their authority over the younger men.

Peace was finally restored but only after a blood bath in which nearly two hundred Kapaukus were killed. It proved to be one of the worst native uprisings that had ever occurred in New Guinea, and oddly enough, in the area where the missionaries had been the most successful in preaching the gospel of love. Some of the Alliance workers were discouraged by the lack of deep response on the part of the Kapauku population. Both the rebellion and the need for force in quelling it were crushing blows to the missionary endeavor. It was true that only a small percentage of the tribespeople had been involved in the rioting. The Kapaukus who were friendly to the foreigners were filled with revenge against their own people. With primitive cruelty they expressed the hope that the government would exterminate the entire native population of Obano. When the missionaries told them they must learn forgiveness, the Kapaukus only snickered and laughed.

It appeared that the gospel cause had suffered a setback from which it might not recover for many years. During the attack, the mission airplane had been destroyed. Now with both craft gone, the future looked black indeed.

Suffering and bitter reverses have ever been the lot of those proclaiming the gospel of Christ. Fortunately, the human instruments of God's redemptive program in Dutch New Guinea did not lose heart. They remembered their vision—the vision that had persisted for more than two decades. One day their patient hope and faith would be rewarded. A converted Kapauku, little known to most of the missionaries then, would be the instrument God would use to reach other tribes with the gospel.

11

YEARNING FOR HAI

The Uhundunis live in secluded valleys, pushed back perhaps by the more self-assertive tribes; unlike the prosperous Danis, they have only a few pigs and scraggly gardens, which cling precariously to the narrow hillsides. The Uhundunis are the unwanted men of the mountains.

They rate the lowest on the tribal scale. The proud, warlike Danis put themselves at the top; the wily Kapaukus come next; the lazy Monis third; and below them are the Uhundunis, the underdogs.

On the surface the Uhundunis carry on like other New Guinea tribes. They engage in warfare, are polygynous, and still live in the Stone Age, employing stone axes, knives, and chisels. The men are often traders who travel great distances to do business. The women tend the gardens and keep the home fires burning.

The Uhundunis mortally fear the evil spirits that dwell in the swift mountain streams, that lurk in the fogs hanging eerily over the valleys, and that speak frighteningly in the loud thunderbolts that strike suddenly. From early childhood until old age, these tribespeople must constantly seek to appease the spirits by offering them the blood of pigs, or by planting certain types of trees in the village yard or along the trail.

Sometimes traditional chants, handed down from their fore-fathers, are sung to ward off the boding evil. In other songs they express their yearning for "heaven" in wistful verses such as the one recorded by Gibbons and Larson in the Ilaga Valley:

> *"O Friend, up in the sky is a large boat on a great lake,*
> *A-wai-wae,*
> *And to this wonderful place we want to go,*
> *A-wai-wae, A-wai-wae."*

This is sung as a solo by the lusty bass of an informal Uhunduni chorus. The soloist holds the last note as his companions join in:

> *"Kwau kwoa, kwau kwao;*
> *Wey wai, wey wai."*

This simple chant with its distorted views of heaven nevertheless reveals an important characteristic of the Uhunduni people: a deep abiding hunger for a better and higher spiritual life. They seem to have more "soul" than the other tribes. It probably explains why they were the first group to respond promptly and in great numbers to the Christian message with its promise of eternal life.

It is necessary to understand the deep-seated emphasis on *hai*, a better kind of life, which dominates their tribal myths. The stories concern individuals searching for *hai*, which was believed would one day arrive in their midst suddenly and mysteriously.

This wonderful new plane of existence would be brought by god-men or deities who would come to them from the outside world. According to the myths, their own tribal leaders would champion these godlike beings and present the gift of *hai* to the tribespeople at the appropriate time.

It was against the background of these popular legends that Gib-bons and Larson arrived in August, 1956, in the Ilaga Valley and commenced work among the Uhundunis. Because of their white skins and the fact that they came from the outside world, the missionaries immediately were regarded as demi-gods. When they began to preach the Christian gospel with its promise of eternal life, their identification with the *hai* myths was complete. It was a long time before the Uhundunis could be convinced that the missionaries were mortal men.

Larson and Gibbons were warmly greeted by the Uhunduni chief, a little man with a bushy black beard who was named Den. He could not do enough for the missionaries. He brought them pork and sweet potatoes. He helped them build their first station near his village of Kunga on the south side of the Ilaga. When Larson and Gibbons preached through interpreters, he hung onto every word. It was apparent that he was deeply moved by the gospel story.

Den's son, Noanbudema, was a muscular youth with bright eyes and a friendly disposition like his father. Samuel, as Noanbudema came to be known, was soon very useful to Gibbons as an interpreter and language informant. The missionaries learned that he had just returned to his native village before they entered the Ilaga. The youth had run away from a Roman Catholic school on the coast where he learned to speak Malay.

Gibbons had picked up Malay while he was stationed at Enarotali. Thus he was able to start preaching immediately to the Uhundunis, using Samuel as interpreter. This relationship deepened the friendship with Den, who began to share his heart yearnings with the missionaries.

First Den told Don Gibbons a strange tale that he had heard from his grandfather, Mukumede, who all of his life had sought to discover *hai*.

Mukumede, the story went, had gone hunting for wild animals in the forest on the hillside above Kunga. He tramped through woods all day but failed to find any game. By late afternoon he had reached the top of the ridge, still without success. Weary and hungry, he sat down under the ledge of a rock. He feared that he would die.

As he sat there, he started to doze. But he was suddenly awak-

ened by a huge bunch of bananas which fell at his feet. He quickly
ate the fruit, wondering what spirit had been so kind to him. But
he was still thirsty and there was no water on the ridge.

At that moment a fountain of water sprang forth from the rock
and began to flow right by his side. He drank until he had quenched
his thirst, and also filled up several drinking gourds that he found
nearby. Then the fountain stopped flowing as quickly as it started.

Mukumede rushed home to his village to tell his people that he
had experienced the beginnings of *hai*.

On his deathbed years later, Mukumede called his family about
him, including his grandson, Den, and said,

"I have not found *hai* although I have sought it for many years.
In your lifetime perhaps you will find the thing we have all looked
for."

Den was deeply moved by his grandfather's prophecy, for there
is a deep sense of nearness and kinship among the Uhundunis. One
does not act primarily as an individual but as part of a family or
clan.

Just before Gibbons and Larson arrived, a favorite cousin of
Den had died. The cousin was a young man of about twenty-one,
just ready to enter into a life of usefulness, when he was fatally
stricken. Den was greatly shaken by his loss. He could not believe
that there could be illness without cause or purpose. He sought
diligently to discover the reason for the death of his kinsman, in-
quiring first of local fortune tellers, next walking many miles through
the mountains to consult with the famed necromancers of the
Dem tribe, then with others among the Monis. Yet Den never
found the answer. He came back to Kunga defeated, and with his
faith shaken in those who have contacts with the spirit world. He
was wrestling with this spiritual problem when the missionaries
arrived.

Gibbons and Larson followed the normal pattern of treating the
sick with penicillin and other medications, always praying over each
patient and telling him the essentials of the Christian message.
Within ten days Den saw stubborn cases of yaws cleared up, in-
curable cases for primitive medicine. Den and his fellow tribesmen

attributed the "magical" physical cures to the gospel preached by the missionaries.

A regular procession of events was preparing Den to become a Christian: his family's concern for attaining *hai;* his own quest for the meaning of life and death; the physical healings that occurred before his eyes; and the promise of eternal life.

However, the first Uhunduni to confess faith in Jesus Christ was his son, Samuel, who probably knew more of the gospel message than anyone else because he had repeated it so often as he served as Gibbons' interpreter. Samuel had heard the misionary tell of the Fall of man and the demands of a holy God as expressed in the Ten Commandments. He and his people did not need much preaching to convince them that they were sinners. They knew that. Gibbons concentrated on presenting Christ as the Redeemer of mankind and the Saviour of all who would come to Him for forgiveness.

Samuel, like his namesake of old, responded to that divine invitation and confessed Christ as Lord and Saviour in March, 1957. But he had a problem. He confided to Gibbons, "What should I do about those three pigs I stole a couple of years ago? Now that I'm a Christian, what must I do about this?"

Gibbons suggested that Samuel make restitution by repaying the three men from whom he had taken the pigs. It turned out that two of the men had moved out of the Ilaga. Taking a steel ax, the precious wages of a month's work, Samuel went to the one still living in the valley, and said,

"You didn't know who stole that pig of yours that disappeared two years ago, but I do. I killed it and ate it. Now that I'm a Christian, I want to pay you for it."

The Uhunduni was thoroughly embarrased. He wanted no payment because he knew he was guilty of the same offense.

"Do you think I have never stolen a pig?" he asked. "Do you think I should accept this payment when I have stolen pigs from so many others and have never repaid them?"

But Samuel insisted, thereby demonstrating the genuineness of his profession of faith. And the incident was noised throughout the entire valley.

It was about this time that a party of about twenty Kapauku traders arrived from the Wissel Lakes area. Leading the expedition was Widi-ai-bi, a warm-hearted Christian Kapauku in the prime of his life. He earned his living by trading but spent all of his free time preaching the gospel. He knew that Gibbons and Larson had come to evangelize the Ilaga Valley, and now he and his friends wanted to help.

Already the strands of spiritual kinship between the solid missionary work among the Kapaukus and its extension into the other parts of New Guinea were becoming evident. Kapaukus Elisa and Ruth Gobai had served as front-line missionaries in the dramatic entrance into the Baliem Valley. But the contribution to be made by Widi-ai-bi in the quieter conquest of the Ilaga would have even greater significance.

Widi-ai-bi had made a clear-cut confession of faith in Christ back in 1951. He had been deeply stirred by the preaching of Zaccheus Pakari, the early Kapauku convert, in meetings held in the Lake Tigi area south of Enarotali. From the start Widi-ai-bi had suffered persecution because he allied himself with the Christian cause. He had seen his house torn down, and was beaten by those opposed to his stand as a believer in Christ. But these fierce winds of opposition only proved him to be a more faithful witness. He went everywhere telling people about Christ just like one of the disciples in the Early Church.

Now he had come to help the missionaries in the Ilaga Valley, and on the side was exchanging some of his cowrie shells for Dani pigs to meet expenses. Widi-ai-bi could not speak Uhunduni, but some bilingual natives came to his aid. Through these interpreters he told the Uhundunis of how he had become a Christian and of the subsequent change it brought to his whole life.

"This news the white men give you," he said, "is not only good for them; it's good for 'real' people too. It's for the Kapaukus, the Danis, and the Uhundunis."

There was no doubt that the Uhundunis, already prepared by earlier parts of a spiritual mosaic, were deeply impressed by hearing a tribesman testify to the powers of Christ. They listened attentively and began to have earnest discussions among themselves. At first two hundred came to the services, and soon that figure jumped to five hundred. Whenever a meeting was announced, the Uhundunis flocked there, singing as they came, and eagerly drank in this new but intriguing message.

During the month of May the Uhunduni leaders continued their long conferences dealing with the minute implications of becoming Christians. In their tight-knit cultural pattern, it never occurred to them that this was a message they could accept or reject as individuals. They always had done things together. It was not likely that they would start a new trend at this important juncture. If the message was good for one, it was good for all.

No one could accuse them of acting on a sudden emotional impulse, bulldozed by the wheedling or cajoling of the white men. Actually, the missionaries at this stage hardly knew enough of the native language to convey anything but the simplest of concepts. Every one of the tribal elders had an opportunity to present good reasons for not accepting the Christian message.

"Shall we lead our families into this new way?" they asked one another. "If we get rid of our charms and fetishes, will the evil spirits become angry and destroy us through sickness or war?"

Yes, war—there was a big problem. Some of their most important fetishes had been regarded as essential in waging successful war. What if they burned them?

This was not an academic question. They had suffered much in recent years from devastating wars that raged throughout the Ilaga Valley, and they still were not sure of peace. "If we burn our war fetishes and our enemies do not burn theirs," they asked logically, "what will become of us?"

They already knew that some of their own Uhunduni tribespeople, south of the Carstensz Range, had destroyed their fetishes under the influence of a Roman Catholic guru named Moses. Thus it was not a new idea exactly.

Furthermore, Widi-ai-bi told of the spiritual movement among his own Kapauku people back in 1950 and 1951 when more than one thousand had renounced their charms and fetishes and expressed their determination to follow in Christ's way. Widi-ai-bi had preached strongly about the necessity of breaking with the pagan past, that it was impossible for a Christian believer to retain talismans. He must take one course or the other.

Gibbons carefully explained to Den and the other Uhunduni leaders that embracing Christianity would make many demands on them: it would involve repentance; require restitution of stolen goods; put an end to demanding and accepting war payments—a deeply etched part of their traditional culture.

The Uhundunis wanted to know how they should destroy their charms. Gibbons told them that this was a problem they must solve. They first considered throwing the magic articles into the river, then reasoned that other natives might salvage the valuable cowrie shells and use them for their own gain; or the discarded weapons might be taken by their enemies and used against them. Ah, they said, why not haul them all away in the mission airplane?

There was no doubt that the superstitious Uhundunis had some fear about even picking up the charms to dispose of them. It would have pleased them mightily if someone else were to undertake the spooky job. Their lifelong fear of evil spirits could not be eradicated overnight.

"Why don't we take one of those [fifty-gallon] drums that your things came in and have the man in the airplane take them away?" they asked. "As he flies out to the coast, he can shove it out of the window in some area where no one is living."

When this plan was turned down, the missionary told them about the story in the Book of Acts dealing with the conversion of the soothsayers at Ephesus. When those men were converted, Gibbons said, they made a fire and burned their magical books.

This method of destruction pleased the Uhundunis. Now they were nearing the moment of final decision.

On Saturday, May 25, the Uhundunis conducted large group meetings most of the day. All the important men took part in the deliberations. Gibbons met with them that afternoon and reassuringly said that Christ would meet their needs if they would trust Him wholly and break with their old way of life.

The next day Gibbons preached to nearly one thousand Uhundunis on the text, "Choose you this day whom ye will serve" (Josh.
24:15). "God can see your pretenses," the missionary declared.
"He is not like the evil spirits you think you can frighten with a
little fence across the path. This God sees everything; you cannot
deceive Him."

Following his message, Gibbons asked his listeners to remain
seated if they were not sure God was able, or if they were afraid, or
if they thought they could deceive God. But if there were those
who wanted to follow Him, they were to rise and meet in a group
near the missionary. To Gibbons' amazement, two hundred and
twenty-five men, women, and teenagers gathered together in a
separate group. Leading the crowd was Den, who now knew that
he had found the true *hai* for which he had sought so long.

Gibbons had counseled the leaders for days on the meaning of
the gospel, that it was the sacrificial work of God's Son upon the
Cross that provided the basis for their salvation, that through His
resurrection they could share in His life for strength and power.
He also explained that commitment to Christ meant that they
should cease dependence on their charms and fetishes. It meant
breaking with the old life.

"We will follow the Lord," said the first band of disciples.

The young men of the tribe then walked over to the men's house,
tore down the fetish shelves, and used them to make a fire. Then
one brought hot coals from the hearth and carried them over to the
clearing where the crowd had gathered. They began to pile their
fetishes, charms, and magic articles upon the blaze. Some were
personal charms; others, village fetishes. It was a strange collection
of objects—little round stones that were used to insure successful
gardens, whole nets covered with pigs' tails, stone axes and adzes,
knives that represented male or female ancestors, long strings of
shells, broken spears and bows and arrows taken from dead
enemies.

As the group of Uhundunis watched the embers die, there was
jubilation among those who had taken the step of destroying

their most precious possessions to declare their faith openly in their newfound Lord and Saviour.

This was the first mass fetish burning in the central highlands. To those who gathered that day at Kunga, it may not have been greatly significant, but it was a bright omen of a spiritual movement that would sweep through the valleys of the Ilaga, into the Boega, the Sinak, and the North Baliem, and ultimately into the Grand Valley and throughout a large share of Dutch New Guinea.

12

THE DANIS RESPOND

The Ilaga Valley, located halfway between the Wissel Lakes to the west and the Grand Valley of the Baliem to the east, forms the hub of a wheel of valleys. The rivers in the valleys are like spokes running to the north and east, to the south and west. Gordon Larson felt that "the area of a hundred valleys" was the new theater for missionary extension.

With the opening of the Ilaga Valley airstrip, the previously impenetrable "hundred valleys" now might be reached by the light airplanes as soon as airstrips could be constructed and outstations manned by missionaries. Because of the rugged character of the terrain, suitable airstrip sites were at a premium, but events that happened in the Ilaga one day would have echoes in the myriads of surrounding valleys.

From the very first contacts with the people of the Ilaga, it was apparent that the Uhundunis were eager to hear. The cocky Danis, however, responded to earnest preaching with scoffing and laughter.

Gibbons and Larson soon learned that whereas there were about twenty-five hundred Uhundunis in the Ilaga, there were at least seventy-five hundred western Danis in the same region. These Danis had migrated to the Ilaga from the Baliem and they had kinfolk in all the intervening territory.

After consultation with Gibbons, Larson decided that he and his wife would establish a mission station at Elamaga in the center of a large Dani settlement. Accordingly, he moved his family from Kunga to the new location on the north side of the valley not far from the airstrip.

Thus Gibbons would continue the work among the Uhundunis and Larson would concentrate on the Danis.

When work was started on the Ilaga airstrip, the Danis lived up to their reputation for being strong and aggressive. Led by two of their chiefs, Opalalok and Nokogi, they worked industriously, sometimes in groups of several hundred, for a period of six months.

First evidence of any spiritual concern on the part of the Danis developed during the long weeks the tribesmen were clearing the landing site.

Opalalok, it turned out, was the father-in-law of Den, the Uhunduni leader who became one of the first Christian converts of his tribe.

Through this family relationship a bridge had already been built between the two tribes. The deep interest in eternal life which had seized the Uhundunis was channeled from Den and his family to Opalalok, one of the most influential men among the larger Dani population.

From time to time Opalalok and Nokogi would call Larson aside, and squatting behind a bush, interrogate him in whispers. They wanted to know more: "Who is this Jesus? When do you expect Him to come? Do you mean He can give us life that will last on and on?"

Then there were other less theological, more practical questions: "What will happen when the sun goes up and down again after one year? Will our potatoes all rot in the ground? Will our pigs die? Will we die? Will sickness come?"

The Ilaga Danis were deeply impressed when their valley neighbors of the Uhunduni tribe took the step of faith and burned their fetishes, but the Danis were not ready to follow at that time. They still had many questions, and their tightly-knit family-centered social structure made it difficult to act as promptly as the more loosely aligned Uhundunis.

"We want to burn our fetishes, too," the Danis told Larson, "but we must wait until our relatives from the North Baliem River visit us."

By this they meant that they could not think of burning charms and fetishes until they had consulted with leaders of their clan in the North Baliem area. They also wanted full settlement of the fierce warfare that had raged in the Ilaga and surrounding valleys for three years.

The Larsons left on furlough in the summer of 1957 and returned a year later. By this time at least five hundred Uhundunis had destroyed their charms and some had been baptized. But Gordon Larson and his wife, Peggy, were not eager to push the cautious Danis into action until the latter were thoroughly convinced in their hearts that it was the right course.

The key to the Dani tribe proved to be Den's father-in-law, Opalalok. The other Dani leaders had been saying that they would burn their charms, but again and again at the last minute they backed off.

Opalalok continued to show interest. After Sunday church services he questioned the missionaries at length. He was concerned about the implications following a break with historic "securities." What would happen if the Danis abandoned spirit appeasement by killing the magical, or ceremonial, pigs? They had depended upon charm magic to gain wealth. What would happen to them under the new order of things? Special charms, like the one called "Mother of the sweet potato crop," had been the talisman on which they depended for agricultural success. Must the women abandon the sorcery that enabled them to cast spells upon their husbands' enemies? And above all else, what about the war fetishes that possess the spirit and power of one's warrior ancestors and bring victory in battle?

In time Opalalok had all his questions answered. He was convinced that the Lord Jesus Christ would be protector and provider for him and his people. Once he reached this decision, he was eager to declare his faith in Christ by publicly burning the symbols of the old culture. It was a long step of faith for an illiterate tribesman with no previous contacts with the Christian world and its message. He told the hesitant Dani leaders, "I have decided to hold a burning. If you men want to hang back, I am going to do it anyway."

So it was that in December, 1958, the first burnings took place in Opalalok's settlement. Three other villages in the valley soon followed the example of Opalalok's people. It was not long before many more clan groups became interested. Within a year twenty-five different settlements had joined in these public testimonies to faith in Christ and a willingness to renounce the old religion. Some of the gatherings were made up of fifty or sixty people, others numbered two or three hundred. By early 1960 a large share of the Dani population in the valley—maybe thirty-five hundred to four thousand people—had been involved in the burnings.

When a community announced a charm burning, the believers from other areas would gather with them. Marching in a company, the visiting Danis would sing and dance to express their joy at this latest evidence of God's power in their midst.

Larson realized that there were mixed motives behind the charm burnings. Like the Uhundunis, the Danis had myths with religious significance. In ridding themselves of their magical past, some undoubtedly thought that they were opening the door for *natelan katelan,* their expression for eternal life, that literally translated means "my outer skin, your outer skin." By this idiom they referred to the shedding of the outer skin, and they linked this to the story of the race between the snake and the bird. To the Danis the snake, which sheds its skin year after year, is the symbol of eternal, or at least non-ending, life. Thus *natelan katelan* meant "we've shed the outer coating of death and will keep on living forever."

According to the legend, the snake and the bird had engaged in a race across the valley at the beginning of time. Since the bird, who died, won the race and the immortal snake lost, the people were deprived of their original eternal life. "Oh, why did the snake not win?" the Danis still ask.

When the missionaries came and talked about Christ, the Son of God, as the Creator and Redeemer who was able to restore true life to man, the Danis linked the message to their myth and the messengers to Bok, their god-man ancestor. In their strange legends Bok came up out of a hole in the ground at a spot in the Baliem Valley between Seinma and Hetigima. As Bok came forth he walked westward, standing the mountains in their places as he traveled. His footprint still may be seen, say the Danis, in a stone of the North Baliem near Tiom and Maaki. Bok finally disappeared when he reached the coast and now lives on the other side of the ocean.

In the Dani concept, the ocean is an extended river that surrounds the entire island. The world, as they know it, is confined to their island, which is encircled by a wall with the sky overhead as a roof. They have vague ideas of the north and south coasts of New Guinea, but have no conception of the distance from east to west. In their little world, the sun climbs a tree in the morning, crosses the sky during the day, then crawls down a tree at night and goes underground. The sun is regarded as a sort of female deity and the moon a male that watches over her during the night.

When Bok arrived in those far-off days, he brought along with him "real" people, the Danis, who accompanied him out of the ground loaded down with the original sweet potatoes, the taro, the tobacco, sugar cane, pigs, and dogs. The Danis then moved westward and settled in various areas.

Originally a man and his younger sister were born into one moiety, and another man and his sister belonged to the opposite moiety. Thus they became the original ancestors of the two moieties of the clans that continue to exist.

With these myths in the background of their thinking, the Danis regarded white men, and the missionaries in particular, as the descendants of Bok who had come to restore their *natelan katelan*.

There were other motives, too. The Danis, trapped in a pattern of warfare waged regularly every two or three years, had seen as many as two or three hundred men perish in a series of battles. They longed to rid themselves of this incessant carnage that was tied in so closely to their sacred ancestral war charms. By destroying these, some of the natives undoubtedly thought they would be freed from the bondage of war.

Dani tribal structure is like a tree with many branches. The actions of a given branch, a village, would involve the other parts of the tree, their kin in related villages. When one part of the clan therefore decided to burn their fetishes, their relatives followed the normal pattern of wanting to act in concert with them. Thus the fetish burnings spread eastward from one kinship group to another.

There were other naïve or even foolish incidents connected with the burnings. The natives of a place called Jygetenok in the Ilaga came to Larson, saying they wanted to burn their charms because they believed that God had dropped a mysterious stem of red berries out of the sky. They interpreted this as some sort of divine signal for them to start action. Larson used the opportunity to explain the real significance of turning away from magic, and in due time a number of the group became devout believers.

So it was that there were those who did not understand at first the full implication of what they were doing. Larson soon realized, along with Gibbons, that once the tribespeople took the charm-burning step, they next needed instruction in the Christian faith. A regular pattern developed: as soon as a group would burn their charms, they reported the following Sunday to the mission station for instruction. Within a year Larson was meeting every week with a throng of two to three thousand Danis who showed an intense eagerness to learn. The missionaries, who had suffered sneers and laughs and brutal attacks upon their expeditions, were impressed by this about-face of the western Danis.

Church gatherings in the early days of the movement were festive occasions, patterned after the taro or sweet potato feasts. The groups began to assemble on Sunday morning around ten o'clock. The men would march together from their villages in the valley,

stopping at the men's houses in villages belonging to their clan al-
liances. They would proceed to church, laughing and singing as
they went. When they reached the clearing near the mission station
at Elamaga, they usually marched or danced about in a circle,
shouting. This was their way of showing their joy on the Lord's
Day before the church service.

The earlier arrivals, perhaps one thousand or more, would race
back and forth in the churchyard for a distance of one hundred
feet, repeating the performance as they chanted monotonously. At
first they showed little taste in their singing, employing words that
were hardly compatible with a service of worship. One song, for
example, consisted of a refrain which threatened an enemy that his
intestines would be spread about the landscape. Eventually, cor-
rections were made in this type of singing, but the Danis still had
much to learn about Christian doctrine, and they had not yet
composed their own hymns of praise.

Some of the missionaries in New Guinea have been critical of
these rather boisterous pre-service dances that have become a part
of the liturgy of the native church. Others, perhaps more familiar
with the ways of the people, believe these cultural manifestations
will be modified as the young church progresses in the faith. In
the first years of the church's growth, Larson feels, it would be as
wrong as abolishing the song service in the Sunday evening meeting of an American evangelical church.

There were other problems with Dani singing. Since many of
the tunes were related to courtship rites and contained suggestive
language, the Danis were understandably reluctant to use them for
worship. On the other hand, the missionaries were loathe to introduce Western music which had little meaning, certainly at that stage,
for the new converts. In time, the Uhundunis developed their own
hymnody and the Danis followed their example. For the tribesmen,
singing became a natural and important part of their worship.

After preliminary activities came to an end, the Danis would
sit down in orderly fashion, the men on one side and the women
on the other. They would turn eagerly to hear what the missionary
had to say.

"Teach us the original thought," the Danis would tell Larson. He then would repeat the Creation Story, which was followed by the account of man's Fall, the birth of Christ, some of Christ's miracles, His teaching, His death and resurrection, and the giving of the Holy Spirit.

As the crowds of new believers increased, Larson realized that it would be physically impossible for him to instruct the hordes who were willing to walk in the "Jesus way." He consulted with Don Gibbons, who had been faced with the same predicament in trying to conduct mass indoctrination classes. Both men knew that this kind of mass teaching was not thorough enough.

Thus Gibbons early in 1958 had extended a call to some of the baptized believers to attend a "witness school" which offered concentrated instruction for four hours every day for a period of three weeks. Gibbons thought forty or fifty would respond. Instead, two hundred turned out on the very first day. This was the beginning of the method to be followed as the missionaries sought to increase their effectiveness in discipling the tribespeople in the Christian faith and life.

Larson had asked for twenty couples to attend the first witness school for the western Danis, and to his amazement, exactly twenty couples responded. Three or four of the couples then dropped out, chiefly because they were not qualified intellectually, but the majority of the original group became strong leaders in the native church. Later, ten of the men were ordained as ministering elders, serving as itinerant preachers.

Instruction in the witness school, commencing in June and continuing until January, was not confined to classroom work. On weekends the witness men visited different villages in the valley to teach those who were eager to know more about the truth of God. Generally, the preachers conducted their services around the central cooking pit.

Larson found that the converts taught in this manner and baptized promptly, developed more rapidly as Christians. Thus as soon as the witness men could prepare the new converts, they questioned them before the village elders on matters of doctrine and personal ethics. The missionaries had always emphasized that proper life conduct was just as important in the Christian life as sound doctrine. When the witness men and local leaders thought the people were ready for baptism, their names were presented to the missionary, who supervised the final questioning. Then the candidates were baptized. By employing this system, the infant church early became involved in evangelistic outreach, and its own people were discipling others in the faith. There was therefore little imported Christianity. The church grew in its own cultural background.

Baptism now represented a substitute for the heathen initiation ceremonies. In a very real sense it conveyed the idea of being initiated into the church of Jesus Christ. Thus baptism became a proper symbol of identification with Christ and only those who were earnest about their faith sought to be baptized. There were no wholesale baptisms, no pressure for the people to join the church.

During the period of the first witness school a good half of the Dani converts were baptized. Sometimes there would be groups of as many as one hundred who took this important step with the Lord. Only by employing the capable services of the witness men was the church able to grow so rapidly and yet sturdily in a short period of time.

In the not too distant future native witness men would play an historic role in New Guinea's evangelization. In the providence of God, these Stone Age tribesmen would implement the final phases of Jaffray's great dream.

13

STRUGGLES IN THE BALIEM

While spiritual history was being made in the Ilaga Valley, the missionaries in the Baliem were still struggling with the physical obstacles of pioneer work. In the single year of 1956, six new missionary couples had set up housekeeping in the Baliem Valley.

Among them were Henry and Bernice Young from western Canada; Edward and Shirley Maxey of the Chicago area; Ben and Ruth Karcesky of Pennsylvania and New Jersey; Tom and Frances Bozeman of Florida; Donald and Glenna Anderson of western Canada; and James and Dolores Sunda of Alabama. The Bozemans and Maxeys had arrived earlier in the year and had already established themselves at their stations.

The decision to send so many missionaries in one year was based on the intense desire of Alliance officials to occupy the Baliem fully and open up a string of airstrips and mission stations in the principal Dani population areas.

Most of the Baliem missionaries could each write a full-length book on the experiences of their first year or two on the field. It took a hardy breed of men and women just to endure the tribulations of getting settled at new stations and adjusting to the strange customs of the Danis.

Some of the new workers were able to report stories of success. Others made slow progress and at times were bowed down with discouragement. But in spite of the hardships all of the missionaries were united in their great sense of mission. Above everything else they wanted to win the natives of Cannibal Valley for Christ.

The Youngs had been assigned to the important new station of Pyramid Mountain, located at the upper end of the Baliem Valley in the midst of a great concentration of Dani villages. Their station was to become a more significant center than the Youngs or anyone else imagined. But the early days did not foreshadow anything like this.

Henry Young, a husky timberman from British Columbia, had been a member of the missionary party that constructed the airstrip at Pyramid. Aided by others, he had built the aluminum house in which his family was to live. His wife, Bernice, a farm girl with training in nursing, cared for their little family that increased by three during their first term. She also treated the Danis for their various illnesses and injuries, became fluent in the native language, planted a huge garden, and kept house.

The Youngs pitched into their missionary duties with real enthusiasm, but it was lost on the Danis. The couple had their patience tried in a hundred ways. First, native thievery nearly drove them to distraction. The Danis took everything around the mission station that was not tied down.

On one occasion a group of Danis came to the front door of the mission home to sell a bunch of bananas. While they talked to Bernice Young, their confederates stole everything on the clothes line in the backyard.

The missionaries were also harassed by the mercurial temperaments of the tribesmen. Their moods ranged from a friendly or cautious acceptance of the newcomers to belligerent hostility. Their smiles turned to anger in a flash. The Young were kept on the alert at all times.

The problems of communication were great. Some experiences

were more amusing than serious. Bernice Young thought that it would be pleasant to have a fire going in the cookstove before she arose in the morning. Conesquently, she wound up the alarm clock, set it for an early hour, then instructed her Dani houseboy that when the bell rang in the morning he was to build a fire. She got up the following day, pleased to find the fire burning merrily —but in the midst of the flames, already well cremated, was her alarm clock.

Particularly trying was the activity of Duguarek, the local witch doctor, who not only stole things from the Youngs, but blandly confessed to thievery. The missionaries found the situation frustrating because the man had status in his tribe and there was no way to punish him. To make an issue over the persistent stealing might even start an uprising. Duguarek's fierce temper flared easily, and on one occasion he threatened them with his spear. The Youngs asked their friends to pray for the witch doctor.

This proved to be the answer to their dilemma. After a while they noticed a marked change in Duguarek. He came to the mission station and sought to make overtures of peace. For the first time a Dani in their area was showing signs of repentance. Eventually, he returned most of the things he had stolen. Then to top it all, he bought two pigs and staged a feast to make amends for the articles he could not return.

Warfare raged near Pyramid. On one occasion a Dani, who worked in the Youngs' garden, dropped his digging stick and picked up his spear to join his tribesmen in a battle. Henry Young walked up to the battlefield in time to learn that their faithful worker had been killed by an enemy warrior who had chopped him to pieces with an ax.

In another larger engagement the Pyramid Danis went to war against their traditional enemies in a neighboring valley. Thirty of the local Danis were killed and ten of the enemy.

The Youngs were appalled by the needless carnage that took so many men in the prime of life. They knew that widows and orphans were mourning in the nearby villages and maiming themselves in their grief.

The pig feast was always a big event. Henry Young wrote of his observations to friends in Canada:

"The Danis are busy getting ready for the coming pig feast. Old houses have to be reconstructed and new ones built. Firewood is cut and stacked in great piles for this festive occasion which takes place once in two or three years—the time when everyone gets more pork than he can eat. They anticipate it like a youngster who looks forward to Christmas, and for months before it is the main topic of conversation. What takes place during this three months of killing and eating pig, we hope to share with you, although we lack complete understanding of their culture.

"First, there is a huge slaughter of pigs. This ends the period of mourning for all the women who have lost their husbands in battle or in other ways. They can now remarry and eat certain vegetables that have been restricted. Following this ceremony come the weddings of the younger girls. At the pig feast all of the eligible girls are married either to young men taking their first brides, or to older men, according to prestige and wealth, taking new brides. One man we know is taking his tenth!

"It is customary for the man to carry his bride off to his village. He doesn't see her again for two or three weeks. In the interval the women of the husband's village remove the girl's grass skirt and replace it with a fiber skirt of the married woman. Then she is 'draped' with nets that hang down her back. Pigs are killed and she places some of the pork in a carrying net that is draped in front of her body. When all the pork is eaten, they have a village sing and the bridegroom comes and sits by his bride. Then the husband's family provides the payment demanded for the girl.

"The exchange of live pigs comes next. In one village we saw eighty-five pigs exchanged on a single occasion. Now the magical pigs are killed in ceremonial fashion with only the important men present. The following day the men's pigs are killed. On these first two days, no women are permitted to be present. It is only on the third day when the women's pigs are killed that they may watch.

There is always singing and dancing throughout the nights of the pig feast days.

"The cooking of the last of the pork is quite a sight. Some pieces have been kept since the first day, so by then the pork is spoiled and full of maggots. The Danis eat what they can and throw the rest to the few remaining pigs.

"During the pig feast the boys of eight to ten are initiated into the clan. We understand there is quite a ritual connected with this. Finally, comes the ceremony of chasing the spirits of the pigs over to the enemy. The natives all carry switches, and at a given signal they thrash the air. Then there is the ceremony that brings the pig feast to an end."

On their first Christmas in the Baliem, the Youngs arranged a pig feast for their Dani friends. Henry Young describes the big event:

"Not one particle of the pig is wasted, except that they singe off the bristles. In the meantime rocks have been heating which are placed in a pit in the ground. This is lined with banana leaves and native grass, and then parts of the pigs are placed in the pit. In between layers of pork they place native spinach. Then on top of everything more hot rocks are placed along with more leaves and grass. The pork is allowed to steam for two hours. By the time we had finished our own Christmas dinner, three hundred Danis had gathered for their feast. What a sweet sound that many Danis make as they noisily chew on dripping fat. I managed to eat some with them. It's best to eat and not look at what you have in your hand."

It was difficult to tell whether the missionaries or the Danis were more confused by the other's cultural habits. On one occasion Bernice Young went out to her bamboo cookhouse to find that one of her houseboys, his body smeared with pig fat and charcoal, had fallen asleep by the stove. When she looked closely, she found he was lying on one of her clean tea towels and using another for a covering. She woke him up and told him that he was not to use her towels as bedding. He looked up at her with his sleepy eyes and said,

"But, Mama, I was real careful. I put the rag you clean the

stove with down on the floor first so the towels wouldn't get dirty."

On another occasion an unruly Dani threw a rock at the mission airplane propeller. Had it reached its mark, another craft might have been put out of commission.

Gradually, the attitude of the Danis changed toward the Youngs and the stealing ceased. Some of the natives listened to the gospel message, but there was not much response to it. Their language informant, Labini, asked many questions: "When will Jesus come? Will He come to the Baliem? Will I see Him? Who will go up to His home? How will they go? In an airplane? If I am saved, will I go? What will happen to those who reject Christ? If I reject Him, will I be punished forever?"

Henry Young tried to reply to every query, but it was not until three weeks later, when they were working on a passage of Scripture, that Labini expressed a desire to accept Christ. He prayed with the missionary and became one of the first converts at Pyramid.

Attempts to get a village school program started were as difficult as the rest of the missionary effort. Young finally was able to enlist a class of seven adults and children by promising them that he would buy garden produce from those who came to school. Classroom work was a new experience. As one pupil sought to pronounce a vowel, for example, the rest of the class would burst out laughing and make side remarks. The men in the class became embarrassed when the women and children began to learn faster than they. This meant that a special men's class had to be held in another part of the village. Eventually, the students of both classes found that they could read their primers prepared by the missionaries, and they were beside themselves with joy. This was the dawn of the literacy work in the area, and in succeeding years the desire to read would become an important by-product of the Christian missionary effort.

The teacher never knew what would happen during a lesson. One day, after Young had presented a devotional message, a woman ran into the courtyard with her husband in close pursuit. He was angry because his wife had not fed the pigs. The Dani picked up a big rock and hurled it at her, but fortunately it missed. He left the courtyard, muttering to himself; his wife quietly joined the class.

Young had scarcely resumed his teaching when another angry man appeared. The missionary approached him, but the Dani motioned him to be quiet, then picked up several lumps of dry clay and began to bounce them off the back of one of the women in the class. He shouted to his wife,

"Why aren't you out in the garden? Get to work."

The missionary reprimanded the husband so sternly that he joined the class and thereafter became a regular attendant, listening eagerly to what the teacher had to say.

Setting up the mid-valley station at Tulim, halfway between Hetigima and Pyramid, was the task of the Maxeys. Coming from pastoral duties in Chicago to the rigors of a primitive field was not easy.

Leaving his wife at Hetigima, Maxey and a party of missionary men traveled by boat up the Baliem River to the Tulim site. On an earlier survey trip Maxey had been narrowly missed by an arrow shot from the riverbank.

As the missionary party began the Tulim airstrip, they discovered that a portion of the land was taboo territory. The local chief, supported by a small group of followers, ordered the construction work to stop. Bromley, one of those aiding Maxey, sought to reason with him, but without success. The leader continued to shout his threats.

Maxey and his comrades wondered what to do. Should they give in to the angry Dani and halt work on the vital airstrip?

They were asking this question of themselves when a faction of the tribe, opposed to the chief, came to the tent where the missionaries were encamped.

"Don't leave now," a tribal spokesman told Bromley. "That's the way the chief talks all the time. He was just telling you to stop work on the airstrip so you could stay here."

Shortly after this Adrian, a Christian Biak boy who was helping the missionaries, came into camp with his face alight.

"We can proceed with the airstrip," he said. "I just received permission from the chief. He only says that we have to work the taboo end of the strip ourselves."

Adrian then related his experience with the unfriendly chief. The headman had invited the Biak native to examine one of his sick pigs.

"It was an animal and I didn't know what to do," Adrian reported. "If it had been a human being, I'd have given it a shot of penicillin. But all I could do was pray that the pig would get well."

While he was in the chief's company, Adrian told him that the missionaries needed the airstrip and that their presence in the valley would be beneficial.

"Well, why do they have to make it so long?" was the next question. Adrian explained that the airplane required that much space for landing.

The following morning the chief sought out Adrian and said, "I am astonished at the results of your praying. That pig ate potatoes this morning." The work on the airstrip proceeded.

The Maxeys and their two children lived for several months in the original 12 by 18 foot tent that had earlier served as the shelter for the original landing party at Minimo. The Maxeys' stay in the tent was lengthened because the taboo scare made it difficult to get a sufficient number of local natives for the airstrip. Work on a permanent home had to be deferred until the landing field was completed. It was a happy day when their new aluminum house was finished and the Maxeys could live more normal lives.

The establishment of the station at Tulim meant that the Baliem Valley was occupied now in three strategic areas.

In the midst of missionary trials Myron Bromley waxed eloquent in a letter describing the area:

"The view of this valley from here is magnificent. Unlike the view from either end, one can see the whole jagged rim of limestone mountains which rise beyond the green border hills that circle the valley floor. The house I built at the other end is visible as a gleaming point in the midday sun, and the bold outline of Pyramid Mountain just obscures the buildings and airstrip beyond it. Directly behind us are the nearly vertical green palisades which mark the Valley's main salt well and also the low saddle over which the plane flies to enter the pass."

Linguist Bromley could speak soulfully about his surroundings, but the Tulim Danis were less than intoxicated by the presence of the strange white men in their section of the valley. One day Bromley inquired about the spicy, fragrant flowers the natives were wearing in their noses in place of pig tusks. One candid lad admitted the awful truth: they just could not stand the body odor of the missionaries! "You stink," said the boy. "Why is it that after a few days here, I stink too, and can't wash it off?"

Perfume and lotions did not improve the odor of the missionaries so far as the Danis were concerned. They found these positively sickening.

Another time when a fleshy white visitor was traveling at the head of a group of missionaries on a long tiresome trek in the hot sun, the Danis implored the missionaries to ask the foreigner to march at the end of the line. They preferred that he remain to leeward!

But Ed Maxey had a friend in Wenekali, a chief with a red-streaked beard, who showed favors to the missionaries from the day they arrived. His favorable attitude greatly increased when the mission doctor was able to save the life of his youngest wife and her firstborn son. There had been serious complications following the baby's birth.

Dubbed "Redbeard" by the missionaries, Wenekali could not do enough for his new friends. He helped them greatly on the language, providing Bromley with normal conversational idioms. Sometimes he grew restless after protracted periods of language coaching, but he never lost his friendly spirit toward the newcomers, bringing them gifts of fresh-killed pork and produce from his gardens.

On one occasion when Bromley and Ben Karcesky were wandering around near Wenekali's village, he called out and invited them into his roundhouse. The next hour was spent in a friendly chat and a sharing of steamed sweet potatoes.

Other Danis maintained a "go home" attitude toward the Maxeys, blaming the presence of their chickens, their rabbits, and their wind charger for a drought that was plaguing the area.

The Maxeys had spent nearly a year at Tulim when Darlene Rose visited them. She brought comfort and encouragement. With her own background of experience she was able to sympathize. She described her visit as follows:

"This is Tulim—where you cannot disassociate yourself from their war and victory dances. This afternoon we gathered in the Maxeys' living room while the natives from villages all over this area gathered on the hill back of the house. With much yelling, chanting, body gyrations, shaking of spears and gesturing with bows and arrows, they rushed down the hill just outside, causing the house to tremble. They were running to their dancing ground which lies between the house and the airstrip.

"Mr. Maxey flipped on the tape recorder and above the offbeat chanting of the Stone Age savages outside the window arose the voice of Dr. A. W. Tozer, noted Alliance pastor whom Maxey had assisted in Chicago, 'I am the vine, ye are the branches.' I closed my eyes and felt the spirit of worship close in upon me, shutting out other sights and sounds as if it were a Sunday morning in Chicago. Again I thought of what a privilege it would be to sit under a ministry like that week after week. 'You will never know what the vine is like, how sweet the sap that flows through it, until you have tasted the fruit of the branches. Neither will this world ever know how sweet Jesus, the vine, is until they have seen and tasted from our lives the fruit of the Spirit . . .' I opened my eyes to see again through the window the forest of spears, fancy headdresses and red-mud-smeared bodies that were running back and forth in a frenzy of excitement. As their chanting crescendoed across the space into the living room, I knew with a great surge of joy that I would rather be here than anywhere

else in God's universe; yes, even in Tulim; and that if these
precious Dani people were ever to know the sweetness of Jesus,
it would be through tasting in our lives the fruit of the vine."

Ben and Ruth Karcesky, a dedicated young couple from the
East, were assigned to a new station at Seinma in the narrow
gorge into which the Baliem River flows from the valley. Like
their fellow missionaries, the Karceskys felt the sting of native
opposition before they were able to move into their new home.
Seinma was located four or five miles south of Hetigima in the
rugged limestone country on the opposite side of the river.

The Alliance missionaries had been eager to lay claim to the
gorge area with a huge Dani population of fifteen thousand or
more. Tom Bozeman, early in 1956, had spent several days at
Sienma, living in one of the men's houses and becoming better
acquainted with the people. They were traditional enemies of
the Danis living near Hetigima.

When Ben Karcesky, accompanied by Adrian, set out to construct the airstrip, he was stopped by Ukumhearik, the big chief,
at the rattan bridge crossing the Baliem just below Hetigima. The
chief threatened them if they took another step.

"You go back," Ukumhearik shouted, "or I will kill you and
all the foreigners in my area."

One of his wives attempted to placate him and to intercede for
the missionaries. This so infuriated Ukumhearik that he took up
his bow and shot an arrow into his wife's thigh. Thus he gave the
missionaries a graphic demonstration of what he might do to them.

Karcesky, still unable to converse freely in Dani, felt it was
the better part of valor to return to Hetigima. Bozeman then besought Ukumhearik to let the work on the airstrip proceed. Ukumhearik gave in reluctantly. But when Karcesky started off a second
time to begin his task, Bozeman received word that Ukumhearik
now was threatening to cut down the rattan bridge so the missionaries could not reach the territory in which the airstrip was
located. Bozeman, running several miles to the river, talked
Ukumhearik out of destroying the bridge. A third time Karcesky

G. Larson

The first and most difficult task faced by New Guinea missionaries is to learn the unwritten tongues of Stone Age savages. A phonetic alphabet is painstakingly constructed from recorded conversations with native language informants. Peggy Larson, being greeted with her children by a friendly group of Ilaga Danis (above), has helped develop with her husband a literacy program to enable tribesmen to read the Bible in their own tongue. Below, missionary Walter Post teaches a language class in the Bible School at Enarotali, where the entire New Testament has been translated into Kapauku; portions of Scripture have been printed in Uhunduni, Dani, and Moni.

E. W. Ulrich

Alice Gibbons

Tribal fetishes are burned in a huge bonfire by Uhunduni natives converted to Christianity. The tribespeople were more eager to hear the gospel and follow the Christian way after destroying these objects of primitive magic and superstition: charms and amulets, weapons of enemies slain in battle, strings of beads and shells.

Uhunduni Christians thatch the roof of their new church at Kunga, where hundreds turned to Christ in a mass movement that transformed their way of life.

Alliance Witness

Henry Young and a native elder conduct a baptism service at a Dani village near Pyramid Station. Converts receive instruction in basic Christian doctrines before baptism, and must show evidence of changed lives before being admitted to church membership.

At church services, Dani Christians offer to God their only valuable possessions—sweet potatoes and cowrie shells. These are divided among native preachers—"witness men"—who assume full responsibility for the leadership and administration of these vigorous, self-sustaining churches.

Alliance Witness

E. W. Ulrich

A communion service in Kapauku territory is led by a native pastor, who distributes sweet potatoes and raspberry juice to the congregation as substitutes for bread and wine. Members sit or squat on the earthen floor of these crude church buildings—men on one side, women and children on the other.

Ruth Gobai, shown here with her daughter Dorcas, is a Kapauku Christian who accompanied the first missionary expedition to the Baliem Valley. The presence of a woman in the landing party convinced Dani warriors of the missionaries' friendly intentions and assured a peaceful welcome.

E. W. Ulrich

Nokogi, a powerful chief in the Ilaga Valley, was one of the first Danis converted after hearing the gospel preached by missionary Gordon Larsen. His example led many tribesmen to reject pagan superstition and follow Christ.

fierce-looking church elder f the Uhunduni tribe, adired among his people for s Christian leadership and xample.

Oswald F. Emery

Danis gather for a huge open-air service to hear a sermon preached in their own tongue by a "witness man" (left), a converted member of their own tribe. These native pastors can recite long scripture passages, quote the Apostle's Creed, and tell hundreds of Bible stories—even before they have learned to read. Converted savages like the tribes-

Oswald F. Emery

The light of the gospel shines in the eyes of a Dani Christian attending a Bible class.

headed for the rugged gorge country. When they reached the airstrip site, the only area for miles around that lent itself to a landing place, the local chief, who only a few days before had killed a native leader, told the missionary team the airstrip could not be built. The territory was taboo. Again Karcesky was thwarted in his efforts.

A new airstrip site was located north of the original area and Karcesky finally settled down to his construction job. Assisted by a thousand natives, the work went forward speedily and was completed within three weeks. On the day the Karcesky family was flown into the new station, three thousand Danis were on hand to greet them.

The Karceskys soon made the acquaintance of the friendly Seinma chief named Lukubalik (Crazy), who, unlike most Dani headmen, had but one wife. It was not long before Lukubalik and his spouse, Kebu-he (Crazy Woman), were invited to have dinner with the missionaries. The Karceskys had eaten often with the natives, but this was the first time Danis had dined in the home of the new missionaries.

Kebu-he, like a normal wife, tried to make simple conversation, and refrained from taking too much food. The couple tried white potatoes, but soon showed their preference for the more familiar sweet potatoes and ribs of pork. They were so fascinated with the saltcellar that they overseasoned their food.

When they had finished eating the pork, their hands were greasy. No napkins were needed for the visitors. Lukubalik rubbed his hands on his arms, then politely offered Karcesky his adze handle to use as a napkin. The Dani couple wanted Ruth Karcesky to use her hair to absorb the grease. She refused this suggestion gracefully and instead permitted the grease to be rubbed on her arms. By this time the Karcesky children wanted to try out Dani manners. They were restrained by a stern warning from their parents.

Noticing the grease that was still left in the platter, Lukubalik used it to smear his entire body.

The party was quite a success, except when Karcesky asked

the blessing. He looked up to find that the chief was sitting with his hands over his ears. Lukubalik did not want to hear the words spoken to Jesus.

Like their chief, the other Seinma natives proved to be friendly and co-operative. When one of them stole some things from the Karceskys, the tribespeople forced the thief to return them. But they listened apathetically to the gospel, grinning and snickering as they stood around during the services. Their women were strictly forbidden to hear the words of the missionaries.

The Karceskys were not unlike other missionary families with their share of illness. Ben Karcesky suffered a serious attack of rheumatic fever that brought him weeks of pain and forced him into inactivity for a longer period.

When the Andersons arrived in New Guinea, they were flown first to Pyramid station to work with the Youngs until they could establish their station on a hillside above the Ibele River.

After the Andersons joined the Youngs at the airstrip, one hundred curious Danis followed them to the mission station. En route the native women pinched Mrs. Anderson's arms until they were red.

A few days later, war broke out between the villages to the east and west of Pyramid. Even before the Danis, working nearby, had left the station with loud war cries, the air was filled with flying arrows. However, the main battle was fought a mile to the west. At the finish, three men were reported to have died, and the wounded Danis tramped back to the mission station for treatment. This was only the first baptism of fire for the Andersons.

A few months afterward, the Andersons' Dani gardener shouted, "*Endoktin, kenigen* [Anderson, look]!" He pointed to clouds of smoke billowing from the hillside in the nearby Wolo Valley. The missionaries learned that the Pyramid Danis had slipped out during the night and raided the Wolo section. They caught the local chief in his garden, chopped him to pieces, and scattered his body about the landscape. Then they proceeded to plunder and pillage the villages. The war party, however, suffered a number of casualties. Some of the dead were brought back, including the local chief's son. The Andersons then were witnesses to a full-fledged Dani funeral, with hideous wailing, chopped-off fingers, and mourners who covered their bodies with clay.

Not all of the new missionary couple's experiences were so revolting. Don Anderson recorded the reactions of Bad News, a local chief, when he was flown to Hollandia and caught his first glimpse of civilization.

In preparation for the journey, the Dani had endured the ordeal of taking a bath and donning clothes for the first time in his life. When he climbed into the airplane and felt the sensations of take-off, he seemed to be quite frightened. He was also confused. Unaware of the speed at which he was traveling, he had gone most of the way to Sentani when he asked if they had passed certain landmarks near home.

"Once when the pilot was reporting his position by radio," said Anderson, "Bad News nudged me and asked, 'Is he lost?' "

The Dani was plainly relieved when the plane landed at Sentani.

When they took the chief down to the ocean, he picked up a discarded bottle and drank a large draught of salt water. Then he refilled the bottle to share with friends back in the valley. Neither Bad News nor four of these friends who welcomed him on his return seemed to suffer from the sea water.

On the coast Bad News was only slightly impressed by horses, cows, deer, or acres of fruit trees, but when he saw a large coastal pig, he became very excited. He wanted to make a deal for the pig on the spot.

Later in the afternoon he came staggering up to the mission headquarters at Sentani with a whole car spring over one shoulder. He wanted to take all the good steel back to his people to make axes. He finally settled for some of the leaves.

Back in the Baliem Bad News had great stories to tell his people. Anderson rejoined his wife at Pyramid.

The Andersons had seen much violence during their first two years in New Guinea. When they finally settled at their new Ibele station, they discovered they still faced other perils.

In January, 1959, a Dani woman committed suicide by walking across the boundary line into territory occupied by opponents of the natives living near the Andersons' station. The woman was speared instantly by the enemy, and this act precipitated a battle. At first the missionaries thought they would not be affected by this native incident, but once the Danis were aroused they thought of other grievances that were annoying them. The Andersons then picked up a rumor that the tribespeople had a score to settle with the white man dating back to 1939 when the Archbold expedition had encamped nearby. The natives had nursed a grudge against outsiders for seventeen years!

At six o'clock on a Sunday morning fighting broke out about three hundred yards from the mission station. The enemy had moved in before daybreak for a surprise attack on the Ibele Danis. The Kapauku workers living on the Ibele compound came to the Anderson home for protection, and the mission family engaged in prayer. They could hear the shouting and screaming of the warriors as they waged the battle against their native foes. Any moment the Andersons felt the mission station would be besieged. They read Psalm 91 together, then waited some more, but the expected attack never came to pass.

The Sundas were scheduled to establish work in what was known as "Pass Valley," or more properly, the Wosi River Valley. This was the valley leading up to the pass through which the airplanes flew to reach the Baliem. Sunda, short but wiry, was a second generation Czech who had been reared in the South. He had met his capable, cheery wife, Dolores, a native of Alabama, while they were students at Bible school.

In most of the advances to establish new stations, the Baliem Valley missionaries teamed up. It was decided that the survey party to the Wosi area would be headed by Tom Bozeman. Others accompanying the expedition were Myron Bromley, James Sunda, Fritz Veldkamp, a Dutch administrative officer, and seven Kapauku carriers. It was in the Wosi Valley of the Oranje Mountains in 1945 that the United States Army paratroopers had constructed the glider strip that aided the rescue of WAC Corporal Margaret Hastings and two companions. Outlines of the clearing were still visible from the air when the missionary party arrived in the summer of 1957.

Aside from the warning of a young Dani that the people in the Wosi Valley would kill the missionaries if they sought to enter the area, everything seemed favorable for the journey. The missionaries had had many contacts with the Wosi people, who often came to Pyramid station for treatment of yaws and other ills. In July, 1956, and in May, 1957, some of the missionaries had visited the glider strip site, and on the latter occasion one old man had invited them to visit him.

By mid-afternoon the party had walked from Pyramid to the point where they were to cross the Baliem River. They were ferried across on Dani rafts. Nothing in the attitude of the villagers whom they met as they moved forward gave an inkling of what was to transpire. The Danis asked if the party had come to stay, and the missionaries replied that they were going to visit Keakwi, an important local chief. They advised the expedition to camp that night at the glider strip site because they had been informed that there might be fighting in the valley. That had been the missionaries' plan.

The campsite was only a short distance from them when the missionaries saw two men with spears erect standing near a village. Bromley left the trail to greet them, but they showed no friendship. Since this was not an uncommon response, the group continued on its way without concern. Suddenly, before they realized what had happened, the marchers were surrounded by warriors screaming battle cries. The carriers nearest the missionaries threw down their packs and scattered.

Bromley, most familiar with the language, tried to talk with the angry crowd. Some of the Danis, who had tagged along with the missionary party from the river crossing, said, "They want to fight with us; pay no attention to them. Let's go back to our village."

The missionaries began to withdraw slowly, but soon all of

them were running. Their pursuers threw clubs and rocks that struck some members of the group. Spears landed alongside the trail. Several of the Kapauku carriers were grazed with arrows, and one arrow went through Bromley's shirt, narrowly missing him. Bromley decided that the main purpose of the attackers was to frighten the missionaries so badly that they would never return. But there were others among the natives who seemed eager to kill the white men on the spot.

An older native, apparently from the same area as the attackers, shouted at his henchmen,

"Don't hurt them; they'll talk about us."

He must have felt that injury to the white men would bring serious reprisals upon the Danis. He was trying to hold back the hotheads of his village.

Veldkamp, the only armed member of the expedition, fired five shots into the air, but this seemed only to enrage, rather than frighten, the screaming mob.

Tom Bozeman heard one Dani yell as he sprang over a fence in their direction,

"Let's kill these fellows. Let's get rid of them. Chase them out. Kill every one of them."

Bozeman looked over his shoulder in time to see a Dani cock his arm to throw a sixteen-foot spear. Bozeman grabbed Bromley by the shoulder and they both ducked. The spear hit the ground in front of Tom. For a moment he thought it would be a fine souvenir, but he abandoned the idea immediately.

Sunda and Bozeman were now running side by side. Both were exhausted and out of breath. Bozeman glanced back to see that Veldkamp had fallen on the trail. Veldkamp yelled as the attackers closed in on him. One of the Danis raised his spear to kill him. The frightened man cried, "Help me. Don't leave me. They'll kill me." With that Bozeman wheeled around and headed right toward the Danis, raising his arms and yelling at the top of his voice. Momentarily the Danis were distracted. Bozeman grabbed Veldkamp's hand and jerked him to his feet. As they started to run again, a Dani threw a spear that hit Bozeman's foot. Fortunately it did not pierce his boot.

The fleeing men ran on until they had reached a wooded area. Bozeman looked back again just in time to dodge a huge rock thrown by a Dani. It struck Sunda in the middle of the back, seriously injuring him. But he kept running.

In the woods just ahead, Bozeman saw a Dani lying in wait for him. As Bozeman came nearer, he tossed out some mirrors he was carrying, shouting,

"Take these mirrors."

This quick action caught the Dani by surprise. As he bent to pick them up, Bozeman ran past him. Upon reaching the banks of the Baliem River, he was too exhausted to go another step. He decided to hide in the reeds. Just as he dived into them, he saw a Dani woman searching for him. He managed to elude her by squirming down the muddy riverbank. He heard the footsteps of the Danis. One shouted,

"We've got two of them; we've only one more to go."

Bozeman's heart sank as he wondered if his companions had been killed. Then he peered through the reeds and saw Bromley approaching nonchalantly along the trail. The arrow was dangling from his shirt sleeve.

Joining him, Bozeman said,

"Pull that arrow out of your sleeve. It makes me nervous."

They walked on together and reached a point about fifteen minutes from the place where they expected to reach the Baliem. But they first had to cross a ditch on a slippery log. Bozeman fell from the log into the slimy ditch about eight or ten feet deep. The missionaries could hear the Danis yelling in the distance. Bozeman tried to extricate himself but the slimy sides of the ditch prevented him. He struggled about, getting more panic-stricken by the minute.

"Don't worry, Tom," Bromley said quietly, "Jesus is with us today."

"Well I know that," Bozeman said impatiently, "but I want to get out of this ditch."

Bromley reached down as far as he could and Bozeman grasped his arm. With this help he was able to scramble out. They walked down to the waiting raft and crossed the Baliem. Then they discovered that Veldkamp and Sunda had reached the other side of the river ahead of them.

Sunda and Bozeman, tired, distraught, and aching in every muscle, slogged on through the darkness. Sunda's back was giving him pain, and Bozeman now realized that the spear that had struck his foot made him lame. The two injured men finally lay down on the ground. They felt they could not go on. Each man placed his hands on the other and prayed for healing. After an hour they got up and continued their journey.

Tom Bozeman declares that the strength and energy received from the Lord enabled them to walk all the way back to Pyramid station. The survey party into the Wosi had not succeeded in its mission, but every man was grateful to have been spared. They had survived one of the most harrowing experiences of their lives.

"Surely God and He alone is to be given the praise for restraining the violence of those men," Bromley said.

Perhaps James Sunda had been restrained from accomplishing his own plans that he might witness something greater at the hand of the Lord.

At this stage and for some time following, the spiritual successes of the Baliem Valley were few. When three Dani boys began to pray regularly at Hetigima, it was regarded as such a major event that Einar Mickelson cabled the news to New York.

The warfare at Hetigima continued to decimate the Dani ranks.

In August, 1958, Bozeman wrote:

"Yesterday there was a big battle across the river in which two were killed and several wounded. I went today to treat some of the wounded and try to save their lives. One of the wounded men had been speared four times. Only the Lord can help him. My heart goes out to these people as their lives consist only of fighting and trying to get revenge over their enemies. I went up to a nearby hill where several hundred Danis had gathered to dance and sing over the victory they had won. When I reached the hilltop I saw the corpses of the enemy dead covered with grass. I was horrified, for one of the men was a friend of mine whom I had visited just two days before. I was really heartbroken to see his body so broken and spear-ridden. What was worse, the people were getting ready to cut up the corpses and eat them. They had built fires and were working themselves up into a great frenzy."

Bozeman had launched a primary school at his station, but he soon ran into difficulties. Ukumhearik, the smiling villain, persuaded the school children to go home. Said the chief,

"If you follow Jesus, you will stop fighting. Then the enemy will take advantage of you and come over and kill us all."

In one village Bozeman asked the people to decide for Christ and not wait any longer. A son of the local chief said he wanted Jesus to "treat" his heart. Then his father said he wanted to pray, too. A tropical rain fell and Bozeman thought the meeting was over. But the chief called him into the men's house and said, "Wait a minute. There are some men here who want to pray." Others followed the example of the chief and his son. It was the beginning of a turning to Christ, but other villagers were held back by their deep fear of Ukumhearik.

There were times when it seemed that the big chief would relent. On one occasion he came to Bozeman's station and listened attentively and respectfully during an entire gospel service. In front of all present, he said,

"I want to pray, but I don't understand it. I want to learn more."

But when great numbers later turned to the Lord in the upper Baliem, Ukumhearik seemed more eager than ever to hold on to his fetishes, and to prevent his people from discarding their charms.

One of the bright notes in the Baliem story came in the winter of 1957 when Myron Bromley attended a linguistic institute in Melbourne, Australia. There he met a slim, dark-haired Australian woman, Marjorie Jean Teague, a physician with eyes turned toward the mission field. Bromley knew that his bachelor days would soon be over. They were married a year later and spent their honeymoon on a furlough to the United States.

14

OTHER VALLEYS HEAR

It was in the strategic Ilaga Valley of central Dutch New Guinea that the native population initially embraced Christianity in great numbers.

First, the Ilaga Uhundunis had turned to Christ in a mass movement. This spread across the valley to the Western Danis.

But now Don Gibbons wanted to convey the gospel message to the Uhundunis in another area—the secluded Beoga Valley to the north that he and Larson had visited back in 1954. At that time the natives had been eager listeners and the missionaries had promised to return.

The arrival of John Ellenburger, a trained linguist, and his wife, Helen, in the Ilaga in October, 1957, meant that Gibbons could be free to make a visit to the Beoga, which had been on his heart so long. Ellenburger a slightly built man who appeared younger than his years, had been reared in Africa by missionary parents. His wife was a trained nurse whose parents were missionaries to Cambodia.

Accompanied by Kama Kama (Nothing Nothing), an Ilaga

Uhunduni convert, Gibbons trekked through the high pass to the Beoga. When they arrived they went first to the home of Kama Kama's aunt. She literally jumped with joy to see her nephew, a favorite, and threw her arms about him in welcome. That night Gibbons and Kama Kama stayed at the men's house in the main village, where Kama Kama proceeded to tell the Beoga Uhundunis gathered about the fire how their kinfolk in Ilaga put their trust in Christ.

"Now I have told you how we have believed in Christ," Kama Kama said to his audience of intent listeners, "and I have explained how we meet to hear the good news every Sunday. But I know you have a question in your mind. You are asking yourselves, 'What will you do when trouble comes?' I want to answer this by telling you a story.

"Once there was a man named Job who had many pigs. Some were camel pigs and some were sheep pigs and there were other kinds of pigs, too. Also, he had sons and daughters. He believed in this Creator I have told you about and he followed Him. One day Job had word that all of his sons and daughters had died and that all of his pigs had been stolen. And what did Job do? Job continued to serve God, and that's our answer.

"We have not accepted this message just so we may have a good time here on earth, or just so our people will not be sick. This is eternal life and we will follow God whatever happens. Even last month my own little son and many other children died in a great sickness. But are we going to turn back to our old ways because of that? Certainly not. That used to happen in the old days, too. Now we are going to serve God whatever happens."

Gibbons spent three weeks in the Beoga Valley. Everywhere he and Kama Kama went they were well received by throngs eager to hear the gospel. Like their kinsmen of the Ilaga, the Beoga Uhundunis seemed already prepared in advance to commit themselves to Christ. As Gibbons and Kama Kama headed back to the Ilaga, the final words of their native hosts were, "You must come again right away."

When Gibbons told his wife how well they had been received

and how responsive the Uhundunis were to God's message, she declared, "You must return, and this time I'll go with you."

Thus it was that Don and Alice Gibbons a few weeks later set out together. It was a difficult trip for a woman, but Alice Gibbons proved her mettle. She made her arduous trip without complaints. Their route the first day, one never before traversed by an outsider, took them to the lower valley of the Ilaga River. It was in this area that Larson and Gibbons had been well received the day after raiders attacked their expedition.

First camping place of the missionary couple was near a village in friendly territory. They were soon surrounded by a large crowd of Danis, many of whom were suffering from yaws. The missionaries decided they would linger in the area long enough to treat some of the victims of the dread disease. In a single day Alice Gibbons administered penicillin to one hundred and twenty people. Afterward her husband preached to a grateful throng. Then they taught the natives a gospel song.

Very weary, the couple retired to their sleeping bags. During the night they were awakened from time to time by repetitious singing of the newly-learned hymn. When the sun broke over the eastern peaks next morning, the native singers were still expressing their joy.

Touched by the deep interest of the villagers, the missionaries stayed on for another two days, ministering to the physical and spiritual needs of the hospitable people.

As they continued their journey, the pair faced the most rugged part of the trail. It was so steep that many times during the day Don Gibbons had to lift his wife bodily or pull her up by the hand. When they reached the crest of the mountains, their altimeter recorded eleven thousand five hundred feet.

In another day of walking they reached the upper part of the Beoga Valley and came into a Uhunduni settlement. One of the chiefs in the welcoming party called Gibbons aside.

"Come over here to the grass," the chief said. (Important matters are always discussed on the grass.) "You have told us the gospel is for us. You have said we must burn our fetishes, if we are going to believe in this God. Tell me, when are we going to get the date for a burning?"

Gibbons was not prepared for such a drastic proposal. He knew that the chief had heard the gospel on only three occasions on his previous visit two months earlier. Already the Uhunduni leader wanted to leave his old ways and turn to Christ. But Gibbons could not believe that this could happen so soon.

"No," said the missionary to the chief, "don't burn your fetishes yet. I'll come once more before I return to my home across the sea. You take your fetishes and tie them up, and do no more spirit worship. When I come back, if you have a single mind to follow Christ, then you may burn the fetishes."

With this parting charge Don and Alice Gibbons left for their home in the Ilaga.

When Gibbons made a third trip to the Beoga in February, 1958, he was accompanied only by Ellenburger. The Uhundunis, who had been eagerly waiting for them, declared,

"We have desired the Lord for this long time. We have one mind to follow the Lord. We won't let you go this time until we have burned our fetishes."

Out of an estimated population of three thousand Uhundunis in the immediate area, about fifteen hundred participated in mass burnings of fetishes to signify they were done with their heathen past and were now ready to trust and serve the Lord Jesus Christ.

As they burned the strange nets on which pig tails were sewed, the bows and arrows of slain warriors, the strings of ancient cowrie shells that had been handed down from generation to generation, the tribespeople danced about the pyres with obvious joy.

Sometimes they would stop dancing abruptly to review the decision they had made. They reminded one another that they no longer had fear of the spirits. Then they talked about their new responsibilities as Christians—what they must do and what they must cease doing now that they were believers. Then they would resume their dancing.

The missionaries realized that some of those among the huge gathering were prompted by mixed or false motives. But they also recognized that in a close-knit society such as the Uhundunis, where everyone's business was known, it would not be long before they were singled out. One man secretly buried all his charms but one in an adjoining valley. Then he ostentatiously burned the one. When he later applied for baptism, the native believers refused to consider him for acceptance in the church and carefully explained the reason to him. Similarly, if a man walked upright, the people of his own village and those for miles around the valley knew about it. Their clear testimony concerning one another attested to the genuineness of their commitments.

A Beoga man accused Den, the Ilaga Valley Uhunduni chief, of retaining some of his magic articles. "He has a very powerful sun fetish which he keeps in his carrying net," the accuser declared. When Den was questioned, he denied the charge and showed Gibbons the contents of his net. Den finally realized that the man had ignorantly mistaken a compass for an offending charm.

The Uhundunis, whose background was steeped in the appeasement of spirits, did not at once understand all the issues of the Christian life. There was much to know about the Bible, and considerable effort would be necessary before they could read God's Book. But they soon were able to pray.

"My, how he prays!" a visiting Kapauku said of one of the new Uhunduni converts. "He prays before he goes to bed, when he gets up, before he eats, and among the unbelieving Danis."

Nor did the Uhundunis of either the Ilaga or the Beoga immediately demonstrate a concern for other tribes. Their traditional resentment of the overbearing Danis led them to say, "They don't love the Lord, and they never will. Let them go to hell." But in time this pharisaical spirit departed and the Uhundunis began to pray for their enemies.

Gibbons was overjoyed with the way the Uhundunis in both valleys had received the gospel. He and his wife could now depart on a long overdue furlough, leaving their work in the capable hands of the Ellenburgers.

However, when Don and Alice Gibbons left New Guinea in the spring of 1958, they were not to return for nineteen months.

On reaching the United States Gibbons was stricken with infectious hepatitis. It was a recurrence of the disease that he had first contracted while the Ilaga airstrip was being built. Now the attack was more severe and physicians ordered months of bed rest. Finally the tall apostle to the Uhundunis recovered, and with his wife and small daughters, returned to the Uhunduni station in the Ilaga.

At the Alliance field conference that year, it was decided that the Ellenburgers should remain at Kunga to carry on translation work, and Don and Alice Gibbons would establish a new mission station in the Beoga Valley. By this time the Missionary Aviation Fellowship had taken over the flying program of the Christian and Missionary Alliance. Also, the possibility of building an airstrip in the Beoga had been reappraised and approved by MAF pilots.

Gibbons, accompanied by Ellenburger, journeyed to the Beoga to construct the new airstrip and build a home for his family. Work on the airstrip was hindered by many frustrating delays. Heavy rains halted the undertaking, but more exasperating were the interruptions caused by Uhundunis who wanted immediate instruction in the faith.

"Stop a minute," a Beoga Uhunduni would say. "Help me with this Scripture verse. I've almost learned it but I don't have it quite straight."

Gibbons taught the leaders gospel stories which they memorized to relate to others. This took still more time from the airstrip. He was likewise constantly interrupted when he started to build his home. Ellenburger had been obliged to return to his station in the Ilaga. Gibbons continued his task alone.

"Wait, now, you listen to me," one of the natives would say. "I want to repeat the story to you. See if I tell it right. I don't want it to be wrong when I go to my village. Don't go and build that house. It can be built tomorrow. Just sit down and listen to me, then you can go back to your work."

It was because of these informal instruction sessions that Gibbons decided there must be a school for witness men in the Beoga like the one that had been so successful in the Ilaga.

After many months Gibbons, aided at times by Ellenburger on return visits, and some of the natives, completed both the Beoga airstrip and mission station. Then he moved his wife and family to the Beoga and the missionary program began to move in high gear.

The witness school developed in this way: Every Friday morning men from various parts of the Beoga would gather to hear Gibbons teach them a gospel message. Then he would drill them in memorizing Scripture portions. After the morning sessions the witness men would travel to six points in the valley to conduct Sunday services. Thus the church in the Beoga Valley began to grow without direct missionary supervision. Essentially, the Christians were nurtured by hearing memorized sermons delivered by unlettered preachers.

From the start the Uhundunis exhibited real enterprise in reaching those who did not attend the Sunday meetings. The leaders would ask one another, "How can we get a crowd together so we can tell them about Jesus?" Perhaps one man would say, "I have a large piece of ground that needs to be cleared. Of course, I'll give a feast when people come to work on the land. When they are eating the feast, we'll preach to them."

Or another man would suggest, "I have a big field of taro that is ready to be harvested. We have always shared our taro feasts. But this time, instead of someone making a speech about war plans or discussing a stolen pig, let us tell our friends about Jesus."

Eighteen men and their wives enrolled in the witness school that in time would enable primitive tribespeople to carry the Christian message into the "hundred valleys" of the vast interior. Classes were held every day from Monday through Friday. They would spend Saturday and Sunday at their preaching stations, then travel late into the night to be back for classes on Monday morning. Occasionally, this meant trekking long distances in tropical downpours. But the witness men joyously went about their tasks and reported the conversion of hundreds of their people who had not yet seen a missionary. In some instances native elders were appointed to care for the flocks in between visits of the witness men.

There were two major developments that gave great impetus to the Christian program with the tribe living in both the Ilaga and Beoga Valleys:

Don and Alice Gibbons had started a literacy program that was enabling the Uhunduni witness men to read. Simultaneously, John Ellenburger was beginning to translate the Gospel of Mark into the native language.

Using the methods of Frank Laubach and other literacy experts, the missionary couple in the Beoga had started to prepare primers for the Uhundunis. These consisted of mimeographed booklets illustrated with line drawings of familiar New Guinea objects and actions. The natives soon learned to form sounds that were associated with certain phonetic symbols. Slowly they were able to pick our phrases, then sentences. In a period of fifteen months perhaps a dozen Uhundunis were able to read the Bible in their own language.

Ellenburger had accumulated a large collection of Uhunduni words and expressions in notebooks that were carefully catalogued. Using native language informants, he then began the tedious job of translating the Gospel of Mark. He sought constantly to find Uhunduni expressions that conveyed the meaning of the New Testament expressions.

By mail, delivered by the MAF plane, the Ellenburgers and Gibbons shared their work. Primers produced in the Beoga were sent to the Ilaga; Scripture portions translated in the Ilaga were dispatched to the Beoga.

Just as there was co-operation among the missionaries, there was an interchange of native workers. Since the Ilaga witness men's school had started first, Uhundunis trained there became the first full-time pastors to serve the six growing churches in the Beoga. Next, elders of these congregations were appointed. They joined with the pastors to handle the disciplinary problems arising in the infant churches. They were called upon to counsel husbands and wives having domestic difficulties; to settle disputes over the ownership of pigs or gardens; and occasionally to excommunicate erring church members. Even though their knowledge of the

Scripture was limited, the new pastors and elders demonstrated an amazing ability to deal with the problems of their people.

One of the picturesque new Christians was Wa Me, a polygamous chief in the Beoga, with five wives—two Uhundunis, one of the Dem tribe, one of the Ndauwa tribe, and one a Dani. Since Wa Me could speak three of these languages and one wife was bilingual, he managed to communicate with all five of them.

Even though one arm had been completely crippled by an early attack of yaws, the chief was a rugged warrior. He told Gibbons that the arm had become permanently bent in a way that actually aided him in using his bow. He boasted of his prowess in war against his enemies in the Ilaga. But he began to inquire about Jesus Christ. Sometimes he would travel with the missionary for three and four days when he went on preaching tours. Finally, he indicated that he wanted to become a Christian.

One so deeply involved in the older cultural patterns of war violence, wife beatings, and hatred could hardly be expected to turn into a saint overnight. But in spite of his background, Chief Wa Me joined the growing band of zealous witnesses for Christ.

Another man, who had been baptized early, came one day to ask the missionary to baptize his wife. Gibbons wondered if the woman believed in Christ and had learned the catechism.

"She hasn't learned it well," the husband admitted.

"But it's your responsibility to teach her," said the missionary.

"She doesn't speak my language," said the Uhunduni.

"What language do you speak?"

"I speak Uhunduni and Dem."

"When you talk to her, does she understand clearly what you've said?"

"No, she doesn't."

"But, what about when she talks to you?"

"When I understand her, I reply, but when I don't, I just say 'yes, yes, yes.' "

The pastors of the Beoga area are now fully supported by the offerings taken each Sunday in their churches. At the opening of the service, the people file forward in long groups to present their offerings to the Lord: sweet potatoes, sugar cane, bananas, cowrie shells, an occasional ax or suckling pig. There are actually two offerings, one for the pastor, made up of gifts of the congregation, and the other for the witness men, contributed by the pastor and his wife and the wives and children of the witness men. Sometimes accumulated offerings of shells are sent to Kapaukus working in the Baliem Valley or to other Christian efforts in the highlands. Thus the missionary vision is growing.

Developing the native hymnody is a story in itself. Attempts were made at first to introduce Western sacred music, but the words and the tunes were so foreign to the Uhundunis that the whole effort was soon abandoned.

Tunes from the old culture, especially those without evil connotation, were adapted for new native hymns and songs. Some of these were compiled by the missionaries with the assistance of the natives, but others were composed by the people themselves. The hymns include the story of creation, the birth and death of Christ, as well as a few of the Bible stories that interest them.

Ellenburger says that the Uhundunis sing more than any tribal people he knows about. Their strange music is actually a chant. One of the men sings the melody; the second man harmonizes, singing about a fifth note above the melody which carries the main words of the song. All the others join in responses to the various phrases. The nearest equivalent in English is the popular rendition of "Old MacDonald Had a Farm."

Sometimes as the men sit around the fire at night one of them will sing out a thought that has been burning in his soul all day. Another will add to it. Soon all will be singing heartily, and the next Sunday they have a new hymn to present.

When the Uhundunis come together for a communion service they sing these words, as they break sweet potatoes in place of bread, and use raspberry juice instead of wine:

"We love Jesus very much,
He died for us.

Jesus took the sweet potatoes and returned thanks,
Jesus took the sweet potatoes and broke them.
Jesus' body was broken for us, like the sweet potatoes are
*   broken;*
His body was broken for you, His body was broken for me.
We love Jesus very much.
Jesus took the drinking gourd and then he returned thanks.
The contents of the drinking gourd are like Jesus' blood.
His blood was shed for me, His blood placed in payment
*   for you.*
His blood washed my sins, His blood took all your sins away.
Jesus died for us.
We are gathered together here,
We are thinking about the death of Christ;
We are thinking that Christ will come in the future;
We, who are Christians, will be taken to heaven by Christ;
We love Jesus very much.
He died for us."

The strong sense of mission which had grown in the hearts of the Uhunduni Christians of the Beoga Valley soon was to bear spectacular results in another part of New Guinea—the populous Dugandoga Valley.

Eager witness men from the Beoga had traveled about thirty miles westward to the Dugandoga, about half the distance between their own remote valley and Homejo, the Moni mission conducted by Bill and Gracie Cutts. In line with their witness pattern, the Uhundunis had ranged that distance to locate kinsmen living in the Dugandoga. As soon as the message was shared, the people of the new area were quick to respond.

When news of this awakening reached Gibbons, he decided that such a population area deserved missionary direction. He quickly communicated with Larson, and in a matter of days they had received an official okay to make an investigation of the region.

Arriving at Hetadipa, one of the largest settlements in the Dugandoga, they found a congregation of new believers. The two missionaries were warmly received by the people who had just concluded their weekly church service in a clearing near the village.

"This place is getting too small for our services," the natives told them. "We are already preparing a larger meeting place so that increasing crowds may hear."

The missionaries found that the valley was densely and predominantly populated by Monis, but there were also numbers of Danis, Uhundunis, and Ndauwas living in the same area. They discovered that for a period of six months four fairly large groups had been meeting regularly, and that within two months four new congregations had been formed. In addition to these eight groups, the tribespeople said, there were still many others eager to hear the gospel.

Larson and Gibbons were able to buy a long strip of land by the riverside, the only level ground for miles around. They paid five steel axes for it. Aided by the Hetadipa people, they began to clear the ground for an airstrip. Since the valley was settled chiefly by Monis, they decided to recommend that Bill and Gracie Cutts move there and build the new Hitadipa station. In the three weeks they worked on the landing field, Gibbons and Larson spent more time answering questions than in physical labor.

"We have already waited too long to burn our fetishes," the people declared. "We must do it now."

"Why don't you wait until your new missionaries arrive?" Gibbons asked. But it did not satisfy them.

"What is the use of waiting that long?" they persisted. "Must they see these burnings? We have been bound with these horrible things too long."

No further effort was made to restrain them. Thus when Cutts and his wife arrived, they were happy to find that a goodly number of the Monis had already burned their charms. Since the missionaries were acquainted with the Moni tongue, they were able to start their teaching program soon after they had a roof over their heads. In no time the church at Hetadipa grew both in numbers and in understanding.

It was a delightful and unexpected experience for Bill and Gracie

Cutts to work among the warmhearted Hetadipa natives after having spent so many years with the unresponsive Monis at Homejo. The new converts showered their love upon the missionary couple, loading them down with more garden produce than they could possibly eat. When payment was offered, the cowrie shells were spurned. The people just said, "We are hungry for God."

At Homejo neither pay nor any other inducement could persuade the Monis to help in the construction of the mountaintop airstrip. But it was so different at Hetadipa where the effervescent new converts gladly offered themselves for work on the landing field. They wanted to do it for the missionaries and "as unto the Lord."

The Dugandoga believers entered the Christian life with zeal, if not with full knowledge. After they awakened in the morning, they would pray aloud in their houses perched on the hillside. As they came outside, they would cry out across the valley, "We have just prayed."

They were quick to judge the faults of their fellow Christians. If they presumed a man was guilty of some offense or an action they believed unbecoming to a Christian, they would say to him, "Don't you put any potatoes in the offering today. Your life isn't right."

As rapidly as they could, the missionaries sought to curb this type of pharisaism, but they tried also to encourage the overzealous converts to continue their faithful witness to others.

Gracie Cutts tells about the amusing memory methods practiced by her new pupils. If she were teaching a verse with ten parts to it, she would rehearse the phrases one by one. As she reached the third phrase, a youth would jump up and run out of the schoolhouse as though he had a hot potato in his hand.

When she continued on a bit, another lad would run out, holding two of his fingers. By the time she reached the end of the memory portion, only two or three would be left in the schoolroom.

She found that the pupil who learned the first phrase would later share it with all the others; the next boy would share his portion;

until finally the group had learned the entire passage by aiding one another.

Bill and Gracie Cutts had labored for years at Homejo with only a weak church to show for their efforts. But at Hetadipa the results were gratifying. Since the work of evangelizing had been taken over by the tribesmen themselves, the missionaries now could spend their days as pastor-teachers, feeding the lambs and sheep hungry for spiritual food.

15

THE PROPHET JABONEP

An unlikely chain of events had characterized the spread of the gospel in Dutch New Guinea from the very beginning.

It was as though Robert Jaffray had ignited a long fuse that continued to burn for twenty years. Sometimes the spark spluttered, or seemed to go out, as during the war years; then it raced on again steadily, inexorably, though unseen.

The missionaries who succeeded Jaffray and Deibler had been dedicated to the same cause, that of reaching the New Guinea tribes, but the onward movement of events transcended human concern and effort. Incidents happened which were not prompted by missionary direction; nevertheless they fitted into the divine plan.

Widi-ai-bi, the Kapauku trader who preached to the Uhundunis in the Ilaga, had been one powerful force in advancing the cause of Christ. Then came Den, the Uhunduni chief, and Opalalok, his Dani father-in-law.

In the summer of 1959 several incidents occurred which were to have great future significance.

216

Gordon and Peggy Larson had launched their witness men's school to train the western Danis for Christian leadership. Among those enrolled in the school was Jabonep, a Dani leader with great natural gifts. Jabonep stood out from the crowd, not because of his appearance, but because he was a "born preacher." Originally he had lived at Maaki, a village in the North Baliem River district, which lay to the east halfway between the Ilaga and the Grand Valley of the Baliem. Many of his relatives were still living in that area.

At this time a difficult struggle over *je-wam* (war settlement) arose between two clans within the Ilaga. The group demanding payment was a village of baptized Christians. Those obligated to make payment included natives whose commitment was not as far advanced.

Both groups in the controversy had relatives in the North Baliem. Since *je-wams* involve all the members of a clan regardless of where they live, settlement could not be made until kinfolk living in the North Baliem approved. Discussions had been long and tensions rose over the terms. Most of the bargainers on both sides hoped that a proper solution of this case would end the *je-wam* pattern forever.

Jabonep, sensing the spiritual implications involved, decided that he, as one of the clan members, should make the eighty-mile journey to visit his kinfolk in the North Baliem. He would discuss the *je-wam* case and at the same time would tell his relatives about the great turning to Christ in the Ilaga Valley. He felt called upon to conduct the trip as a "prophet" of the new order.

Undoubtedly, his decision to go was influenced by his close association with Jyybittu, another Dani Christian stalwart, who was one of the local chiefs and also deeply involved in the Ilaga *je-wam* issue. He had known Larson longer than most of the others. When the missionary, sick and depressed, had languished for three weeks in the distant settlement of Ugwimba, he had received assurance from the Lord that he would reach the Ilaga in spite of all obstacles. In addition to this inward confidence, Larson had been warmly greeted by two visiting Dani chiefs from the Ilaga, Jyybittu and Bokoby, who urged the missionary to continue his journey into the land he sought to enter. In a sense it was like an experience of an Old Testament patriarch. Not only had the Lord given the promise, but He had sent His messengers as its incarnation.

These Dani leaders had maintained their friendship for Larson and were sympathetic to the fetish burnings, even though Bokoby still had not publicly declared his faith in Christ. Jabonep, on the other hand, gave more than congenial consent to the gospel and what followed in its wake. He had attended many of the services in the Ilaga. He had listened with enthusiasm to the discussions of the evils of war and the need for doing away with the *je-wams*.

In the witness men's school Jabonep had learned the central message of the gospel well, but he did not absorb all the details of doctrine. There was no question, however, about his deep devotion to Christ nor of his yearning to preach.

Thus it was that Jabonep, the first "prophet" of the western Danis, left for the North Baliem in November, 1959, accompanied by other tribesmen from the Ilaga. As they visited various settlements on their eighty-mile journey, Jabonep succeeded in leaving these impressions with the people: that the Ilaga had received the real message of *natelan katelan* (eternal life); that the first step in obtaining *natelan katelan* was the burning of fetishes and charms; and that the rite that seals eternal life is baptism.

Whether Jabonep did not succeed in making the message clear, for which there seemed to be some evidence, or whether the people heard wrong and garbled it, was not completely determined. There was no doubt that in some areas the Christian message was quite twisted. One impression that gained considerable acceptance was that if the Danis baptized their older women, they would become young again. Others understood that those who were baptized would never experience physical death. The Ten Commandments took on certain accretions, such as, "Thou shalt not eat a certain kind of sweet potato."

Jabonep was nevertheless a powerful preacher; everywhere he went he made disciples, and these in turn made other followers— all absorbing some tenets of a garbled message. In every area one constant theme was drummed: "Let us put away war and all our systems of magic and sorcery so that we may follow the true way of *natelan katelan*. Where the "Jabonep gospel" was proclaimed in the vicinity of the mission stations of the evangelical societies such as the Australian Baptists, the extreme teachings were corrected by instruction provided by the missionaries.

But Jabonep's journey was by no means a failure. Indeed he was a forerunner of dramatic developments that would be felt throughout the mountains of New Guinea. As he proceeded eastward in the North Baliem Valley, Jabonep reached a point near Pyramid station in the Grand Valley. He was preaching to a Dani settlement in the area.

Henry Young, the Pyramid missionary, heard about Jabonep, even though first reports were badly twisted. Young had carried on his mission work for nearly four years with indifferent success and many discouragements. Now, facing his first furlough, he had confided to friends that he and his wife, Bernice, had little to show in the way of spiritual results. They wondered what they would tell their supporting churches when they returned to Canada.

It was early in December, 1959, when Young was awakened one morning by a few of his schoolboys. They were shouting to one another about some exciting news that had reached them from the North Baliem. This was the strange story they were telling:

A short, blind man had arrived in a neighboring village. He had been shot when Archbold's party explored the Baliem Valley in 1938. Although a bullet had passed right through the blind man, he had remained alive.

He had left the North Baliem area many years earlier, but now he had come back. On his way the waves of the Baliem River had parted and he walked across a dry ground. He was now planning to stay for a while near Pyramid, then would return to his home. But no one knew where that was.

It had been said that if this strange man were to die, his family would not cremate his body as was the tribal custom. Instead, they would throw him into the river. As soon as he hit the water, he would come to life and go on living forever.

Continuing their wild tale, the Pyramid Danis told Young that when the blind man came to life and left the area, the spirits of the dead would be visible.

Young had never seen the natives of his vicinity so excited. He could readily understand their interest after hearing the reports. He had had enough experience with primitive people to recognize that they did not always get their facts straight. He also recognized that some of the incidents in the stories of the blind man were twisted versions of Bible stories.

When the Pyramid Danis asked him if he would like to see the amazing stranger, Henry Young needed no second invitation. He was as curious as the natives. He set out with a group from his area to the settlement where the man was holding forth.

Young discovered that the "blind man" was actually three men—Jabonep and two other Ilaga Danis. They explained that they were seeking to locate family fetishes in the North Baliem. Now Jabonep was telling his relatives and friends about the Christian message. From settlements in the vicinity a crowd of fifteen hundred had jammed into the village yard to hear him.

Jabonep stopped in the middle of his sermon and invited Young to speak. But the missionary, skeptical because of the weird tales he had heard, declined the opportunity. Instead, he set up his tape recorder to make an accurate account of what was being preached.

True to Dani custom, the Ilaga men were slow in getting started, but once they were under way, they delivered their messages with the speed of machine-gun fire. Then one of them concluded by asking the multitude to bow their heads in prayer. They did so reverently, something Young had never before witnessed. Usually the Danis of his area showed little respect and often jeered following a service. After the people were dismissed, Young noticed that instead of standing around for the customary visit, they proceeded directly to their homes. They seemed deeply engrossed in their own thoughts.

Young invited the speakers to preach the following day at Pyramid. There another crowd of three thousand gathered eagerly to hear the Ilaga men present the same message that they had been given the previous day.

Jabonep opened the service with this prayer:

"Greetings, our Creator, greetings. Today we who are gathered here at Pe-nungalo [Pyramid], where the tuan has built his house, give You our greetings, our Creator. The tuan knows about You and what You have done for us. He has told these people about You, but they have not listened, and we have come. We are telling them about Your talk. We are telling them carefully. Before we did many things badly, but today we don't do those things any more because we have heard Your talk. Since I have heard Your good talk, I want to tell these people here about it. You have given Your good disposition to us, our Creator; those who do badly will be cast out. Your disposition is good, our Creator. Today we have been satisfied. You have given Your knowledge to the tuan. I have finished talking with You. Your eyes are like the stars, our Creator."

Despite the earlier reports of a confused message, Young found that the sermon was doctrinally accurate. He was for the first time hearing Dani speakers giving out the Word of God in the power of the Spirit.

From that time forth there was a complete change in the attitude of the Pyramid Danis, who came daily to be instructed in the Christian faith by the missionary. They sat respectfully and listened intently to every word. There was no more jesting or lightness. Several stolen articles suddenly turned up at the mission station.

The inhabitants of one entire village declared they were going to follow in the way of the Lord. Two other village groups, who had been bitter enemies, made peace and both became eager to hear more of "Jesus' words." Eatlek, the second most prominent chief in the area, declared that Jesus had treated his heart; and he brought his wife and children to be instructed. Disputes among the people were being settled without violence.

One elderly man that had given Henry Young considerable trouble announced with a glowing face that he was now a Christian and that he and the missionary were going to heaven together.

All this happened in an area where there had been faithful proclamation of the gospel for several years, but only listless response
from the natives. As the Pyramid Danis heard the gospel from their
own tribespeople, they began to turn to Christ in great numbers.

In a village where all had turned to Christ, a man died. Instead
of the usual wailing and gloomy chanting, everyone was quiet and
orderly at the funeral. No taboo pigs were killed to appease the
spirits; no one had smeared mud on his body; no fingers were cut
off or heads beaten with rocks. Instead, the believers were rejoicing
because they would see their departed loved one in heaven.

Jabonep and his friends returned to the Ilaga. He had witnessed a
great turning toward God both in the North Baliem River area and
at Pyramid in Grand Valley, but he had left confusion in some
places and aroused the opposition of some of the missionaries in
others.

In the North Baliem at Maaki he had refused to co-operate with
the Australian Baptist missionaries, or to identify himself with
their message. He conducted services in some villages against the
wishes of the Baptists, who at that stage were extremely skeptical
of encouraging the people to dispose of their fetishes.

Even though the messages he had given at Pyramid were Bibli-
cally accurate, as the tape recorder indicated, Jabonep in other
areas had identified Mary with Eve, and this resulted in wrong
teaching about the person of Christ. Furthermore, his disciples
perpetuated the error as they preached at Bokodini and Kelila,
Unevangelized Fields Mission stations, and at Kaga-paki, the
Swart Valley station of the Regions Beyond Missionary Union.
Thus the gospel moved ahead of the missionary too rapidly.

In the minds of many natives the Ilaga became known as the
source of the message of eternal life. Because it already had developed into an important trading area for axes and salt, the Ilaga
was confusedly regarded almost like heaven.

It was because of these developments that the missionaries of
the area where Jabonep had preached invited Gordon Larson to
visit them and aid in correcting doctrinal error. They also wanted
his counsel on the handling of fetish and charm burnings. This

urgent S O S call followed earlier requests that Larson lead a party of trained witness men to preach all through western Dani territory from the Ilaga to the Baliem.

Thus it was that Larson agreed to make the long preaching trek with a band of witness men from the Ilaga training school. This would be the march of a small army of Christian soldiers whose only weapon was the gospel and its liberating power. They would be the instruments God would use in the final stages of the spiritual conquest of the Grand Valley of the Baliem.

16

THE FIRES AT PYRAMID

Conducting a party of ten witness men from the Ilaga Valley eastward to the North Baliem River Valley and beyond posed no small problem for Gordon Larson. Yet he was eager to lead such a pilgrimage, since he knew the effectiveness of native preaching.

But even Larson had no advance knowledge of the impact his band of Danis would make upon their kinsmen in the Grand Valley of the Baliem and elsewhere. The eighty-mile round-trip trek of the itinerant preachers would revolutionize the lives of thousands of Danis.

Larson wanted to confer with some of the missionaries who were skeptical about the mass movement that had begun in the Ilaga. Workers were concerned also about the value of Jabonep's teaching which had resulted in odd versions of the faith.

Accordingly, Larson met with two Dani leaders, Jeebit and Jyybittu, and completed the arrangements for the spiritual expedition. Since there had never been a preaching mission such as this, the missionary and his Dani aids had no precedents to help them in their planning.

Jeebit, a village chief with great ability for organization, was responsible for the business details. Jyybittu, Larson's good friend, was a strong lieutenant and an able preacher. There were many delays chiefly because relatives of the witness men predicted that the marchers would be imperiled as they passed through hostile territory en route to the North Baliem and beyond.

But in spite of these warnings, a company of forty people, including the witness men and their wives, and extra carriers of food and supplies, left the Ilaga on January 22, 1960. Nearly everyone in the party had to carry a load of sweet potatoes, rice, salt, trading items, or other articles.

An all-day climb through a jungle brought the marchers to a settlement called Li-baka, on a ten-thousand-foot plateau. They slept there that night. Next day westbound travelers brought the ominous word that warriors from the adjacent Sinak Valley were lying in wait on the trail just ahead. This report seemed to confirm the earlier fears' of the witness men's families.

The leaders of the expedition decided to send back to their home valley for an armed escort party. Meanwhile, the marching group encamped a second night in the cold mountains.

On the third day one hundred Ilaga warriors joined the waiting witness group. The fighting men were led by Takanit, a notorious chief who had a reputation for being a kind of Robin Hood. He fought the strong and protected the weak. Later other Danis joined the company which now had swelled to three hundred people.

Accompanied by Takanit's men, the pilgrimage moved forward That night they camped at Akadukume where the Ilaga, Sinak, and Baliem pathways meet. They found a crowd of one hundred fifty fellow Danis, westward bound, who had stopped to catch shrimp and cook sweet potatoes. It was a peaceful meeting, although, according to tribal custom, Takanit's men conducted ceremonial war maneuvers.

As the eastbound procession started out next morning, the warriors went first, then the carriers, the women, and the preaching team. The line stretched out single file for a mile. In order to avoid giving the enemy warning of their presence on the trail, they had been committed to silence and a regimen that permitted rest stops only every hour and a half.

When Larson casually began to eat a snack, he was sharply reprimanded by his native companions. Did he not understand that all of them must eat at the same time?

The line of marchers, weighted down with their loads, plodded on through swamps, over knolls, through wooded areas, like a convoy of trucks laboring up a hill in low gear on a hot day. Forsaken gardens and former village sites were reminders of Dani settlements that had been raided by Takanit in 1954 after Larson and Gibbons were attacked on their survey expedition. Stone markers represented the number of deaths in that raid. Larson counted one hundred thirty-two. Small wonder that the Ilaga party proceeded cautiously.

When they came to the West Baliem, they discovered a Dani settlement on the opposite bank of the river, but there was no bridge. They could see a group. Kaga-paki, one of the witness men, shouted across to them, "We have come to bring you the living words. Would you like to hear them? You are our relatives. We have not come to make war."

This brought an invitation for a delegation to cross the river. The natives with him said, "Larson, you go first." Whereupon he stripped to his shorts and swam the swift icy mountain stream. Kaga-paki, who said he had never swum before, accompanied Larson.

The villagers welcomed the two men and immediately built a fire in the open to keep them warm. Larson soon found that his Ilaga companions had no real intention of following him.

It was growing late in the day. Larson and Kaga-paki walked to the men's house with their hosts to spend the night.

"Oh, Larson," one of the villagers began, "your men are the ones who killed my younger brother in the Takanit war back many moons ago, and now you are in our men's house. I want to follow Jesus, but my heart feels very bad about my dead relatives."

Larson explained that all this had happened before the people in the Ilaga came to know the Lord.

The evening meal was already in progress in the houses surrounding the village compound. Kaga-paki nevertheless insisted that the entire village, women included, gather in the courtyard to hear the gospel story. With half-eaten potatoes in hand and crying babies in the arms of mothers, the village population heard Kaga-paki relate the account of the Creation, the Fall, the stories of Christ, and the Ten Commandments. While he stepped out momentarily during a brief pause, the people said, "My, his words are strong." The service went on until midnight, with everyone giving rapt attention. It was the first of many such sessions that would be conducted in villages on the route of the witness men's journey.

The next morning Larson and Kaga-paki swam the river again and rejoined their friends who had camped by the riverside. Takanit and his men had decided that there was no need of their services, so they headed back to the Ilaga.

The party of witness men continued to march. That evening they reached their first objective in the North Baliem, Tiom, an Australian Baptist station. Larson and his group were welcomed by Norman Draper and Dean Mountford, two of the workers who had been disturbed by Jabonep's visit and subsequent developments. It was at this center that the Dani "prophet" had been most uncooperative with the resident missionaries.

At Tiom the witness men's team had their first great crowds. A throng of three thousand attended the first Sunday service, and similar numbers gathered each time meetings were held.

The Larson party concentrated on rectifying the distorted messages, hewing strictly to the heart of the gospel message. To prove the fallacy of the taboo on certain sweet potatoes, the witness men ate some before the crowd in one service.

After the marchers left Tiom they came into a part of the North Baliem Valley highly reverenced by the natives. It was the fabled pathway of Bok, the mythical god-man who reputedly had left a footprint in one of the stones when he walked westward just before "real" people came into being. Larson examined the footlike impression and decided that the "print" in the stone was a freak of nature. One of the witness men had a different explanation. It had been made by God, not by Bok, he said solemnly.

At Maaki, the pilgrimage caught up with Jabonep, who was fervently preaching what he believed was the unique message of the Ilaga. But he responded to correction. Also, when he was criticized for having accepted cowrie shells and beads from the people, he surrendered the gifts without complaint to one of the Australian missionaries.

Jabonep affectionately said farewell as his fellow witness men left Maaki. They would pass through a few more villages and then would reach the point where the North Baliem empties into the main Baliem River. Just ahead was Pyramid station, the major goal of their journey. They could see the distant rocklike mound that was the landmark of the upper end of the Grand Valley.

The witness men quickened their pace, jabbering to one another in their excitement. They finally came to the long, swaying rattan bridge across the Baliem that took them to the gentler slopes on which Pyramid station was built. They were met by crowds of eager Danis who had been alerted on the progress of the long march, and who welcomed their kinsmen from the Ilaga with handshakes and warm embraces. Henry Young and a group of other Alliance missionaries who had arrived for the visit of the Ilaga preachers strode out to greet Larson and his companions.

It was late in the afternoon, so the witness men and their wives and others in the party were sent to a nearby Dani settlement. Larson joined the Youngs in their mission home.

For a number of weeks—actually since Jabonep's visit—several of the influential tribesmen had been planning a charm burning. Young had advised them to wait until the arrival of the Larson party. Therefore, on the following two days, a Friday and Saturday, Larson, Young, and the Ilaga Danis talked informally to local leaders of the native settlements.

The missionaries said plainly that only those who fully understood the message should proceed with the destruction of their talismans. The others should postpone action. But a large number of Danis told them that they would burn their fetishes next day.

Larson and Young asked, "What will you do if, after you have burned your fetishes, your pigs die or your people take sick?"

"We would come to the missionaries for medicine and ask Jesus to treat us," they replied confidently.

The missionaries were convinced that the natives of the Pyramid section were determined to go ahead with the ceremony. Larson told the tribesmen that if they did burn their magical articles, they should include everything. Nothing should be withheld.

Next morning the sun rose gloriously, coming up slowly over the hills rimming the east. It was Sunday, February 14, 1960. The gardens surrounding the Pyramid compound were filled with familiar North American flowers—zinnias, marigolds, and sweet peas. There were also tropical shrubs and trees that had been planted by Bernice Young to make the lovely hillside a little Eden.

The Danis began to gather about eleven o'clock, singing and dancing in formations of clan groups. They proceeded to the clearing on the hilltop not far from the Youngs' aluminum house. The tribespeople were carrying their previously prized objects that were so intricately related to their animistic religion. There were magic stones that, rubbed on the bodies of the sick, would restore them to health; bows and arrows of vanquished foes; pig tails and desiccated organs of animals; and strings of beads and cowrie shells. The charms and fetishes were piled together on what would become a pyre seventy feet long, four feet wide, and two feet high.

Soon a crowd of five thousand or more was milling about. The men were wearing their most cherished necklaces and gaudy feather headdresses. Their faces and bodies had been freshly smeared with pig grease, and soot was carefully added to enhance the traditional facial make-up. Even some of the women, usually more drab than the men, were decked out in their best beads, head-dresses, and carrying nets. There was one great difference in the normal appearance of a Dani crowd: a complete absence of war weapons—bows and arrows and spears, except those that had been thrown upon the pyre.

It was not until two-thirty that afternoon that the jubilant pre-service dancing and singing halted. The throng sat down quietly to hear the message of God. Larson, like a football coach before a big game, briefed his witness men. He urged them to stress the essential elements of the gospel.

Thrilled by the huge crowd, the Ilaga witness preachers made it plain that charm burning in itself had nothing to do with salvation of the soul, and that *natelan katelan* would not come to them as the result of the burning. Then they explained the Christian meaning of eternal life as well as the significance of the death and resurrection of Christ. Finally, they said that burning of the charms, should they insist on carrying it out, was merely a step toward the gospel.

The spokesmen compared eternal life with a seed that would grow in the heart only if there were commitment to Jesus Christ and a putting away of sin and unbelief.

Throughout the speaking period, the natives operated their own brand of public-address system. Scattered throughout the crowd were Ilaga Danis of the preaching mission who served as relay men to pass along the message spoken by the central preacher.

Now the Pyramid Danis declared through their leaders that they wanted to proceed with the charm burning. They asked that their missionary, Henry Young, ignite the great pyre. This he did at their insistence, even though he later was criticized by missionary colleagues for participating. As the flames shot up, the crowd sang and danced with joy.

The Pyramid missionaries estimated that about half of the Danis living in the immediate area had joined in the ceremony, and the following day another three thousand, representing all but ten per cent of the population, disposed of their charms at a second burning.

Gordon Larson and others had hoped that the movement begun at Pyramid would sweep through the entire Baliem Valley. He had expected that the Danis at other points would want to break with their fetish worship and embrace Christianity.

Accordingly, a few days after the Pyramid ceremonies, he flew with a group of Ilaga witness men to Ibele station, closest to Pyramid. But the chiefs of the Danis in that area had other ideas. They said flatly that they were opposed to burning their charms. Their threats against the preaching party became so intense that

THE FIRES AT PYRAMID

Larson, after conferring with Don Anderson, the local missionary, decided to leave.

Damot Dek, one of the opposing chiefs at Ibele, said, "If this message had come from the place [in the lower Baliem Valley] from which our people rose out of the ground, we would hear it. But since it comes from the tail end of things [the Ilaga], we cannot receive it."

During the Pyramid burnings a party of Danis asked the witness men to visit Tulim in mid-valley, but Larson decided against it. The charm burnings took place in the areas where kinship ties were the strongest. The Danis of the Ilaga were related to the Danis of the North Baliem and the contiguous area of Pyramid, in the Grand Valley, but the dialect boundary there became the limit of the mass movement. This was further demonstrated when North Baliem native Christians carried the gospel to their kinfolk in the Kulukwi region below Hetigima. Tom Bozeman later would find great response at Kulukwi in the Baliem gorge.

Missionaries were not all agreed in their thinking about the mass movement and the charm burnings. With concern for the future of the gospel and a desire to follow what they felt were more tried and true methods, some of the Alliance missionaries had sincere doubts about the spiritual quality of the movement which began with such wholesale burning of charms. They feared that the impetuous response of the people might actually block the advance of the true faith.

These questionings and concerns had understandable explanations. In the history of evangelical missions, the chief pattern of evangelism has been the proclamation of the redemptive message of Christ with a strong emphasis on individual response. One Alliance leader has said, "God never intended . . . to use wide-gate evangelism to win narrow-way Christians." The quotation was employed as an argument against the mass movement.

Those who were most involved were conscious that many who burned their charms did not fully understand the implications of the act even though the missionaries sought to make the gospel plain. Where a close-knit, tradition-bound society behaves as a unit, the followers inevitably "go-along" with the leaders. Thus some of these followers had no real personal conviction.

Larson, back at the site of the two huge burnings, found that the people had already appointed representatives to attend a new witness school to be held at Pyramid. Only those who had burned their fetishes and openly declared their faith in Christ were eligible. A man must have only one wife and be possessed with an earnest desire to preach. At first eight couples met these requirements and began to build a special village on the outskirts of the missionary compound. Later they were joined by three other couples. The school men and their families were to be supported by offerings of shells and sweet potatoes in the Sunday church gatherings.

"Naturally we are thrilled and yet we stand in awe, somewhat fearful of the tremendous task of teaching and training the lives before us," Henry Young declared.

Larson and his company of preachers also visited stations of the Unevangelized Fields Mission at Kelila and Bokodini in valleys north of the Baliem. They also visited Katu-paka, the Regions Beyond Missionary Union station in the Swart Valley.

Everywhere the Ilaga group went they were heard by thousands of eager Dani-speaking natives. In every instance there were great charm-burning ceremonies.

Larson and his preaching team returned to the Ilaga after a forty-six-day trek that had taken them to the principal mission stations of all societies working in Dani territory. Out of a population of at least one hundred thousand Danis, about twenty-five thousand had heard the preaching of the Ilaga witness men, and perhaps fifteen thousand had taken part in the charm burnings. Following the burnings, adult witness schools were established at four new centers: Pyramid, Kelila, Bokodini, and Katu-paka.

It was not easy to assay the results of the Ilaga witness men's pilgrimage for some weeks. But then it became plain that a large share of the Dani tribe had been affected by their gospel message. Thousands of former pagans had turned from their idols to worship the true and living God.

From that time forth the missionaries would continue to instruct their eager converts in the Word of God. Later many of the Danis would read the Scriptures in their own tongue and would worship in churches that would spring up in the mountain valleys.

The main fact was that Christianity had come to Cannibal Valley. The long-awaited spiritual conquest of the Baliem had begun. True, there were still many thousands to be reached for Christ. But now the gospel could be proclaimed with the much more effective voice of the Danis themselves.

17

MARTYR OF KULUKWI

On a beautiful morning in the spring of 1961, Tom Bozeman stepped outside his home at Hetigima to drink in the cool air of dawn and to look out on the lush Baliem Valley.

The secluded pocket in the mountains to which Bozeman had come five years before stretched to the northwest for a distance of forty miles. He could see the Baliem River, fed by dozens of mountain streams to the north and west, flowing down the center of the valley. Winding through the dewy grasslands like a coiling brown serpent, it rushed past Hetigima on its right bank into a narrow rocky gorge for thirty miles. Then it leaped from a palisade several thousand feet down to the swamps of the south coast, and emptied into the sea.

Later in the day Bozeman and a companion would visit a settlement in that gorge. He entered his small four-room house, a transplant of American comfort to Cannibal Valley half a globe away.

As Bozeman walked into the combined kitchen and dining room, he smelled the pungent odor of frying bacon. His wife, Frances, was preparing breakfast for him and their visitor, David Martin, a

234

smiling twenty-six-year-old Canadian. A Regions Beyond Missionary Union worker from the Swart Valley, Martin had spent the night with the Bozemans. After breakfast he and Bozeman were planning a hike to a new mission opportunity among Dani people living in the gorge country, more than twelve miles to the south. They had no idea then what they would experience before the day was over.

While the missionaries sat at breakfast, they heard a knock at the door, and three natives entered the house.

"*Nerok,*" said the Danis in greeting, shaking hands all around. Their perfect white teeth glistened against their black make-up. Then they sat on the clean linoleum floor.

Bozeman told Martin, "These are the three men from Kulukwi, the settlement we'll be visiting today. They hiked up yesterday afternoon just to accompany us on the trail. They have become Christians in recent weeks."

Martin, who had been present when Larson and his band of witness men preached at Katu-paka in the Swart Valley, was told that Danis from the North Baliem River district had carried the gospel to Kulukwi. As in other parts of the highlands, the gospel had reached the large settlement in the gorge below Hetigima as a result of native evangelistic efforts. Bozeman had been invited to the area because the people wanted instruction in the Christian faith after they had ceremonially broken with their old culture by burning their fetishes.

Following the mass movement at Pyramid, there had been attempts by both missionaries and natives to preach to the Baliem Valley people in other areas. But Ukumhearik, the treacherous chief, and other Dani leaders had thwarted all such attempts. Finally, the Danis from the North Baliem had skirted around the entire Grand Valley to reach their kin in the gorge area, where their preaching met with good response.

Bozeman had been visiting the Kulukwi on weekends for several months. On these difficult twenty-five-mile round-trip jaunts, he had found a population of about fifteen hundred Danis living there. Now he would take Martin to see the area. They assembled the men who would make up the party.

Led by their native escorts, Bozeman and Martin began their journey. They were also accompanied by Anthon and Daniel, Papuans from the New Guinea coast, who were employed at Hetigima. Four Danis from a nearby village served as carriers.

The hikers walked up the slope of the hill past the landing field. They followed the rough trail that soon brought them to a ridge marked by outcroppings of white limestone. They skirted abandoned sweet potato gardens grown over with weeds and underbrush. From time to time they could hear pigs rooting for food. The men all watched apprehensively. They knew the peril of an animal's rushing out to gore a man suddenly and viciously without warning. It had been near this very spot on the trail that Bozeman a few months before rescued a native woman who had been attacked by a wild boar and left bleeding with a dozen deep lacerations from the animal's scimitar-shaped tusks. Bozeman had killed the enraged boar with the last cartridge in his shotgun after pumping a half-dozen shells into the charging animal. It had fallen dead only inches away from his feet.

Because of the uneven path cluttered by boulders, tree limbs, and frequent holes half-filled with water, the men had to be wary. Now they passed through a grove of eucalyptus trees with their gray-green leaves and fragrant odor. As they neared the crest of the hill, Bozeman and Martin could see the outlines of the Baliem Gorge to their left and could hear the river rushing through the narrow rocky channel.

Now the trail plunged downward toward a deep ravine—the first of a score or more that they would have to cross on the five-hour trek. At times the men were forced to hold on to the low evergreen shrubs or long tropical vines to keep their footing.

At the bottom of the ravine a mountain torrent rushed northward to join the Baliem. A single six-inch log was the only bridge over the twelve-foot stream. The Danis raced across, then looked back to watch the missionaries balance themselves as they proceeded slowly and cautiously.

Bozeman told Martin that the Kulukwi natives had insisted on burning their fetishes even though both the Hetigima missionary and Myron Bromley had tried to discourage them. Bozeman said,

"We discovered that their settlement is surrounded with unfriendly villages violently opposed to the burnings. We warned the people that destroying their spears and bows and arrows would leave them defenseless if their opponents were to attack.

"There are two men who have been the leaders of the movement, Alikat, the chief, and his brother, Selanuok. They were the first to respond to the gospel when they heard it. I told them their people needed further instruction in the faith before destroying their magic charms. Selanuok's answer to that was, 'You come down and teach us.' "

"So you and Myron couldn't gracefully back out with such a wide-open invitation?" Martin asked, as the missionaries paused to rest briefly in the shadow of a huge rock.

"Right. You see how tough this trail is—it must be the worst in the whole Baliem area. Round trip from Hetigima to Kulukwi is just about twenty-five miles. You have to travel up one slope and down another, and one of the mountain peaks we have to cross is a good seven thousand feet high. In only a few weeks on this trail I wear out a pair of these boots. Yet Selanuok or someone from Kulukwi makes the round trip every week to accompany Bromley or me over the trail and help us carry our belongings. We generally go down weekends like this and usually have a crowd of from fifteen hundred to two thousand out for the preaching service."

"We have the same experience in Swart Valley," Martin said. "We found that when the people got rid of their fetishes, that was only the beginning. Now they live to hear the Word of God. This is part of the same movement that we have observed."

The spokesman for the Kulukwi Danis interrupted the conversation. "Boatman," he said, "we still have much of the trail ahead of us. You know the enemy villages are there, too. Let us move on."

"You are right, Medwi," Bozeman agreed. "We still have many miles to travel."

The missionaries climbed the side of the ravine, pulling them-

selves up the steepest places by grasping the roots of a stunted evergreen that covered the area. Sometime they had to crawl over huge
boulders or walk through stretches of "broken bottle" limestone—
sharp rocks with jagged edges that threatened to cut their shoes
to pieces.

Throughout the morning the missionary party repeated the performance of climbing up a slope only to descend into another
ravine with its rushing stream, log bridge, and tangled vegetation.
The hike became a grueling test of physical strength. Again and
again the white men tripped on the tangle of vines and roots that
conspired to halt their progress.

It was nearly eleven o'clock when the men struggled to the top
of the seven-thousand-foot limestone peak that marked the high
point of their trip. They had been traveling about three hours.

The hikers could look out upon the panorama ahead of them.
They could see the long winding line that marked the course of the
gorge. On either side of the indentation that only hinted at the
rocky chasm below, the virgin forests of tropical hardwood and
dark casuarina covered the hillsides. Interspersed among the trees
were the dead-white outcroppings of limestone rocks weathered by
centuries of tropical storms.

"That valley to the south of us is the Kulukwi. We'll be following
the trail right down there in an hour or more. In a little while the
trail takes us through the enemy villages that are opposed to the
charm burnings," Bozeman said.

"Any danger from attack? Martin asked. Tom looked thoughtful.

"I can't deceive you, Dave. There are some pretty rough cus-
tomers among them. The rumors have been flying thick and fast
lately. They have been threatening to kill Selanuok and Alikat,
they want to drive the North Baliem witness men out, and they
have no use for the white missionaries."

After a brief rest, the file of hikers commenced the last part of
their trip. They descended the mountain, sometimes sliding and
falling on the way. Finally, they came to the bottom of the ravine
and to the largest stream yet encountered. It was perhaps eighteen

feet wide, and two long logs formed the only crossing. Nearly twenty feet below, the maddened waters churned and boiled with a frightening roar.

"This is the bridge I hate to cross," Bozeman admitted to his companion. "Even the natives take their time here. These Danis are sure-footed, but occasionally one of them slips from this bridge and is drowned. It's a suicide leap for unhappy wives, too."

The missionaries gingerly picked their way over.

After climbing to the top of the opposite side of the ravine, they were able to look out across the neat Kulukwi, a miniature Baliem Valley with less arable land and many more rocks and boulders. Through the valley ran the Kulukwi River.

"We know the enemy villages are just ahead," one of the Kulukwi Danis told Bozeman. "But they will not attack us when you are with us. They have fear that you are ghosts."

The trail led into a clearing—the first sign of habitation since the group had left the mission compound early that morning. The settlement was surrounded by a five-foot fence with a stile. This was the only trail and it ran directly through the settlement.

Naked little Dani boys, wearing shorter gourds as befitted their age, came running up with grass-skirted girls trailing shyly behind. They begged for cowrie shells.

Their elders appeared resentful and sullen. One of the younger men made threatening motions toward the marchers with an arrow in his hand. But he did not attack. In a few tense moments the missionary party passed through the enemy village.

In other settlements farther on there was no evidence of hostility, but the warm Dani smiles were missing. No incidents marred the half mile or more through the opponents' territory.

It was nearly one o'clock in the afternoon when Bozeman and company, bone-tired and footsore, reached the main part of the Kulukwi. At last they were among friends. They found the new converts enjoying a huge pig feast. That day they had killed the last of their "magic" pigs and burned a few more of the strange charms that had once meant so much to them. Everyone seemed to be in a joyous mood.

First to greet Bozeman was Selanuok, who shook hands warmly, then threw his arms about the missionary and gave him a bear hug. Selanuok, a well-built young Dani in his twenties, wore several necklaces of cowrie shells and large flat white shells. He bore himself with dignity, for he was, after his brother, Alikat, the most influential man of the Kulukwi group. He was the Dani who had been most insistent that his people break with evil-spirit worship and turn to Jesus Christ.

Alikat, smiling broadly, also greeted the missionaries with warmth. He wore an elaborate fiber net on his head, and the "crown" of white tail feathers of a rare mountain bird set him apart from the rest of the tribal group. In the step of faith his younger brother had shown greater leadership, but Alikat's friendly demeanor evidenced his full accord with the movement toward Christ.

Selanuok presented Bozeman and Martin with two steaming sweet potatoes that must have weighed two pounds or more each. Then he gave them choice pieces of the pork tenderloin that had been steamed for several hours in the village baking pit. He knew this was a portion preferred by his white friend from Hetigima.

As Bozeman and Martin and their carriers joined in the feast, the Christian villagers gathered on a nearby clearing and began to dance.

By the end of the day Tom Bozeman's feet were bothering him. Martin was rubbing the long muscles of his aching legs as they sat near the round house that had been assigned to them as their quarters. They wanted to retire soon after the tropical night fell, for they knew that tomorrow, Sunday, would be a big day.

"Okay, tell us what we are to teach the people tomorrow," one of the Danis said to Bozeman.

"I'll begin early in the morning on that," he replied.

The Danis who clustered about him showed their disappointment and protested, "What's wrong with tonight?"

Bozeman relented. Weary though he was, he rehearsed the leaders in the Bible story of the Resurrection they would preach the following day. Bozeman knew from experience that even a willing pupil such as Selanuok had to be drilled on the "sermon" he would relay to his people. The missionary remembered the time he had spent all day Saturday and a good part of Sunday morning going over the story of the rich man and Lazarus. As the hour approached for Selanuok to preach, he had come over to Bozeman and asked, "Boatman, what was that man's name again? It slipped my mind."

Now Selanuok was preparing to tell his people about the Resurrection and what it meant to be a Christian.

Bozeman finally dismissed his charges and with Martin sauntered over to the house in which both of them would spend the night. They unrolled their sleeping bags and stretched them out on the earthen floor. Just before they retired, they were joined by Selanuok and Alikat.

"I have fear, Boatman," Selanuok said. "We have heard that our enemies on the hillside want to kill Alikat and me and all those who have had their hearts treated by Jesus."

Bozeman suggested they commit the matter to the Lord, and the two missionaries and their Dani friends bowed in prayer. Both of the Danis seemed relieved as they left for their quarters in the main round house nearby.

Next morning the entire community was stirring as soon as the sun was visible over the rim of the valley. Usually the Sunday service started about eleven o'clock, but on that bright morning three hundred villagers had gathered for the service by eight o'clock. They began to chant, praising the Creator for making the mountains and the skies, the pigs and sweet potatoes.

The missionaries were listening to the singing when Selanuok came up to them and said, "Warriors from the enemy villages are coming down to attack us today, and they say they will kill me."

Impressed with Selanuok's obvious distress, Bozeman again prayed with him. This seemed to restore his courage. He joined the singing crowd.

Just then Bozeman happened to turn his head toward the mountainside with its winding trail clearly outlined in the morning light. Near the top of the ridge he saw a band of fully armed warriors ad-

242 CANNIBAL VALLEY

vancing down the hillside. They were marching in groups of a dozen or more, one band following another. They bore long wooden spears or bows and arrows ready for battle.

"Here they come," one of the Christians shouted in terror. Most of the helpless believers, devoid of weapons, watched the advancing warriors with faces frozen in fright. They huddled together.

"Let's keep singing," Selanuok and Alikat told their people. Bozeman and Martin sent up a quick S O S of prayer. The believers continued to sing.

When the missionaries lifted their heads, they saw a mob of perhaps two thousand armed men running down the hillside. The warriors swept into the clearing. Bozeman realized the seriousness of the peril to his missionary friend and the carriers from his station. He warned them to flee. Anthon said,

"I'm not going to leave. If they kill me, I'll just go to be with Jesus. What's wrong with that?"

By this time the missionaries could see the frenzied faces of the warriors. They were shouting threats and filling the air with their war cries. Some were leaping like mad men. They cocked their spears for action, and those armed with bows had their arrows ready to shoot. Nothing could stop them.

"Hide in one of our houses," a villager told Daniel. Fortunately, the Papuan did not obey, for in a matter of seconds the attackers began to set fire to the village houses which were made of wood and straw. The flames were soon crackling, and panic-stricken villagers were running in all directions.

The warriors moved forward, spearing anyone in their pathway. An aged woman fell screaming as the blood of a spear wound gushed from her abdomen. A spear grazed the arms of a youth.

Some of the war party looted the houses, stealing pigs and lesser valuables. Then they grabbed a flaming torch of wood and set fire to other houses. Soon twenty-four buildings were burning to the ground. Cries of the wounded and dying mingled with the hoarse threats of the attackers and the squealing of the pigs.

Hidden behind a rock, Daniel saw the invaders charge Selanuok as he started belatedly to run. A spear stopped him as it passed through his body.

"Jesus, Jesus," he cried as he fell. In a moment he was dead. Already he had entered the portals of glory to experience resurrection joy with his sermon on that subject undelivered. He had become the first Dani Christian martyr.

Anthon, badly beaten, managed to escape by fleeing up the mountainside. Daniel disappeared in the melee.

Bozeman, accompanied by Martin and two of his carriers, ran to the end of the airstrip and entered a wooded area. They found a path that led away from the slaughter. When they broke out of the thicket they came to a clearing where the warriors could see them on the unprotected mountainside. They continued to sprint up the difficult trail. By this time some of the invaders were in hot pursuit. Others were jumping across the creek below to join in the chase. They were gaining on the missionaries. The carriers had now disappeared along escape routes of their own choosing. Both Bozeman and Martin were breathing hard, and utter fatigue and the steepness of the grade forced them to slow down.

"Let's stop and hide," Martin said.

"No, that's the worst thing you can do," Bozeman warned. "There's no such thing as hiding from a Dani warrior."

Martin began to lag.

"Come on, man, you've just go to keep moving," Bozeman shouted as he pushed him forcibly up the trail. Bozeman knew they still had another forty-five minutes of climbing before they would reach the top of the mountain.

Looking back into the valley, they could see the horror below. Men and women were being killed before their eyes, but they could do nothing about it. They could not take time to find out how many had been killed or wounded. They could only try to escape with their lives. The valley was black with the soot-smeared invaders.

With their pursuers only seconds behind them, the missionaries came to the crest of the ridge. Bozeman made a quick decision. He guided his companion off the main trail to a small one leading down toward the Baliem River. They knew from cries above them that they had outwitted the warriors just in time to avoid being ambushed by their opponents who had sought to outflank them.

Continuing for another three hours along the river, Bozeman and his friend finally reached a government police outpost at the entrance of the Grand Valley. The tiny metal building was manned by two Papuan policemen, who appeared more frightened than the missionaries when they learned of what had occurred. They would seek reinforcements before attempting to enter the disturbed area.

By mid-afternoon the missionaries reached Hetigima. They fell wearily upon the floor of the mission home. Frances Bozeman listened to the story of their escape as she hastily prepared food for them. Taking stock of their belongings, they realized they had left their cameras, a short-wave radio, and other equipment in the village. Not until later did they learn that the attackers had smashed all their possessions on the rocks and then tossed them into the river.

By the end of the day both Daniel and Anthon had dragged into Hetigima, footsore and tired, but both were alive. The other carriers filed back one by one. Daniel brought the sad news of Selanuok's slaying. It would be several weeks before Bozeman learned that Alikat had escaped without injury. But Selanuok, the man who had led his people in the way of the Lord, was dead.

It looked like a complete defeat for the gospel advance in the Kulukwi. Ukumhearik, the big chief, added bitterness by saying, "Those Kulukwi people were stupid to burn their fetishes. I told you this would happen."

Tom Bozeman could only nurse his bleeding feet and weep.

Weeks passed by before a party of Kulukwi Danis visited Bozeman at Hetigima. Would he not return to their village and give them "Jesus truth"? The government had forbidden all travel to the troubled area, but Bozeman was able to get the ban lifted.

He made the southward trip in July, 1961, over the treacherous trail through the subdued but still unfriendly villages. Finally, he reached Kulukwi and found that a nucleus of faithful believers were still seeking to demonstrate their faith. He continued to make journeys to the settlement each weekend. The small attendance seemed to confirm his fears that the work at Kulukwi would never prosper.

But Bozeman persisted. By the end of August the crowds began to grow.

Months before, the Kulukwi Christians had begun work on an airstrip. Now a band of volunteers had nearly completed the job. Soon an MAF pilot would trek in to inspect the landing site and airplane service would be inaugurated.

From the beginning it had been a labor of love. "We want to do this for Jesus," the faithful band of believers had told the missionary. They ignored the constant taunts of the enemy group that had perpetrated the savage attack.

Thus Tom Bozeman continued to risk his life every time he made the arduous round trip to Kulukwi. On one journey he was warned by natives that the enemy was planning to ambush him on the trail. He returned home under cover of darkness, once again escaping narrowly.

One morning he awoke to find that during the night his camp at Kulukwi had been encircled with drops of pig blood. The opponents had sneaked in to carry out a ceremony that directed a curse against him.

But Tom Bozeman's joy of working with the eager Kulukwi believers made up for the harassment and threats of death. He knew that he was facing an invisible wall at Hetigima. Kulukwi was such a contrast.

The Kulukwi Christians chided him for remaining at his station in the lower Baliem. "Why do you stay there where they do not want to hear the message? We want you to come and make your home with us."

Despite the bitter opposition at Kulukwi, the crowds grew to a throng of eight hundred who gathered each week to hear the word of God. With such encouragement Bozeman decided it was the time to advance. At his invitation two capable Dani witness men from the Ilaga Valley were assigned to Kulukwi. Thus, should the

246 CANNIBAL VALLEY

missionary be prevented from reaching the valley, the native preachers could carry on.

The cause of Christ had triumphed at Kulukwi. From the blood of the martyr Selanuok the church of Christ had sprung with renewed life.

18

DAWN OF A NEW DAY

In slightly more than a quarter century Jaffray's dream had been realized.

Not only had the major tribes of interior New Guinea been reached with the message of Christ. There had been a wholesale turning of the tribespeople from their animistic religion to an enthusiastic acceptance of Christianity. A spiritual revolution, unprecedented in missionary annals, had transformed Stone Age savages into hearty exponents of the new way.

Jaffray with rare prescience had anticipated that the missionaries would reach the remote New Guinea peoples. No doubt he had thought chiefly in terms of their ultimate spiritual destiny rather than of the immediate and temporal benefits of Christian faith. But already the new order of life gave the lie to the view that the missionaries would destroy an idyllic primitive existence. Actually, in the primitive society there had been much ugliness and sorrow. Instead, Christianity was bringing peace and joy.

In a few short years the ancient culture patterns were being destroyed. The intricate system of charms and fetishes used in the appeasement of spirits was abandoned wherever Christian faith had been accepted. Tribal warfare and the involved war settlements were almost nonexistent. Polygamy and the system of heathen marriage had been shaken. Grisly funeral rites had been replaced by the Christian hope of future life.

The missionaries who had begun the crusade to win New Guinea for Christ had showed remarkable vision as well as courage and dedication, but were not there to share in the victory. Jaffray and Russell Deibler had died before the task was really started. Al Lewis, the able pilot, had perished in the crash of the first amphibian airplane. Others had begun well but had been forced to drop out and return home because of physical disabilities.

Lloyd and Doris Van Stone had sought to resume their arduous duties in the Baliem, but the strain of the work prevented them from completing their second furlough. Einar Mickelson, the sturdy pioneer and persistent advocate of penetration of the Baliem Valley, had left the field because of his wife's serious chronic illness and other concerns.

Of the original Baliem beachhead party only Myron Bromley remained in the valley, faithfully continuing the enormous task of language analysis and translation of the Scriptures into the Dani tongue. The Roses, who had been involved in the missionary operation from the earliest days, had been pursued by recurring attacks of illness. They returned to their beloved valley and ultimately established a new mission station at Sinatma, in the hills above Wamena, the government center.

The Youngs found themselves busier than ever after the mass movement toward Christ that began with the two great charm-burning ceremonies. Young spent his time training the witness men for spiritual leadership. His wife, Bernice, was training Danis to read.

The Maxeys, Andersons, and Karceskys were carrying on at their respective stations, but the natives of their areas resisted the gospel. Tom Bozeman had seen no results at Hetigima, chiefly because of Ukumhearik's steady opposition, but was involved in the phenomonal response to the gospel at Kulukwi.

Not all of the missionaries in the Baliem were agreed about the results of the mass Christian movement. They had misgivings about what they feared was shallow Christianization of society. They preferred to continue traditional missionary methods that emphasized natives turning to Christ one by one. Most of the skeptical workers had cause for their questioning. They had served areas where the most distorted versions of the gospel had been relayed by untaught natives.

Nevertheless, a strong church was being formed in the villages around Pyramid. There was a new hunger among the Danis for the Word of God. Attendance at church services had jumped from listless dozens to hundreds and thousands.

At the slightest provocation, former savages would pour out their hearts in fervent prayer. They prayed in the morning, at noon, and before going to bed. They prayed before they ate, before they took a drink of water. There was ample evidence of a spontaneous fervency of worship and praise almost unknown in even the most devout churches of Western civilization.

Perhaps it was in the moral area that the transformation was most apparent. With one accord the people turned from their deeply embedded patterns of tribal warfare with its horrible cruelty and needless slaughter.

The barbarous customs of funerals ceased and the eerie wailings and hopeless weeping of pagan ceremonies for the dead were replaced by rites marked by Christian hope and the great truth of the Coming of Christ.

Obviously, it was not possible for polygamy to be eradicated in a single generation, but there were beginnings of better attitudes toward women. The brutal wife beatings were no longer the accepted pattern. It was recognized that women could enjoy the grace of God along with men. The new churches themselves ruled that polygamists could not take leadership in the house of God. Also, the discarding of wives at the slightest pretext was replaced by a recognition that God joined a man and woman together in wedlock, and no one should seek to dissolve this holy bond. Monogamous marriage became the mark of the new order. Promiscuity and fornication now were recognized as sin and were so treated in the discipline of the church. The orgiastic singsong was replaced by joyous praise to God and a love for the brethren.

Lying and stealing, so universally approved in the older culture, became recognized as transgressions of the Law of God. The new believers accepted the fact that restitution and repentance were required of them.

All of the practices relating to the animistic culture were classified as evil. Many acts of conduct that seemed harmless enough to the missionaries were outlawed by the native believers familiar with the intricate old culture.

The Lord's Day became hallowed. It was a day for rest and the worship of God. No work could be performed in the gardens. Weaving and simple activities were not permitted by the zealous, and often legalistic, church. In one area a missionary who absent-mindedly pulled up a few blades of grass as he was teaching a Scripture lesson was reprimanded for violating the Sabbath!

While there were some evidences of a pharasaism which drew attention to their separateness, the native believers showed a new spirit of love and a desire to share. The sacrificial offerings of sweet potatoes and cowrie shells from almost destitute people was deeply touching. Visitors to the native churches were impressed by a sense of warm Christian fellowship. Some of the converts lavished gifts on the missionaries as well as on needy tribespeople.

Christian teaching had deep meaning for everyday living. A leading woman convert was chided by her unbelieving neighbors who blamed the Christian movement for causing a potato shortage. She had this reply: "I told them that when the Devil led Jesus into no man's land and told Him to make all those stones into sweet potatoes, He said, 'One can't be good just by eating potatoes. One becomes good by hearing and obeying the Creator's words.'"

Primitive men are not any less intelligent than their civilized fellows. The New Guinea natives often demonstrate deep comprehension of spiritual issues. A tribesman requested that a visiting missionary pray for him.

"What kind of sickness do you have?" asked the Christian worker.

"I'm not sick," came the reply. "I've got bad things inside me."

"What kind of bad things?"

"Not long ago the people here did bad and fought; my younger brother was killed. I have wanted to get revenge. Pray that the Creator will make my heart right and take this desire away."

To some observers the stark twofold objective of the Society— preaching the gospel and building up the indigenous church—may seem insufficient. Perhaps no other missionary organization is more fearful of falling into a rut of institutionalism in missionary effort. Rightly or wrongly, the Alliance program shies from what others describes as the social implications of the gospel. This means that only a minimum of emphasis is placed upon medical missions, education, and agricultural programs.

The Alliance leadership insists that these are the responsibility of government or the national church, rather than on the missionary society. However, circumstances in New Guinea have forced some modifications of these policies.

The Netherlands government has been working hard to extend the benefits of civilization to the interior tribes as rapidly as the tribal areas can be brought under peaceful control. In compliance with the United Nations Charter, it has provided large subsidies for medical, educational, and agricultural work. However, in line with educational practices in the homeland, the authorities have refused to operate public schools; they have turned over this function to the Roman Catholic and Protestant missionary societies working in New Guinea.

Since the Alliance was the largest mission operating in the highlands, it was not possible to delegate the educational task to others. Thus, in the areas near all mission stations and under the society's close supervision, there are village or primary schools which offer three years of instruction. These village schools are taught by Indonesian gurus, instructed in the tribal language or in Malay. The continuation schools, which offer three years of advanced instruction, are conducted in Dutch by teachers who must meet high educational standards. A number of Netherlands nationals, who possess both academic and spiritual standards, have been assigned to this missionary task by the Alliance. With limited equipment and in a Spartan atmosphere, they conduct a very impressive continuation school at Gakakebo on Lake Tigi in Kapauku territory. Supervisor of the society's educational program is Adrian Stringer, a well-trained Netherlands national now serving as a missionary.

Because of the Netherlands government's eagerness to provide medical care in the newly opened mountain areas, funds were provided for a subsidized hospital in the Baliem Valley. The authorities offered to build and equip the hospital and to provide the support of a doctor if the mission would provide the personnel. This challenged the Alliance to veer again from its traditional policy on medical misionary work. Dr. Sytze Smit and his wife, Jopie, a nurse, both Hollanders, were appointed to the New Guinea field in 1957. In time Bethel Hospital, a small but well-equipped institution, was established at Pyramid Station.

From the very start medical treatment offered by the missionaries had been a means of establishing rapport with the native population. With the arrival of a trained physician in the Baliem, the medical and accompanying spiritual ministry moved forward with a quickened pace.

Louis L. King, foreign secretary of the Alliance since 1956, insists that "free medical, educational and economic aid causes the Christians to consider themselves the beneficiaries of the mission. The ineradicable impression is that the mission is the 'Father-Mother,' the great provider, and that the mission's very duty is to look after the welfare of its converts."

Great stress, however, is placed upon literacy programs that develop readers among both adults and children. This is regarded as imperative to the growth of the church which thus may derive first-hand spiritual strength from the Scriptures and be freed of dependence on the foreign missionaries.

The noted literacy expert, Frank Laubach, visited the Baliem

Valley late in 1960. Laubach's presence gave greater impetus to the literacy programs that were already under way in all the major tribal areas of the interior.

While literacy is regarded only in its relationship to the building of a strong church, it is apparent that leaders for eventual self-government are being developed by this means in the back valleys of the mountainous, isolated island.

Translation of the Scriptures into the various tribal languages has been given a triple-A priority, especially since the mass movement has swept so many new believers into the Kingdom. The entire New Testament has ben translated into Kapauku by Miss Marion Doble, linguist stationed at Enarotali. The Gospel of Mark has been translated into Uhunduni by John Ellenberger; into western Dani by Gordon Larson. Portions of the Scriptures have been translated into the lower Baliem Dani dialect by Myron Bromley; and Moni Scripture portions were translated both by Larson and William Cutts.

All these aids to building a strong indigenous church, able to carry on after the missionaries leave, is vitally important. Preparing the church for the rapidly approaching encroachments of westernized civilization that has spread to every corner of the world, is a tense race.

In some ways the perils to the missionaries are as great as when they entered the Baliem Valley in 1954. Ukumhearik, with a smiling face, has been agitating for the expulsion of all white men. Some of his clansmen have killed Kapauku believers working in the area. It is an ominous hint of what may happen to the missionaries.

But those who entered New Guinea dependent upon God continue "preaching the kingdom of God, and teaching those things which concern the Lord Jesus Christ, with all confidence." They know that even though they themselves are expendable, faithful native Christians will continue the work that they have begun.

Acknowledgments

Writing this book involved a trip to Dutch New Guinea where I was warmly entertained by the faithful missionaries of the Christian and Missionary Alliance. I am grateful to them not only for their kind hospitality but for letters, reports, and interviews that provided the documentation for this story.

For reasons of space it was impossible to include the activities of all the workers serving the New Guinea field. A volume could be written about each of them.

Transportation in New Guinea was provided by the airplanes of the Missionary Aviation Fellowship. My thanks go to the officers and pilots of MAF.

One of the extra dividends of this assignment was the fellowship I enjoyed with the Alliance Foreign Department staff in the New York headquarters. They traveled the second mile to provide me with information and assistance.

My wife was a constant adviser who also willingly took time from her busy life to type the manuscript.

When the first draft was completed, I received the expert help of Edward R. Sammis, consulting editor, and Eleanor Jordan of Harper & Row. If the work has any merit, they have demonstrated the truth of the old saying that a book is made in the editing.

RUSSELL T. HITT

JAPEN

Seroei

GEELVINK
BAY

Waren

Mambera

Weinami

Rouffaer R.

Nabire

Homejo   Pogapa   Dugandoga R.

WISSEL
LAKES   KEMANDORA   Hitadipa   Sinak

L. Paniai   MONI   BEOGA VALLEY   DAN

Obano   Enarotali   VALLEY   Beoga

Magode   L. Tagi   Elamaga (DANIS)   W.

Gakokebo   CARSTENSZ PEAKS   ILAGA VALLEY   Balie

L. Tigi   Kunga   Jila

KAPAUKU   UHUNDUNI   NASSAU

Orawaja

Oeta

BANDA SEA   Kokonao

NEW GUINEA MISSION AREA

COVERED IN THIS BOOK